THE ECONOMICS OF MARX'S *GRUNDRISSE*

Also by Adalbert G. Lallier

PEACE WITHOUT HONOUR
SOUVERAINETÉ-ASSOCIATION: RÉALISME ÉCONOMIQUE OU
UTOPIE?

The Economics of Marx's *Grundrisse*

An Annotated Summary

Adalbert G. Lallier
Professor of Economics
Concordia University, Montreal

St. Martin's Press   New York

Scholarly and Reference Division,
St. Martin's Press, Inc., 175 Fifth Avenue, New York, NY 10010

First published in the United States of America in 1989

Printed in the People's Republic of China

ISBN 0-312-02038-4

Library of Congress Cataloging-in-Publication Data
Lallier, Adalbert.
The economics of Marx's Grundrisse.
Bibliography: p.
Includes indexes.
1. Marx, Karl, 1818–1883. Grundrisse der
Kritik der politischen Ökonomie. 2. Marxian
economics. I. Marx, Karl, 1818–1883. Grundrisse
der Kritik der politischen Ökonomie. II. Title.
HB97.5.M3319L35 1989 335.4'12   88–4613
ISBN 0-312-02038-4

To my students, as a challenge, encouragement, and hope for a better world

Contents

Acknowledgements

The attempt to read, understand, and interpret Karl Marx's *Grundrisse*, which is claimed by many to be Marx's greatest work, would have been a far more difficult undertaking had it not been for the inspiration, the encouragement, the counsel, and the steadfastness of the following individuals, to whom I shall be for ever grateful: Professor Marie Lavigne, of l'Université Paris I; Professor Peter Wiles, of the London School of Economics; Professors Jalil Ahmad and Frank Mueller, of Concordia University; Milan Gilmore, for his untiring assistance; and the following past or present graduate or undergraduate students, for their assistance in research, indexing, and proofreading: Vonnie Gilmore, Noriko Haruta; and Julie, for her devotion to the arduous task of typing the manuscript.

Preface

Our basic interest in the *Grundrisse der Kritik der politischen Ökonomie: Rohentwurf*, as the first of the major writings of the 'mature' Marx, derives from the controversy involving the question of the significance of this massive manuscript (980 pages in the German edition of 1953) in the totality of Marx's writings, and, in particular, from our exploration of the origins of Marx's economic reasoning and of his views concerning international trade and international finance.

David McLellan names the *Grundrisse* the 'completest of Marx's works':[1] a work whose scope is much broader than that of *Das Kapital* and whose treatment of themes central to the *Paris Manuscripts* is much more mature because it reveals the synthesis of his ideas concerning philosophy and economics. Günther Kohlmey points to the 'numerous important comments on the theory of international values and on external trade'[2] and claims that this work contains the essential elements of a theory of international values.

The first English translation of the *Grundrisse* was published in 1973, with a Foreword by Martin Nicolaus ('M.N.'), which, it appears, reflects views normally attributed to the *Institut für Marxismus-Leninismus*. In his Foreword, 'M.N.' lauds this work by Karl Marx:

– ' . . . the only outline of Marx's full political economy project . . . ';[3]
– a work which ' . . . challenges and puts to test every serious interpretation of Marx yet conceived . . . ';[4]
– 'the record of Marx's mind at work, grappling with fundamental problems of theory which is the manuscript's most valuable distinguishing characteristic . . . ';[5]
– 'the first scientific elaboration of the theoretical foundation of communism . . . ';[6]
– 'the key elements in Marx's development and overthrow of the Hegelian philosophy';[7]
– ' . . . a sourcebook of inestimable value for the study of Marx's method of inquiry.'[8]

This manuscript by Marx was named *Grundrisse zur Kritik der politischen Ökonomie* by the Institute for Marxism-Leninism. The Institute refers to the manuscript as the result of one of Marx's most intensive writing efforts during the years 1850 to 1867, which began with the publication of the *Class Struggles in France* and culminated in the first volume of *Das Kapital*.

Marx had discussed with Engels as early as November 1851 the intention to commence writing his *Economics*, a work which was to contain three volumes: a critique of 'political economy'; a critique of the socialists; and the history of political economy. In anticipation of this undertaking, Marx had already begun in the autumn of 1850, in the British Museum, his intensive reading of works on money, finance, and recent economic trends. During 1851 he added further writers on money and currency (Bailey, Carey, Jacob, Grey, Smith, Bosanquet, Torrens, Hume, Locke); on ground rent and land fertility (Malthus, Thornton, Johnston); on wages, labour problems, and the theory of value and wealth (Malthus, Carey, Torrens, Owen, Hodgskin), and on colonisation and slavery (Prescott, Howitt). He also gathered relevant statistical material and even proceeded to study algebra in seeking to facilitate his calculations concerning his analysis of capital.[9]

Five months later, in a letter to Engels written on 3 February 1851, Marx revealed that he had reviewed the propositions concerning the price-specie-flow mechanism (i.e. of the 'currency theory') by Loyd (Lord Overstone, Samuel Jones Loyd) and by Ricardo and that he had found wanting their claim that the flow of precious metals determined trade balances and rates of exchange on the international money market.[10]

Soon after, in another letter to Engels (2 April 1851), Marx informed his friend that he was hoping to complete this 'economic shit' in about five weeks and that he would then shift to another science because this one was beginning to annoy him.[11]

In his quest for completion, Marx accumulated twenty-four notebooks of reading notes between September 1850 and August 1853, but his subsequent economic studies were interrupted during 1855 and the first half of 1856 because of additional commitments (mainly political and journalistic) and increasing pressures (family problems). He resumed his studies in June 1856, in 'response to the growing economic crisis and the wave of speculation which were gripping all of Europe', and finally settled down, in August 1857, to write the introduction, which he completed in September 1857.[12]

The contents of what is presently termed *Grundrisse* comprise the following material:

(1) Twenty-four notebooks on economic subject matter and some non-economic topics, written during September 1850–August 1853: commodities, money, capital, wage labour, landed property, international trade, history of technology and inventions, credit, population theory, economic history of states, world market, colonialism, the history of customs and manners, literature, and so on.

(2) Excerpts from Ricardo's *Principles*, written during April–May 1851 and published in part, as supplementary material, in the *Grundrisse*.

(3) A manuscript on theories of foreign exchange, which was written during November 1854–January 1855 and, held by the Institute for Marxism-Leninism in Moscow, remains unpublished.[13]

In addition, the following material was also included:

– a fragment on Bastiat and Carey, written in July 1857;
– a 'new theory of profits' (so named by Marx himself and contained in the fourth of the seven notebooks), which he wrote during October 1857–March 1858, with a few extra pages in May 1858.[14]

The first version of the manuscript was completed by May 1858. It originally included the two main Chapters (On Money, On Capital), the Introduction, and the unfinished fragment on Bastiat and Carey. But Marx was pleased with neither of the two main Chapters, nor with the Introduction. He subsequently redid (twice) the Chapter On Money (late summer 1858). He then rewrote the Introduction and had it published in 1859. Eventually, he also reworked the Chapter On Capital (several times, in two phases) between August 1861 and July 1863. In this revision, he expanded the treatment of capital to twenty-three notebooks (1472 quarto pages), added new material (which was eventually published as Volumes 2 and 3 of *Das Kapital*), and then still some more material, during 1865–67, which was then included in Volume 1 of *Das Kapital*. Finally, he also wrote a new manuscript, *Theorien über den Mehrwert* (Volume 4 of *Das Kapital*).[15]

In the Foreword to the English edition of the *Grundrisse*, the editors-translators compare and contrast Marx's approach in the xviPreface

Grundrisse with that in *Das Kapital*. While the 'inner structure' in *Das Kapital* is deemed identical in its main lines with the *Grundrisse*, Marx is said not to have carried much of the contents from the latter to the former. In their view, in the *Grundrisse*, the maturing Marx placed emphasis on the comprehensive portrayal of scientific thought but with due consideration of the realities of the Europe of his day – a transformation from his 'early' years, when he engaged in the topical coverage of problem areas in philosophy and political economy. In their interpretation, this new, comprehensive approach manifests itself in the treatment of the following topics:

- critical review of the Hegelian method;
- value of labour and the concept of *Arbeitskraft*;
- theory of alienation;
- thoughts concerning the tendency towards accumulation and auto- mation, the counter-tendency of the decline in the rate of profit, and the increasingly passive role of labour in the production process;
- rising contradictions between forces of production and relations of production;
- seminal discussion of the theory of the state.[16]

Marx treats several main themes in the *Grundrisse*, especially scope and method of political economy; Hegel's concept of harmony in the dialectic method; the time dimension.

His treatment of the question of scope and method first appears in the Introduction. As regards scope, he puts emphasis on 'the categ- ory of material life, of political economy'. stating that material production in society is the only real form of existence.[17] With respect to method, he ponders on the direction of scientific inquiry: does the scientist proceed with the dawn of history or does he first study the categories predominant at a certain stage of socioeconomic develop- ment, categories which dominate a particular society at a point of time in history? Should the direction of scientific inquiry proceed from simple general abstract relations towards the analysis of com- plex particular totalities, or should it proceed from the particular to the general?

His preoccupation with scope reveals itself in his 'plan of work'. He has several of these 'plans', in the *Grundrisse* as well as in two of his letters written in 1858, one to Lasalle (22 February) and the other to Engels (2 April). He confirms that his work, a 'critique of bourgeois economy', would comprise a total of six books: Capital; Landed Property; Wage Labour; State; International Trade; World Market.[18] In the *Grundrisse*, he elaborates in more detailed form:

> The order obviously has to be (1) the general, abstract determinants which obtain more or less in all forms of society, but in the above-explained sense. (2) The categories which make up the inner structure of bourgeois society and on which the fundamental classes rest. Capital, wage labour, landed property. Their interrelation. Town and country. The three great social classes. Exchange between them. Circulation. Credit system (private). (3) Concentration of bourgeois society in the form of the state. Viewed in relation to itself. The 'unproductive' classes. Taxes. State debt. Public credit. The population. The colonies. Emigration. (4) The international relation of production. International division of labour. International exchange. Export and import. Rate of exchange. The world market and crises.[19]

Marx is yet more specific early in the Chapter On Capital, where he presents the scope of his work in a somewhat different sequence and in a detailed composition which looks beyond the capitalist era:

  I.   (1) General concept of capital.
       (2) Particularity of capital: circulating capital, fixed capital.
       (3) Capital as money.
 II.   (1) Quantity of capital. Accumulation.
       (2) Capital measured by itself. Profit. Interest. Value of capital . . . .
III.   Capital as credit.
 IV.   Capital as share capital.
  V.   Capital as money market.
 VI.   Capital as source of wealth. The capitalist. After capital, landed property will be dealt with. After that, wage labour. All three are presupposed, the movement of prices, as circulation now defined in its inner totality.
       Then the state. (State and bourgeois society.)
       Taxes, or the existence of unproductive classes.
       The state debt. Population. The state externally: colonies.
       External trade. Rate of exchange. Money as international coin. Finally the world market. Encroachment of bourgeois society over the state.

> Crises. Dissolution of the mode of production and form of
> society based on exchange value. Real positing of individual
> labour as social and vice versa.[20]

We note with interest Marx's prediction of the dissolution of the
bourgeois mode of production and of the form of society based on
exchange value. However, even in the *Grundrisse* he says almost
nothing about the economic organisation of the post-bourgeois era.

As regards Hegel, after referring to him in the Introduction, Marx
eventually dissociates himself after taking issue with Hegel's view:
that the dialectic process is founded on the unity and the identity of
opposites which interact and lead to a harmonious evolution. In his
own interpretation, Marx queries whether dialectics viewed in a
materialistic sense does not constitute a process of change based not
on harmony but on antagonism, the antagonism of the opposites, a
course of action which will lead to violence, an action in the course of
which the unity of the opposites and their harmony will be broken up.
Marx admits that, originally, examples may be found of the unity of
opposites in the sense of Hegelian harmony: this unity reveals itself in
the sphere of simple circulation, where, in the relation between use
value and exchange value, the unity and equality of the opposites is
implied; this being so because

> the relations between individuals are those of liberty and
> equality . . . because the exchange of commodities is based, on the
> average, on the law of equivalence: the products exchanged are the
> embodiment of equal amounts of labour time . . . because individ-
> uals are free to participate or to refuse to participate . . . on the
> basis of free competition . . . because in the market all consumers
> are deemed equal.[21]

Marx points out that in the dialectic process, antagonism constitutes
the essential element: the presumed 'identical' opposite of consumption and production constitutes in fact a contradiction rather than the
harmony based on unity and equality. Since the workers consume
and the capitalists produce, the antagonism becomes visible and
self-evident; in lieu of an identity and a harmony, a contradiction; a
contradiction which leads to antagonism, to disunity, and to a violent
breaking asunder.[22]

With respect to the time element, Marx recognises its importance
in economics in two particular respects: (1) an essential determining

element in the organisation of society; (2) the significant universal expression of motion, of movement, of change, and the requisite towards the full development of man. His perception of time takes on a particular significance in his description of the circulation of commodities in an expanding world market.[23]

So far, Marx's main themes have a universal dimension. However, his *Grundrisse*, like *Das Kapital*, does not contain even one single chapter on matters pertaining to international trade and international finance, a subject which is not even mentioned in the Foreword. Yet even upon a cursory glance, we discover Marx's continuous preoccupation with this vast problem area. As early as the Introduction, Marx deals with Ricardo's propositions concerning the effects of free trade upon grain prices; on wages, rents, and profits; he reflects upon income distribution and class structure; elaborates on exchange, division of labour, and market expansion, as well as on money, exchange, and different levels of economic development.[24] He also discusses the effects of trade between nations on the development of production and the expansion of the world market.[25]

Each of the two main Chapters also contains further explicit statements on these issues. In the Chapter On Money, Marx treats specifically the relation between gold exports and crises, trade imbalances and devaluation during crises. In this discussion he defines value and price and speaks of the determination of values and prices; develops the concept of the double movement of circulation (C-M-C and M-C-M^1) and of accumulation through extended reproduction; elaborates on the role of money as the general equivalent; reflects upon exchange at equivalent prices and exchange under conditions of non-equivalence; and points out the universal character of money.

In the Chapter On Capital, which contains three Sections and several subsections, Marx develops his ideas concerning the production process of capital (with a subsection on surplus value and profit), the circulation process of capital (with three subsections: how surplus value becomes surplus capital; the original accumulation of capital; and theories of surplus value), and the transformation of value into profit. In this Chapter, numerous implicit references to international trade and international finance may be found, mainly in the following subheadings:

– capital and labour; transformation of labour into capital;
– exchange value and use value; value of labour and surplus value; absolute and relative surplus labour time;

- determination of values and prices;
- confusion of profit and surplus value; general rate of profit; transformation of surplus value into profit; fall in the rate of profit;
- realisation process; capital costs and production;
- formation of surplus capital; fixed capital and circulating capital;
  fixed capital and the creation of value;
- circulation and the creation of value; transport costs and circulation costs;
- transformation of the product into money; competition; equality,
  freedom of exchangers; the market;
- devaluation during crises; credit.

Even the Miscellaneous Section in the Chapter On Capital contains a
reference to foreign trade theory: a declaration that commerce with
equivalents was impossible, with an elaboration on Ricardo's views
on money and currency.

In addition, Marx intersperses throughout the *Grundrisse* economic terms typical of classical reasoning on foreign trade; but he
also adds terms of his own, terms which indicate his priority concerns. Thus, unlike in most of his earlier writings, he now uses almost
exclusively the term 'international', especially when referring to
exchange, relations of production, division of labour, relations between states, and economic policy. He also devotes much space to
the discussion of equivalent exchange (pre-capitalist) and non-
equivalent exchange (bourgeois mode of production), their definition
and their significance in the evolution of society. In non-equivalent
exchange, exploitation, expropriation and theft are the rule.

In our exploration of the economics of the *Grundrisse*, we are
faced with several tasks:

First, in consideration of its sheer volume, to undertake a systematic
review of the whole manuscript, with the purpose of narrowing this
work down to the subject matter of concern to economists: value,
pricing, distribution, international trade and finance, equivalence *v.*
non-equivalence, circulation of production and circulation of commodities; economic development and crises.

Second, an analysis of topics in which Marx appears to have had
particular interest: Ricardo on value, rent, foreign trade, gold and
crises; the causes and effects of crises; gold as universal currency;
devaluation, revaluation; capital accumulation; relation between

surplus value and profit; value and price determination; transportation costs. These topics are of interest to us because their study will assist us in accepting or refuting claims concerning Marx's seminal ideas (for example, Kohlmey's statement that Marx indeed had a theory of international values).

Third, to survey Marx's overall reasoning in the *Grundrisse* (in particular, his reflections concerning the 'substructure' and the 'superstructure', the linkage between these two structures and the cause–effect relationships, including the dialectics of this evolution), in order to be better able to assess the claims by 'M.N.' and others (that this work contains 'the first scientific elaboration of the theoretical foundation of communism') concerning the significance of this first major work by the 'mature' Marx.

In all of the cited extracts in this book, the emphasis is as in the original, unless otherwise stated.

NOTES AND COMMENTS

1. D. McLellan (ed.), *The Grundrisse Karl Marx* (New York: Harper Torchbooks, 1971), p. 15.
2. G. Kohlmey, 'Karl Marx Theorie von den internationalen Werten', *Jahrbuch des Instituts für Wirtschaftswissenschaften*, Band 11 (1962), p. 20.
3. Karl Marx, *Grundrisse*, translated with a foreword by Martin Nicolaus (Harmondsworth: Penguin, 1973), p. 7.
4. Ibid.
5. Ibid., p. 25.
6. Ibid., p. 7.
7. Ibid.
8. Ibid.
9. M. Rubel and M. Manale, *Marx Without Myth* (Oxford: Basil Blackwell, 1975), p. 102.
10. Ibid., p. 97.
11. K. Marx and F. Engels, *Werke*, Band 7 (Berlin: Dietz, 1957), p. 228.
12. Rubel and Manale, op. cit., p. 11.
13. *Grundrisse* (English edition), p. 12, note 12.
14. The original Moscow (1939 and 1941) edition of the *Grundrisse* contains the following material:

> Two main Chapters: Chapter On Money and Chapter On Capital; the fragment on value;
> Annexed works: excerpts from Ricardo; Bastiat and Carey;

Index concerning Marx's notebooks (and Marx's index on Ricardo);
Marx's references to the manuscript of 1857–58 and his own notebooks;
fragment of the first draft of *A Contribution to the Critique of Political
Economy*;
the plan of work and of writings envisaged by Marx in 1859;
annotations and sources; bibliography; names of cited authors.

15. Rubel and Manale, p. 150
16. *Grundrisse*, p. 52.
17. *Grundrisse* (German edition), p. 83
18. *Grundrisse* (English edition), pp. 54, 228. *Werke*, vol. 29, pp. 312, 549.
    The French edition (Anthropos, 2 vols) is based on the Moscow edition.
    The German edition (1953) has the two main Chapters, the Introduc-
    tion, and the fragment on Bastiat and Carey.
19. Ibid., p. 108.
20. Ibid., p. 264.
21. Ibid., p. 650.
22. Ibid., p. 247.
23. Ibid., pp. 652–7.
24. Ibid., pp. 95–7, 280–2.
25. Ibid., pp. 100–1.

Introduction

The Introduction to the *Grundrisse* totals thirty-three pages, in four Sections:

1. Production.
2. The general relation of production to distribution, exchange, and consumption.
3. Method in political economy.
4. Forces of production and relations of production.

1. PRODUCTION

In his reflections concerning material production, Marx first highlights eighteenth century notions about the individual in the state of nature *v.* the individual in 'civil society'; next he distinguishes between 'epochs of production' and 'production in general'; finally he takes up the issue of 'natural laws' *v.* 'social laws'. Marx's own examples have a universal dimension, in time (the historical evolution of production) as well as in space (contemporary state of production as seen by the 'political economists': Adam Smith, David Ricardo, John Stuart Mill).

In Marx's view, material production has to do with 'individuals producing in society – hence historically determined individual production. . .'.[1] However, these individuals do not represent the 'natural individuals' of the Smithian and Ricardian hunter and fisherman or the naturally independent subjects of Rousseau's *Contrat social*, but, rather, individuals who reflect the emergence of the new forces of production, individuals who ' . . . appear as dependent, as belonging to a greater whole . . . from the family . . . to the fusions of the clans.'[2] With the disappearance of the fetters of the feudal form of society, the 'civil society' emerges during the eighteenth century. Even though, in this society, the individual appears free of the previous bonds (which, while they lasted, may even have appeared 'natural' to him) in fact he now becomes even more firmly embedded in its ' . . . hitherto most developed social relations'.[3] The individual may now compete freely, but he becomes a political

1

animal whose production is tied to a definite stage of social development, a much higher stage in 'civil society' than in any of the previous forms. There is therefore no point in dwelling any longer on the isolated individual, ' . . . on the production of an isolated individual outside of society'.[4]

In this manner, Marx proceeds to make production a function of social relations in their historic development through their different phases, and the 'human being . . . an animal which can individuate itself only in the midst of society'.[5] 'Production' always means production at a definite stage of social development, that is, 'at a specific historic epoch such as e.g. modern bourgeois production'.[6] Each of these phases has its own characteristics, but all epochs of production also have some traits in common. Marx names 'instruments of production' one such general, eternal relation, a relation without which production could not take place, a relation of which capital constitutes a typical example: 'capital, . . . an instrument of production, stored-up, objectified [vergegenständlichte], past labour'.[7]

In this, the definitional, sense of production, Marx distinguishes between 'production in general', 'particular branches of production', and 'totality of production'. The first is an abstraction, a general category, which brings out and fixes the common element in all epochs contained in the process of historical development. The second refers to a particular production branch, for example agriculture, manufacture, cattle raising. The third involves a level of development determined by the social body, by society, by the individuals living in society, 'a social subject which acts upon he totality of the branches of production'.[8]

Marx is critical of the 'political economists' for their treatment of production: (a) their analysis of the conditions without which production is not possible is 'tautological';[9] (b) their work concerning the conditions which promote production is valuable but further studies would have to be undertaken before this work is elevated to scientific significance, for example the development of competition and of accumulation and their effects on the relation between degrees of productivity and development of individual peoples; (c) their claim that an industrial people reaches the peak of its production at the moment when it arrives at its historical peak is questionable; (d) their statement that wealth is created more easily where its elements are subjectively and objectively present to a great degree is also 'tautological'.[10]

2. GENERAL RELATION OF PRODUCTION TO DISTRIBUTION, EXCHANGE, CONSUMPTION

Marx is even more critical of the political economists' treatment of production in general, and particularly of their proposition that the determination of production is separate from the determination of distribution:

> Political economists pretend [Marx singles out J.S. Mill in particular] that production, contrary to distribution, is subjected to eternal laws of nature, independent of history, while the latter is made out to be a function of social laws; the right occasion to insinuate that bourgeois relations are natural and indestructible. . . .[11]

> On the contrary, in distribution man can permit himself all kinds of phantasies . . . which means a brutal cut between production and distribution and their *real* rapport. Slave, serf, worker, receive subsistence – *fonctionnaire*, landowner, priest, receive their income by different laws, private property and *Faustrecht*.[12]

In Marx's view, this kind of reasoning is 'empty', because it

- separates production (which it deems determined by natural laws) from distribution (which it considers subject to social hazard and chance and their effect on the quantity of production);
- separates exchange, which is situated between production and distribution without having any social significance of its own except its form;
- separates consumption, which it places outside the economy even though it is considered the outcome, the final purpose, of production.

Marx views as misconstrued the classicals' notion on these relations; that production creates objects according to social laws; that distribution divides these objects according to individual needs; and that consumption becomes directly object and agent of individual needs – whereby the social sphere of consumption is abandoned. In the classical set-up, suggests Marx, production represents the starting point, while distribution and exchange make up the middle. But whereas distribution has its source in society, exchange rests with the individual.[13]

Marx's rejoinder is as follows:

- distribution cannot be separated from production, since 'the structure [Gliederung] of distribution is completely determined by the structure of production';[14]
- distribution is an apportioning, not only of products among individuals but also of instruments of production and of humans among different kinds of production, bearing in mind that production itself has its own determinants and preconditions, since it must begin with a 'certain distribution of the instruments of production';[15]
- these determinants and preconditions themselves undergo a process of continuous change and acquire particular relations and characteristics in particular epochs in history;
- interest and profit are the proof that production and distribution are closely intertwined because they figure in the former but also represent forms of the latter:

> To examine production while disregarding this internal distribution within it is obviously an empty abstraction; while, conversely, the distribution of products follows by itself from this distribution which forms the original moment[16] of production.[17]

- Historically, distribution does not appear to be determined by production; but 'distribution' applies to the sharing out not only of products but also of the instruments of production and of the members of society into determined relations of production.
- Even Ricardo, ' . . . a *par excellence* economist of production, affirms that the very theme of modern economics is not production but distribution.'[18]
- Even modern manuals on economics consider capital both a factor of production and a source of production.

Marx's own conclusion: since interest and profit are types of distribution based on capital as well as the means (the method) by which capital is reproduced, distribution appears as a preliminary condition of production as well as of a new productive era; but in fact it is also the fruit of production. The linkage between production and distribution is therefore clearly established, even though the effect of laws upon distribution relations and therefore upon production must be subjected to further study.[19]

Concerning the relation between production and consumption,

Marx queries whether they are directly linked, that is, whether production is directly consumption? He suggests that the Hegelians had no problems identifying production with consumption as an identity of opposites, a complete whole, a unity of opposites, leading to harmony.[20]

However, he terms this issue more complex, since ' . . . between the producer and the products, that is, the production and the consumption, distribution is situated, which fixes by social laws that part that comes to everyone from the mass of products.'[21] Neither is production simply *equal* (emphasis added) to consumption, as claimed by J.B. Say and the 'beaux penseurs socialistes', because, as demonstrated by Henri Storch (*Considérations sur la nature du revenue national*, Paris, 1824), a people does not simply consume its product but also creates other means of production, fixed capital, and so on.[22]

Marx admits that the issue of the *identity* between production and consumption cannot be glossed over. This is because as the individual develops and expends his faculties in the act of production, he also uses up means of production; this means that 'in all stages the process of production is therefore also an act of consumption . . . [and that] 'consumption creates the need for a new production.'[23] Production furnishes the material and the object for consumption, while consumption provides the producers with a motive: 'production produces the object of consumption, the manner of consumption, and the motive for consumption. Consumption likewise produces the producers' *inclination* by beckoning to him as an aim-determining need.'[24]

The relation between exchange and production and between exchange and circulation must also be considered. Marx starts out by stating: 'Circulation is exchange in its totality . . .' and 'there is no exchange without a division of labour, natural or produced by history, where intensity and extent of exchange are determined by the development and organisation of production.'[25]

Marx's overall conclusions may be summed up as follows:

- Production, distribution, exchange, and consumption, even though intertwined, are not identical but distinct members of a totality.
- Production is at the base and is predominant: 'A definite production determines a definite consumption, distribution, and exchange.'[26]
- The distribution of products is unlike the distribution of the agents

of production, the latter constituting only a 'moment of production'.[27]
- 'A change in distribution changes production.'[28]
- But production itself is subject to influence by other moments, that is, as exchange (the market) expands, production increases its volume and diversifies, with the resulting change in distribution, which will also make for a greater concentration of capital, etc.[29]
- It is self-evident that exchange and consumption cannot be predominant.[30]
- But, clearly, in 'an organic ensemble, all factors are interrelated.'[31]

In this Section of the Introduction Marx's reflections have a universal scope, as they involve the 'peoples of the world': 'the development of individual peoples is tied to secular changes in the degrees of productivity.'[32]

3. METHOD IN POLITICAL ECONOMY

In the English edition of the *Grundrisse*, the writer of the Foreword ('M.N.') elaborates on Marx's difficulties with the question of what constitutes the 'proper beginning' of inquiry in political economy. In his initial treatment of this question (*Grundrisse*, Introduction, pp. 100–8), Marx recalls the following:

> the economists of the seventeenth century, e.g. always begin with the living whole, with population, nation, state, several states, etc.; but they always conclude by discovering through analysis a small number of determinant, abstract, general relations such as division of labour, money, value . . . .[33]

Marx considered this approach incorrect when he first looked at it, because the founding element (the population), which may seem concrete, may not be that at all. It could in fact be an abstraction because the economists may have neglected to study the concrete determinants of this founding element and the social relations within which this element functions. Unless such an analysis is undertaken (a population in specific relations, in a specific division of labour, etc.), a further examination of the 'population' in its abstract meaning can only lead to even 'thinner abstractions' concerning the constituent elements on which the population rests, including the classes of which it is composed and its productive undertakings. The same is true of the simple, general notions of value, money, prices, capital, wage labour, exchange, etc., notions which have been derived from an abstract base.

This direction of thought is wrong, claims Marx, because it starts with a *Vorstellung* (a particular *conception* of something that is deemed to be 'concrete', for example population) and yields, necessarily, a *Begriff*, an 'abstract determination' as the end result, whereby 'the idea itself is diluted into abstract notions'.[34]

In countering this direction of thought, Marx submits that the correct scientific method is the one whose thought moves in the opposite (reverse) direction, starting out with more or less firmly established and abstracted notions towards reproducing the concrete by way of thought (of reasoning). This approach begins with the simple, general, abstract relations and moves on to the economic systems at the level of the state, of the exchange between nations, and of the world market, systems which have arisen from the simple relations such as labour, division of labour, need, exchange value, etc.:

> The latter is obviously scientifically the correct method. The concrete is concrete because it is the synthesis of numerous determinations, it is the unity of the diversity. . . . For thought, it is a process of synthesis and a result, and not a point of departure. In our eyes it is the point of departure in reality and hence the point of departure for observation [*Anschauung*] and conception.
>
> The concrete reality is the totality of thoughts, concrete in thought, in fact a product of thinking and comprehending – but not in any way a product of the concept which thinks and generates itself outside or above observation and conception – a product, rather, of the working-up of observation and conception [*Vorstellung*] into concepts [*Begriffe*].[35]

Marx then attempts to demonstrate, with particular emphasis on time as a factor in the evolution of society, the historical existence of the 'simpler categories' as general, abstract genres; and the relation of these simple categories to the more concrete. The latter, Marx considers, are themselves subject to continuous change, from the less developed (pastoral) forms to the 'most developed and complex historical organisation of production (i.e. bourgeois society)'.[36]

As examples, Marx singles out exchange value, money, and labour as three particular 'simple economic categories':[37]

For example, the simplest economic category, say e.g. exchange value, presupposes population, moreover a population producing in specific relations; as well as a certain kind of family, or commune, or state, etc. It can never exist other than as an abstract, one-sided relation within an already given, concrete, living whole. As a category, by contrast, exchange value leads an antediluvian existence.[38]

How about the origin of exchange, asks Marx? Exchange did not originate in a communal society as its constituting element, but in intercommunity trading.[39]

Money, 'this very simple category', plays an extensive role very early but is a preponderant element only in nations specialised in commerce in Antiquity. Not even in Greece and Rome did money attain its full development (premise of bourgeois society). Even there it did not permeate all economic relations: for example the Roman Empire, even at its highest development, had taxes and payments in kind as its foundation, while money was confined to trade and the army but 'never took over the whole of labour'.[40] As a simpler category, money could have predated (historically) the more concrete category, but it could realise its full development, intensive as well as extensive, only with the most developed form of society, the bourgeois society, in which the full development of money is presupposed.[41]

Labour also appears as a very simple category. In its general form – labour as such – this concept is 'immeasurably old'.[42] But in its contemporary economic sense, labour, this pure and simple abstraction, is 'a category as modern as the relations which engender it'.[43] In line with the evolution of the more complex, more concrete forms of economic society, the original abstract notion of labour, in its general form, had, according to Marx, been updated to reflect its conceptualisation in bourgeois society (the society in which capital is the all-dominating economic power): the specific labour (for example, slave labour; agricultural labour in Physiocracy) had become labour as 'the means of creating wealth in general',[44] the totality of objective labour and subjective labour. Marx traces this redefinition to Adam Smith, who rendered labour 'the point of departure in modern economics'[45] by declaring that the abstract universality of wealth-creative activity is based on the universality of labour.

Marx's attempt to show that the 'simplest, abstract, categories' may well have existed historically before the complex, concrete

categories expresses an interesting duality: in spite of their validity
for all epochs, the abstract categories must be conceived of in
reference to each specific epoch, in their particular manifestations, as
the product of their historical relations and valid only within that set
of relations.[46] In his view, these abstract categories themselves attain
universal significance in the course of the development of the increasingly complex historic organisation of production, that of the
bourgeoisie being the most complex and taking on a worldwide
dimension. He concludes that these abstract categories, which obtain
more or less for all forms of society, should constitute the starting
point because they attain universal significance in the course of
evolution. This viewpoint is expressed in his first proposed order of
work:

> The order obviously has to be (1) the general, abstract determi-
> nants which obtain in more or less all forms of society, but in the
> above explained sense. (2) The categories which make up the inner
> structure of bourgeois society and on which the fundamental
> classes rest. Capital, wage labour, landed property. Their inter-
> relation. Town and country. The three great social classes. Ex-
> change between them. Circulation. Credit system (private). (3)
> Concentration of bourgeois society in the form of the state. Viewed
> in relation to itself. The 'unproductive' classes. Taxes. State debt.
> Public credit. The population. The colonies. Emigration. (4) The
> international relations of production. International division of
> labour. International exchange. Export and import. Rate of ex-
> change. (5) The world market and crises.[47]

But Marx is having problems with his own proposed order of work;
in fact, he contradicts himself several times (note the various comments by 'M.N.' in the Foreword to the *Grundrisse*, especially pp.
37–8, and by Marx himself, particularly MEW XIII and *Grundrisse*, p.
881, English edition, and p. 763, German edition). On page 107 of
the *Grundrisse*, Marx states that 'capital is the all-dominating economic power of bourgeois society. It must form the starting point as
well as the finishing point.'[48] On the same page he also states that the
proper beginning is not a chronological account from the dawn of
society to the present, with particular emphasis on those categories
which pervade more or less all societies, but the analysis of those
economic categories which exert a dominating role in a particular
society as distinct from other societies;

The point is not the historic position of the economic relations in the succession of different forms of society. Even less is it their sequence 'in the idea' [Marx refers here to Proudhon's *Philosophie de la misère*, Paris, 1846, vol. I, p. 146]. Rather, their order within modern bourgeois society . . . [that is, capital].[49]

Marx's difficulties with the 'proper' starting point persist right through the seventh notebook of the *Grundrisse*. In its section 'On Value' (p. 881, English edition; p. 763. German edition), Marx begins his recapitulation of the manuscript with the *analysis* of the *commodity* (emphasis added) as 'the first category in which bourgeois wealth presents itself . . . as unity of two aspects [namely, use value and exchange value, editor's note, p. 37].[50] According to the editors of the *Grundrisse* it is this category, the commodity, which forms the starting point of Marx's *A Contribution to the Critique of Political Economy* (1859) and of Volume 1 of *Das Kapital* (1867).[51] In the editors' opinion, Marx's use of the commodity as the starting point renders him more consistent with his own logic, in opposition to that of Hegel:

[The commodity is] a beginning which is at once concrete, material, almost tangible, and historically specific (to capitalist production); and it contains within it (is the unity of) a key antithesis [that is, use value *v.* exchange value] whose development involves all the other contradictions of this mode of production; . . . this beginning constitutes not . . . a pure, indeterminate, eternal and universal abstraction [following Hegel and the earlier Marx] but rather . . . a compound, determinate, delimited and concrete whole – 'a concentration of many determinations, hence unit of the diverse' [as stated by Marx on p. 101] . . . [instead of] the 'pure' (indeterminate, eternal, absolute and universal) beginning . . . it is a materialist beginning, a beginning with the concrete, the determinate, and hence . . . the contradictory itself, . . . a truly dialectical beginning.[52]

Marx's viewpoint as to what constitutes the 'proper' beginning changes once again in his Preface to *A Contribution to the Critique of Political Economy*, which he wrote as a replacement of the first Introduction in the *Grundrisse*:

I am suppresing a general Introduction which I had thrown on paper because upon further reflection [*bei näherem Nachdenken*] any anticipation of yet-to-be-proved results seems to me a distraction, and the reader who wishes to follow me at all must resolve to climb from the particular up to the general.[53]

The editors of the *Grundrisse* interpret this declaration as a rejection of his previously expressed viewpoint: 'that the path of analysis must proceed from simple, general, abstract relations towards a particular whole and constitutes the scientifically correct procedure.'[54]

Summing up the issue of 'where to start?', we are faced with the following Marxian structure of how the direction of exploration is to begin:

He first states that analysis begins with simple, abstract categories over time – exchange, money, labour, value – and in the concrete presence of populations, states, commodities. Then, in 1859, he shifts his position and suggests that the direction should be not from the simple, general, abstract relations, but from the particular to the general, the exploration of complex, particular wholes. Finally, he proposes that bourgeois society represents the proper beginning and, within it, the commodity, as the first category in which wealth presents itself.[55]

In an overall sense, Marx's problem is not unlike that of Ricardo: the oscillation between the abstract and the concrete, the universal and the particular (the nation-state), the deductive and the empirical. While one of Ricardo's main concerns in Chapter VII of his *Principles* concerns the effect on the distribution of precious metals among the nations of the world of the improvement of manufactures owing to trade, Marx speaks of the effect of free trade and protectionism on Germany and of gold exports on France; he also reflects in a universal context on value, price, exchange, and labour. Like Ricardo ('free commerce, . . . by increasing the general mass of productions, . . . diffuses general benefit, and binds together, by one common tie of interest and intercourse, the universal society of nations throughout the civilised world . . .'[56]), Marx states that 'if the market, i.e. the sphere of exchange, expands, the production grows in quantity . . . [and] there is no exchange without a division of labour, natural or produced by history, where intensity and extent of exchange are determined by the development and organisation of production.'[57]

Trade and exchange are one of the 'moments' in the course of this evolution, as well as an essential part in the sphere of simple circulation, of extended circulation and of wealth-creating activity in a worldwide context. In this evolution, the individual simple categories (exchange, money, labour) need not have been equally developed, but they may have been well developed even in societies whose historical progress on the whole had been weak, for example Peru, in which co-operation and division of labour had existed without any trade or money; or others in which exchange with neighbouring countries had existed before exchange was taken up between the individuals in the same community.[58] In this evolution, commodity and commodity exchange become the historically specific, most developed, concrete forms in the most advanced mode of production, that of capitalism. In bourgeois society, money's full development is itself presupposed, while labour becomes the means of creating wealth in general: 'the most general abstraction in the midst of the richest possible concrete development . . . an immeasurably ancient relation valid in all forms of society . . . which achieves practical truth . . . as a category of the most modern society.'[59]

But, unlike Ricardo ('It is in this principle [of perfectly free commerce] and the peculiar powers bestowed by nature which determines that wine shall be made in France and Portugal and other goods shall be manufactured in England'[60]), Marx states that 'the conditions which promote production [and exchange] to a greater or lesser degree . . . would require investigations into the periodization of degrees of productivity in the development of individual peoples . . .'[61]

Moreover, Marx is also critical of John Stuart Mill's view on the distinctness of production from distribution: 'for the Economists' aim is to present production as distinct from distribution etc., as encased in eternal natural laws independent of history . . . '[62] Whereas Ricardo implies that the production of hardware and manufactures is 'natural' to England, Marx views trade and exchange in an evolving sense and as reflecting a development from the pastoral stage to the bourgeois stage, in which capital becomes the 'all-dominating economic power':

> In the succession of the economic categories, as in any other historical, social science, it must not be forgotten that the subject – here, modern bourgeois society – is always what is given, in the head as well as in reality, and that these categories therefore express the forms of being, the characteristics of existence, and often only individual sides of this specific society, this subject, and therefore this society by no means begins only at the point where one can speak of it *as such*; this holds *for science as well*.[63]

Marx's method involves all ages, all countries and all stages of economic development, but with emphasis on those countries which had evolved into the stage of bourgeois society. In this evolution, commodity and commodity exchange become the historically specific, most developed, concrete forms in the most advanced mode of production, that of capitalism; money's full development is itself presupposed in modern bourgeois society; and labour becomes in bourgeois society the means of creating wealth in general: 'the most general abstraction in the midst of the richest possible concrete development . . . an immeasurably ancient relation valid in all forms of society . . . which achieves practical truth . . . as a category of the most modern society.'[64]

4. FORCES OF PRODUCTION AND RELATIONS OF PRODUCTION

In this Section, Marx proposes to investigate the following topics: productive force, relations of production, relations of exchange in war and peace; the influence of international relations (note Marx's use of the term 'international') on derivative (that is inherited, not original) relations of production; the uneven development of material production relative to, for example, artistic development; how relations of production develop unevenly as legal relations. However, these topics remain unexplored in this Section (of only two and a half pages).

5. THE STRUCTURE OF THE BOURGEOIS ECONOMY

In this short section, Marx once again reviews his proposed deliberations concerning political economy and presents an outline in a manner slightly different from that in the Introduction. But the revised structure contains only five sections:

1. Exchange and money, and communities appear as already present and the first exchange appears as exchange of the superfluous only; trade does not have a hold over production and does not determine it: 'It is the available overflow of overall production which lies outside of the world of exchange values.'[65]
2. The internal structure of production (economic relations which are posited as relations of production).
3. The concentration of the whole in the state.
4. The international relations of production.

5. The world market, in which production is posited as the totality together with all its moments, but within which, at the same time, all contradictions come into play and crises ensue; the world market, then, forms the presupposition of the whole as well as its substratum.[66]

NOTES AND COMMENTS

1. *Grundrisse*, p. 83.
2. Ibid., pp. 83–4.
3. Ibid., p. 84.
4. Ibid.
5. Ibid.
6. Ibid., p. 85.
7. Ibid.
8. Ibid.
9. Ibid., p. 86
10. Ibid., p. 97.
11. Ibid., p. 87.
12. Ibid., p. 88.
13. Ibid.
14. Ibid., p. 95.
15. Ibid., p. 97.
16. Ibid., p. 96. According to the editors, 'moment' in Hegel's interpretation means 'element' or 'factor' in a system at rest; to which Marx adds the notion of 'a force, a mass, moving through time' (*Grundrisse*, p. 29).
17. Ibid., p. 96.
18. Ibid., p. 97.
19. Ibid., p. 98.
20. Ibid., p. 93.
21. Ibid., p. 94.
22. Ibid., p. 93.
23. Ibid., p. 94.
24. Ibid., p. 92.
25. Ibid., pp. 99–100.
26. Ibid., pp. 99.
27. Ibid.
28. Ibid., p. 86.
29. Ibid., p. 99.
30. Ibid., p. 86.
31. Ibid., p. 100.
32. Ibid., p. 86.
33. Ibid., p. 100.
34. Ibid., p. 101.
35. Ibid.
36. Ibid., p. 105.

37. Ibid., p. 101.
38. Ibid.
39. Ibid., p. 103.
40. Ibid.
41. Ibid.
42. Ibid.
43. Ibid., p. 104.
44. Ibid.
45. Ibid., p. 105.
46. Ibid.
47. Ibid., p. 108
48. Ibid., pp. 107–8.
49. MEW: *Marx-Engels Werke* (The Writings of Marx and Engels).
50. The editors' interpretation, in the Foreword to the *Grundrisse*.
51. *Grundrisse*, p. 38.
52. Ibid.
53. Ibid. Also in MEW, vol. XIII, p. 7.
54. Ibid., p. 38.
55. Ibid.
56. Ibid., p. 81.
57. Ibid., pp. 99–100.
58. Ibid., p. 102.
59. Ibid., pp. 104–5.
60. David Ricardo, *Principles of Political Economy and Taxation* (London; 1821), p. 137.
61. *Grundrisse*, p. 86.
62. Ibid., p. 87.
63. On p. 170, note 31, Marx's quote of Xenophon's view on natural advantage reads as follows:
    'And the pre-eminence of the land (Attica) is not only in the things that bloom and wither annually: she has other good things that last for ever. Nature has put her in her abundance of stone, etc. . . . . Again, there is land that yields no fruit if sown, and yet, when quarried, feeds many times the number it could support if it grew corn.' (Xenophon, *On Revenues*, Ch. 1, printed in Xenophon, *Scripta minora*, London, 1925, pp. 193–4.) Marx adds the following comment:
    Important to note that exchange between different tribes or peoples – and this, not private exchange, is its first form – begins when an uncivilized tribe sells (or is cheated out of) an excess product which is not the product of its labour, but the natural product of the ground and of the areas which it occupies.
    Marx's statement that a tribe may be 'cheated out' of a product which is not the fruit of its labour but abundant in its area and available as an excess suggests that things may have value even though they may not have been produced by labour – both use value and possibly exchange value to the 'cheaters' (why else would they go through the trouble of buying this product or even of cheating in order to get it?).
64. Ibid., p. 106.
65. Ibid., p. 227.
66. Ibid., pp. 226–8.

Part I
On Money

Introduction

Marx's treatment of money in the *Grundrisse* is contained in the following parts: Chapter On Money, which comprises Notebooks I and II (a total of 125 pages, written during October and November 1857), the Section 'Money as Capital' (twelve pages), and, interspersed with other subject matter, in the 'Miscellaneous' Section (a total of twenty-eight pages). According to Martin Nicolaus, the Chapter On Money deals with a process in which equal amounts of labour are exchanged, that is, with the law of equivalence.

Marx's twenty-three headings dealing with the subject matter of money comprise the following main topics, which will be treated in three concise chapters.

1. Gold exports and crises.
2. Relation between money metals and commodities. Convertibility. Depreciation.
3. Money, value, and price. Labour time as the general equivalent.
4. Money as a means of payment. The general equivalent, its *Preisverwirklichung* and *Verselbständigung* (price realization and attainment of its independence). The properties of money. Quantity of money in circulation and price levels. Money outside of circulation: accumulation, store of value. Money and interest. Money, trade and international trade.
5. Precious metals as money. Coin and world money:
   (1) the national character of coins v. their universal character;
   (2) money in its metallic being and accumulation of gold and silver;
   (3) double metallic standards;
   (4) money and international balances.

1 Money as Means of Payment

A. THE GENERAL EQUIVALENT, ITS *PREISVERWIRKLICHUNG* AND *VERSELBSTSTÄNDIGUNG*

Money is the universal equivalent which is generally acceptable: 'the form in which all commodities equate, compare, measure themselves'.[1] No money is needed if a commodity containing one hour's worth of labour time is exchanged for another with equal labour time (in which case, proposes Marx, the exchange is equivalent and the two commodities are convertible into each other because in such a situation exchange value = market value and real value = price).[2]

According to Marx, in a general sense, all commodities, as values, are equal and therefore exchangeable, and everything can be transformed into money, with certain repercussions:

Because money is the general equivalent, the general power of purchasing, everything can be bought, everything can be transformed into money. But it can be transformed into money only by being alienated [*alieniert*], by its owner divesting himself of it. Thus the so-called *inalienable, eternal* possessions, and the immovable, solid property relations corresponding to them, break down in the face of money. Furthermore, since money itself exists only in circulation, and exchanges in turn for articles of consumption, etc. – for values which may all ultimately be reduced to pure individual pleasures, it follows that everything is valuable only in so far as it exists for the individual . . . For, just as everything is alienable for money, everything is also obtainable by money.[3] . . . There are no absolute values, since, for money, value as such is relative. The involuntary alienation [*Entäußerung*] of feudal landed property develops with usury and with money.[4]

Money is a symbol, a measure, of value because it is labour time materialised in a specific substance and hence itself value. Prices express only the relations in which commodities are exchangeable for one another, the proportions in which they are exchanged for one

21

another. The reciprocal value of, say, potash to cocoa to iron bars is defined by their relative prices: 35 s/ton to 60 s/lb. to 145 s/ton, which means that undenominated units will suffice and that these ratios do not have to be expressed in terms of fixed quantities of gold or silver.[5] But once these proportions are given, commodities become commensurable magnitudes. If these different commodities are already expressed in terms of a particular measuring unit, this unit, the monetary unit, marks the proportion of their values. Through this unit, the various magnitudes of the commodities become measurable. However, this comparison is feasible only if the commodities as well as the measuring unit have one common denominator: the labour time relatively objectified in them: 'The labour time is the real unit, labour time posited as general.'[6]

The measuring unit, be it gold or silver, must itself be a certain quantity of a commodity in which a quantity of labour is objectified. This unit marks the proportion of the values of the commodities. This unit has different fractional parts of an ounce of gold and carries different names in different countries, but the exchange rate reduces all of them to the same unit of weight in gold or silver with a quantity of labour objectified in it. The value of this measuring unit itself is variable, since the same quantity of labour is not always contained in the same quantity of gold, but 'this variability is no obstacle in so far as money is regarded only as measure.'[7]

Why is it, asks Marx, that

> instead of saying this commodity is equal to one ounce of gold, one does not say directly it is equal to x labour time, objectified in an ounce of gold? Why is labour time, the substance and measure of value, not at the same time the measure of prices, or, in other words, why are prices and values different at all?[8]

In answering this question, he recalls that 'Proudhon's school believe it a great deed to demand that this identity be posited and that the price of commodities be expressed in labour time.'[9] But, suggests Marx, the coincidence of price and value presupposes the equality of demand and supply, the exchange solely of equivalents. However, even this presupposition is wrong since the exchange of capital for labour is a non-equivalent one, revealing

> at once that this demand is the negation of the entire foundation of the relations of production based on exchange value. . . . The

commodity in its unmediated presence as use value is not value, is not the adequate form of value; it must be equated to another object. Since commodities, as values, are objectified labour, the adequate value must therefore itself appear in the form of a specific thing, as a specific form of objectified labour.[10]

The values of gold and silver depend on the production time they cost and are expressed in different multiples of fractions of pound sterling, shillings, etc. But these numbers are always the expression of the proportion in which a specific quantity of labour is contained in an ounce of gold (or silver).[11]

Since money, as the measuring unit, must itself be a certain quantity of a commodity in which a quantity of labour is objectified, and since this quantity of labour may vary over time, Marx asks if money is an ideal measure, submitting that the theory of the ideal measure had first been brought up at the beginning of the eighteenth century and again in the second decade of the nineteenth:[12]

> Money is a measure only because it is labour time materialized in a specific substance, hence itself value, and, more particularly, because this specific materiality counts as its general objective one [*allgemeingegenständliche*], as the materiality of labour time as such, as distinct from its merely particular incarnations; hence because it is an equivalent . . . the names, pound, shillings, guinea, dollar, etc., which count as accounting units are not specific names for specific quantities of gold, silver, etc., but merely arbitrary points of comparison which do not themselves express value, no definite quantity of objectified labour time. Hence the whole nonsense about fixing the price of gold and silver – price understood here as the name by which fractional parts are called. An ounce of gold now divided into £3, 17sh, 10d. This is called fixing the price; . . . Now what does this, our 'fixed price of an ounce' of gold, mean? Nothing other than that a certain aliquot part of an ounce is called pence, a certain multiple of this pennyweight of gold a shilling, and a certain multiple of this shillingweight of gold a pound? . . . That, in England, a monetary coin expressed in gold is more than a monetary coin, and in other countries, less? It would be interesting to know what this noble spirit[13] imagines the exchange rate to be?[14]

Even though, in a general sense, all commodities, as values, are equal and therefore exchangeable, and everything can be transformed into money, this is not so with particular commodities: each commodity reflects its own particular properties, its own different labour times. To make each commodity exchangeable, it must first be translated into the form of a universal equivalent which is generally acceptable – money. Payment in money is required in order to make up the imbalance between two commodities if the value of one prevails over that of the other: 'In order to cover the excess of one value over another in exchange, in order to liquidate the balance, the crudest barter, just as with international trade today, requires payment in money.'[15]

Overall, in Marx's view, money represents an exchange value with its own separate existence: money is wanted because of 'its exchange value, whereas the commodities are demanded because of their natural properties, because of the needs for which they are the desired object.'[16]

B. THE PROPERTIES OF MONEY

Marx declares money to have the following properties:

1. Money in circulation:
   (1) *Zahlungsmittel*: measure of the exchange value of commodities, of commodity exchange; means of payment;
   (2) *Tauschmittel*: medium of exchange;
   (3) representative of commodities and hence object of contracts;
   (4) general commodity alongside particular commodities;[17]
   (5) the quantity of money in circulation relates to price levels.

The properties of money in circulation arise from money's existence as exchange value separated from the commodities themselves and itself objectified.[18]

2. Money outside of circulation:
   (1) accumulation;
   (2) store of value.

In this particular role, money emerges 'independent from circulation',[19] even though it appears in itself as a result of circulation. It can be transformed into luxury articles and jewellery, it can be accumulated to form a treasure, it can be stockpiled. But this property already latently contains its quality as capital; it is negated only as a medium of exchange.[20]

1. Money in circulation

(1) Zahlungsmittel (means of payment)

Zahlungsmittel and *Tauschmittel* constitute money's dual character. As *Zahlungsmittel*, money measures the exchange value of commodities. The property of money as *Zahlungsmittel* pertains to circulation proper (money for commodities rather than barter trade or payment in kind):[21]

> Money is the commodity (gold or silver) in which the exchange value of another is expressed; as such, it serves as the measure of the exchange value of the other commodity or, speaking in general terms, of all commodities: if a pound of cotton is worth 8d, then it is worth $\frac{1}{116}$ oz. of gold, which is contained in 8d (at the price of gold of 3£, 17s, 7d, which is its labour-time equivalent). . . . As a measure, money is not expressed as a relation, not as exchange value, but as the natural quantity of a certain material, a natural weight-fraction of gold or silver. . . . Money as *Zahlungsmittel*, as measure, as element of price determination, . . . is required only as an imagined unit once the exchange value of an ounce of gold compared to any one commodity has been determined; its actual presence is superfluous, along with, even more so, its available quantity; as an indicator of value the amount of which exists in a country is irrelevant. . . . [22]

(2) Tauschmittel (medium of exchange)

Money is an instrument, a vehicle, of circulation and, as the medium of exchange, it mediates the exchange of commodities. Monetary turnover and commodity circulation form a two-in-one circular flow: M-C-C-M, the form of circulation in which money appears as an end-in-itself,[23] and C-M-M-C, in which money appears as a pure medium of exchange.[24] Marx terms the former '*Warenzirkulation*' and the latter '*Geldzirkulation*'. As a flow, monetary turnover is the opposite of commodity circulation, but these two flows determine one another.[25]

Marx devotes some time to the question of monetary turnover, seeking to find out the law which determines it. He starts out with emphasis on three aspects: (a) the form of the turnover itself; (b) the quantity of money in circulation; and (c) the velocity of its circulation.[26] He proposes that, overall, 'the circulation of commodities is the original precondition of the circulation of money, even though in some circumstances the circulation of commodities is independent of monetary turnover.'[27] But both circulations are determined by the 'overall character of the mode of production':[28]

> The overall character of the mode of production will determine them both, and will determine the circulation of commodities more directly. The mass of persons engaged in exchange (population): their distribution between the town and the country; the absolute quantity of commodities, of products and agencies of production; the relative mass of commodities which enter into circulation; the development of the means of communication and transport, in the double sense of determining not only the sphere of those who are in exchange, in contact, but also the speed with which the raw material reaches the producer and the product the consumer; finally the development of industry, e.g. spinning, weaving, dyeing, etc., and hence makes superfluous a series of intermediate exchanges. The circulation of commodities is the original precondition of the circulation of money. To what extent the latter then reacts back on the circulation of commodities remains to be seen.
> The first task is firmly to establish the general concept of circulation or of turnover. But first let us note that what is circulated by money is exchange value, hence prices. . . . Thus, actually, the concept of price has to be developed before that of circulation.[29]

What money circulates is exchange value (products of labour); therefore circulation is the process in which commodities are transformed into prices [*Preisrealisierung*].[30] In simple circulation individual interaction reflects self-interest, the reciprocal satisfaction of needs, a situation in which the exchange is between equals (that is, equivalent), since the exchangeable commodity is of one's own labour.[31]

The relation between exchange value, money, and price, Marx views as follows:

(a) Exchange value represents embodied labour time; every exchange value is a particular quantity, a quantitatively different and specific exchange value:

The exchange value of the commodity expresses the totality of the quantitative relations in which all other commodities can be exchanged for it, determined by the unequal quantities of the same which can be produced in the same labour time.[32]

(b) Every exchange value is equal to a particular quantity of money because it expresses price as a specific quantity of money: 'Exchange value expressed as money, i.e., equated with money, is price.'[33]

(c) Positing that exchange values of commodities are prices, commodities are transformed into their monetary expression.[34] Marx labels this process 'the ideal transformation of commodities into money . . .',[35] but he claims that this process is independent of the mass of 'real money, . . . the quantity of really available money being altogether a matter of indifference.'[36]

(3) Money as a representative commodity

Even though it is a general commodity, money is also a particular commodity. As such it comes under the laws of demand and supply. The price of money is brought down by a general demand for commodities against money. However, an equivalent increase in the cost of production (of the exchange value) of gold would leave the prices (that is, the exchange value expressed in money) of the other commodities unchanged.[37]

Is money a commodity or a medium of exchange, asks Marx? Essentially, he argues, it is both, even though followers of the monetary system and partly of the protectionist system adhere to the first and the modern economists to the second view.[38]

As a medium of exchange, is money productive or 'non-productive'?[39] In answering, Marx first sides with Adam Smith: money is not productive if the frame of reference is a particular branch of production; but then he speaks in support of Ferrier, Smith's opponent: money is productive because it creates values, because the money relation itself is a relation of production, and finally because, as capital, money itself is an instrument of production.[40]

(4) Quantity of money in circulation and price levels

Marx devotes particular attention to the question of the relation between the quantity of money in circulation and price levels, in his reflections concerning the historical treatment of this question and in his own analysis of this complex issue.

He commences his treatment by affirming Adam Smith's statement that 'labour is the real and money the nominal measure of value'.[41] Then he reviews the assertion of the 'currency people' (Fullarton *et al.*) and their claim that the value of currency depends on its quantity:

> If the value of the currency is given, and prices and the mass of transactions likewise (as well as the velocity of circulation), then of course only a *specific quantity* can circulate. Given prices and the mass of transactions as well as the velocity of circulation, then this quantity depends exclusively on the *value* of the currency. Given this value and the velocity of circulation, it depends exclusively on prices and on the mass of transactions. In this way is the quantity determined. If, however, the money in circulation is representative money – mere value-symbols – then it depends on the standard they represent what quantity of them can circulate. From this it has been wrongly concluded that quantity alone determines its value. For example, paper chits representing pounds cannot circulate in the same quantity as those which represent shillings.[42]

He then makes reference to James Mill's assertion concerning the rise or fall in the value of money:

> Whenever the *value of money* has experienced a rise or fall, and whenever the quantity of commodities for which it could be exchanged, and the movement of circulation, remained the same, this change must have had as cause a relative increase or diminution of money, and can be ascribed to no other cause . . . The *costs* of production govern the value of gold and silver, like that of all other products.[43]

Marx is severely critical of James Mill's viewpoint, declaring that it 'represents the most formal development of the false theory of prices. . . . The insipidness of this reasoning is quite evident.'[44] In support of this critical view Marx develops five points of refutation, of which the two major ones are presented here, for their pertinence. First of all, he submits, Mill's confusion is clearly shown in his thesis that the value of money diminishes or increases with 'every alteration in the movement of circulation'. Whether one pound sterling circulates once or ten times a day, in each exchange it expresses an equivalent for the commodity, exchanges for the same value in commodities. Its own value remains the same in every exchange, and is hence altered neither by slower nor by rapid circulation. The mass of the circulating money is altered; but neither the value of the commodity, nor the value of the money. In opposition to this view, Marx agrees with Hubbard's[45] proposition: that 'prices must fall because commodities are estimated as being worth so many ounces of gold, and the amount of gold in this country is diminished'.[46]

Secondly, Mill himself admits that with free circulation of money, the value of money is determined by its cost of production – that is, according to his own admission, by the labour time contained in it.[47]

In support of his critique of James Mill, Marx invokes David Ricardo, who himself is 'making a shambles of Mill's viewpoint'.[48] According to Ricardo, 'the amount of notes in circulation depends . . . on the amount required for the circulation in the country, and this is governed by the *value* of the standard, the amount of payments, and the economy applied to accomplish them.'[49]

Furthermore, Marx also recalls Steuart's[50] views on the pronouncements of Hume, Montesquieu, and Locke's three theses concerning the relation of prices and the mass of the circulating medium. According to their doctrine: (a) prices of commodities are proportionate to the mass of money in the country; (b) the coin and current money of a country is representative of its labour and commodities, so that the more or less representation, the more or less quantity of the thing represented goes to the same quantity of it; and (c) an increase in commodities makes them cheaper; an increase in money increases their value.[51]

In his own analytical assessment of this question, Marx labels 'simplistic' the proposition that prices are determined by the quantity of money, since the issue is more complex than this simple proposition implies:

> The quantity of money which is required, then, for circulation is determined initially by the level of the prices of the commodities thrown into circulation. The sum total of these prices, however, is determined *firstly*: by the prices of individual commodities;[52] secondly, by the quantity of commodities at given prices which enter into circulation . . .[53] Thirdly, by . . . the rapidity with which money circulates.[54]

This much is clear, that prices are not high or low because much or little money circulates, but that much or little money circulates because prices are high or low; and, further, that the velocity of the circulating money does not depend on its quantity, but that the quantity of the circulating medium depends on its velocity (heavy payments are not counted but weighed; through this the time necessary is shortened).[55]

Moreover, Marx suggests that this problem involves several issues:

First, in the actual sale, money is only the measure of the price of the commodity; the determination of prices has nothing to do with the actual sale because changes in commodity prices and in commodity quantities in circulation will change the total sum of prices, whereas the velocity of the medium of circulation is determined by 'circumstances independent of itself'.[56]

Secondly, velocity is important, since 'all commodities can fetch a thousand times more money than is in the world if every piece of money were to circulate a thousand times.'[57]

Thirdly, circulation itself may be induced to rise in the following manner: by the increase in the amount of commodities, with prices remaining the same; by the increase in commodity prices, with the amounts remaining unchanged; or by both of these.[58]

Fourthly, with the proposition that prices regulate the quantity of currency and not that the quantity of currency regulates prices – or in other words that trade regulates currency (that is, the quantity of the medium of circulation) and currency does not regulate trade – it is supposed that price is only value translated into another language. But the presupposition is value, and value as determined by labour time. It is clear, therefore, that this law is not equally applicable to price fluctuations in all epochs.

Fifthly, from the general law that the total price of commodities in circulation determines the mass of the circulating medium at a given stage of the velocity of circulation, it follows that at a given stage of growth of the values thrown into circulation, the more precious metal – the metal of greater specific value; that is, which contains more labour time in a smaller amount – takes the place of the less precious as the predominant medium of circulation: for example, the same aggregate sum of prices can be circulated with fourteen times as few gold coins as silver coins. But copper or even iron coin as predominant medium of circulation supposes weak circulation.[59] A distinction must therefore be made between coins used for larger payments which can pass only at their intrinsic worth (for example gold coins as medium of exchange) and subsidiary currency (for example silver and copper markers, which are not minted in the relation of the value of their substance to the value of gold – that is to say, they appear only as money-symbol, even though they may still be a relatively valuable substance).

The gold coin, as the medium of circulation, is full-bodied money, the equivalent, which realises prices and accumulates as independent value. But subsidiary mediums of exchange whose intrinsic worth is much less than the equivalent can never solidify as realisation of price and must therefore be rendered acceptable in payment, by law. Their relative share is very small because the small retail traffic of everyday life requires exchange on a very diminutive scale, a scale which gold could not serve because it would have to be divided into excessively small fractions if it is to serve as the equivalent of the commodities traded in this retail traffic. The value of the subsidiary currency is something that exists outside of itself; its quantity can be issued only such as to meet the demand for the small retail trade; it cannot therefore accumulate. Its nominal value can never be compared with its intrinsic value. In this case, it is not the quantity of circulating medium that determines prices but prices that determine the quantity of this circulating medium. If too much circulating medium were put into circulation (in relation to that required by circulation) it would be depreciated and its value would fall.[60]

Finally, the value of the medium of circulation will fall if there are no outlets which will permit circulation to shed the superfluous quantity – that is to say, if it cannot change from its form as superfluous quantity into the form of value for itself. However, suggests Marx, apart from artificial hindrances, prohibition of melting down, prohibition of export, and so on, this can happen only if the circulating medium is merely a symbol and does not itself possess a real value corresponding to its nominal value, and hence cannot make the transition from the form of circulating medium into that of the commodity in general, 'and shed its stamp; if it is imprisoned in its existence as coin'.[61]

Marx ties in the quantity of money required for circulation with (a) the short run and (b) the longer run. In the short run a certain mass of payments must be made simultaneously, and the quantity of money required for this circulation is determined by 'the sum total which starts from the simultaneous points of departure in circulation, and by the velocity with which it runs its course. . . . '[62] In the longer run, circulation is based on demand which can be paid for in money;[63] however, the quantity of the circulating medium is exposed to many ebbs and floods. These flows make for an average level of the quantity of money in circulation because 'the permanent changes are only very gradual, and take place only over longer periods.'[64]

What happens, inquires Marx, if the price of a commodity cannot be realised (because the demand is not backed by money)? In this case, the commodity 'cannot be transferred into money; it appears devalued, de-priced.'[65]

2. Money outside of circulation

(1) Accumulation and hoarding; (2) Store of value

In Marx's reflections concerning accumulation, he considers the role of money as instrument of production.[66]

He defines accumulation as 'essentially a process which takes place in time'.[67] The accumulation motive is due to 'self-denial, . . . self-sacrifice, . . . economy and frugality . . .'.[68] But what is important is that 'accumulation is a form . . . antithetical to circulation.'[69]

Marx is concerned about the effects of accumulation. The accumulation of goods and services is not yet the accumulation of capital, even though it has that appearance. To lead to an accumulation of capital, the accumulation of goods and services would have to be re-entered into circulation as a means of accumulation.[70]

Even though it is the result of circulation, accumulation involves money – that money which takes on an independent existence outside of circulation, as treasure, as goods and services, as luxury articles. Accumulation 'already latently contains the quality of money as capital.'[71]

As store of value, money manifests the property of 'wealth': that is, of satisfying every need, money being the embodied form of wealth, the general material representative of wealth, 'an intense object of desire, of greed'.[72]

Storing up money is an expression of the drive to wealth, but its by-product is safety. Gold and silver are particularly suitable for accumulation because they are enduring, whereas the other commodities are perishable.[73] Metals are also accumulated because of their greater rarity as well as for their unique character as instruments of production *par excellence*. It is a treasure which 'neither rust nor moths eat up':[74]

The accumulation of gold and silver, of money, is the first historic appearance of the gathering-together of capital and the first great means thereto; but, as such, it is not yet accumulation of capital. For that, the re-entry of what has been accumulated into circulation would itself have to be posited as the moment and the means of accumulation.[75]

The piling up of gold and silver had been going on since Antiquity, as priestly and royal privilege, to display overabundance, but later it becomes political. As means of general wealth, accumulation is deemed to make one richer the more of such wealth one possesses. However, accumulation also means withdrawing money from circulation, the not using of money as money, the antithesis between the real needs of production and the supremacy of money.[76]

The seriousness of Marx's concern about accumulation is evidenced by his sarcastic reference to the Mercantilists and by his statement that to accumulate money does not mean to increase it:

> when one considers the anxiety involved in the doctrine of money in particular, and the feverish fear with which, in practice, the inflow and the outflow of gold and silver are watched in times of crisis, then it is evident that the aspect of money which the followers of the Monetary and Mercantilist System conceived in an artless one-sidedness is still to be taken seriously, not only in the mind, but as a real economic category.[77]
> The notion that to accumulate is to increase it, . . . turns out again to be false. If the other riches do not also accumulate, then it loses its value in the measure in which it is accumulated.[78]

In fact, argues Marx, the independence of accumulated money is a 'mere semblance'.[79] This is so because its value depends both on demand and supply, and on variations in its specific costs of production. 'An absolutely secure wealth, . . . it is something completely external to me, the absolutely insecure, which can be separated from me by any accident.'[80]

However, Marx points out another aspect of the hoarding principle: that in which money functions as independent value, apart from the striking form in which it appears necessary as one moment of exchange resting on money circulation. This is so since everyone needs, besides his own commodity, the medial quantity, a certain proportion of the 'general commodity'.[81]

(3) Money and interest

Marx ties in money with interest when he reflects on the evolution of money wealth v. agricultural wealth. There are two historic forms of interest: (1) usury, in the pre-bourgeois forms of production (that is, the stage in which capital does not yet seize possession of production, small-scale agriculture or handicrafts, where capital is subsumed under the individual workers or families of workers); (2) lending of capital to wealth which is engaged in consumption, whereby the income – and often the land, too – 'of the landed proprietors accumulates and becomes capitalized in the pockets of the usurer.'[82]

Marx reopens the question of the origin of interest and of the linkage between interest and profit at the end of the *Grundrisse*, in response to the propositions of Proudhon, McCulloch, Ramsay, *et al.* To start with, he states:

> In regard to interest, two things are to be examined: *Firstly*, the division of *profit* into interest and profit. (As the unity of both of these the English call it *gross profit*). The difference becomes perceptible as soon as a class of monied capitalists comes to confront a class of industrial capitalists. *Secondly*: *Capital* itself becomes a commodity, or the commodity (money) sold as capital. Thus it is said e.g., that capital, like any other commodity, varies in price according to demand and supply. Then these determine the rate of interest.[83]

The form of interest is older than the form of profit. Historically, the form of industrial profit arises only after capital no longer appears alongside the independent worker. Originally, profit appears determined by interest. But in the bourgeois economy interest is determined by profit, and profit must be large enough to allow for payment of interest. Occasionally, interest rates charged to workers are so high that the worker ends up being a debtor even after restituting the capital.[84] How did profit first arise? In Marx's view:

> Interest must have become so depressed that a part of the surplus gain could achieve independence as profit . . . The important thing is that both interest and profit express relations of *capital*. As a particular form, interest-bearing capital stands opposite, not labour, but rather opposite profit-bearing capital.[85]

Profit-bearing capital is the real capital; interest-bearing capital is in turn the purely abstract form of profit-bearing capital.[86] Money is the form of realised capital plus its realised surplus value. That value is realised and measured in money. Therefore, interest as well as profit express themselves in money. When one party cedes his commodity and the other party makes his payment only later, the need for money for this purpose constitutes a chief historic source of interest.[87]

NOTES AND COMMENTS

1. *Grundrisse*, p. 142.
2. Ibid., p. 140.
3. Ibid., pp. 838–9.
4. Ibid., p. 836.
5. Ibid., pp. 791–2.
6. Ibid., p. 794.
7. Ibid., p. 793.
8. Ibid., p. 794.
9. Ibid.
10. Ibid., p. 795.
11. Ibid., p. 796. In Marx's view, confusion surrounds the question whether giving names to specified and unchangeable fractional parts of the money substance amounts to assigning to money the role of a unit of measure – i.e. denominating it – or to fixing the price of money. Clearly, the latter had to do with the mass of the circulating medium and the amount of labour time contained in the metal as well as the mass of commodities in circulation.
12. Ibid., pp. 834–9. According to Marx, the issue both times was whether or not debts of state, and other debts, contracted in depreciated money, should be acknowledged and paid back in full-valued money. Marx assesses specifically the cause and effects of the depreciation of the pound sterling (the lowering of its gold content) and the battle of words between Locke and Lowndes concerning the state debt contracted, in depreciated money, during the years 1688 to 1695 (depreciated because the full-weighted money had been melted down and the lightweight remained in circulation). On pp. 834–9 Marx reviews the evolution of Roman money, including the reduction of the silver content in Roman coins and the price ratio between silver and copper; he also reviews the evolution of the various currencies in medieval Europe.
13. Marx refers here to a letter to the editor of *The Economist*, 13 March 1858.
14. *Grundrisse*, pp. 791–4.
15. Ibid., pp. 142–3. We must note here that Marx's statement about the

possibility of a trade imbalance which can be rectified only by payment in money, even if the trade is accounted for by the labour theory of value, goes well beyond Ricardo's assumption that the value of imports and the value of exports (both expressed in terms of labour-day units) would balance out. This proposition by Marx raises an interesting question: does a negative trade balance imply that non-equivalent exchange must have taken place, and, if so, will a subsequent transfer of funds, in payment for the imbalance, render the trade transaction ex-post 'equivalent'?

16. Ibid., p. 147.
17. Ibid., p. 146.
18. The editors' translation of '*vergegenständlicht*' is 'objectified', a poor translation which does not reveal the depth and intensity of the interaction, during the production process, of labour and capital in transforming the component inputs into a final product which has use value and will enter circulation as exchange value.
19. *Grundrisse*, p. 216.
20. Ibid., pp. 216, 508.
21. Ibid., p. 187.
22. Ibid., pp. 203–7.
23. Ibid., p. 215.
24. Ibid., p. 208.
25. Ibid., p. 186.
26. Ibid.
27. Ibid., p. 187.
28. Ibid.
29. Ibid.
30. Ibid.
31. Ibid., pp. 236–7.
32. Ibid., p. 188.
33. Ibid.
34. Ibid., p. 190.
35. Ibid., p. 191.
36. Ibid.
37. Ibid., p. 200.
38. Ibid., p. 214.
39. Ibid., p. 215.
40. Ibid., p. 216.
41. Ibid., p. 864.
42. bid., p. 878.
43. Ibid., p. 868.
44. Ibid.
45. Quoted from G.J. Hubbard, *The Currency and the Country*, p. 44.
46. *Grundrisse*, p. 869.
47. Ibid., p. 870.
48. Ibid.
49. Ibid.
50. Steuart, Sir James, *An Inquiry into the Principles of Political Economy* (Dublin, 1770), vol. I, pp. 166–203.

51. *Grundrisse*, p. 871.
52. Let us recall Marx's definition of circulation: *Vergegenständlichung* of exchange values; the goods which enter into circulation being 'produced as exchange values, not as immediate use values' (p. 198).
53. Marx adds that the sum total of the commodity prices is determined by the prices of the individual commodities and by the quantity of commodities at given prices which enter into circulation (p. 194).
54. Velocity is a 'negative moment; it substitutes for quantity' (p. 194).
55. Ibid., p. 195.
56. Marx does not explain this statement, except to emphasise that the quantity of mediums of circulation must be capable of expanding and contracting (p. 213).
57. Ibid.
58. Ibid., p. 814.
59. Ibid., p. 810.
60. Ibid., pp. 811–13.
61. Ibid., p. 813.
62. Ibid., p. 195.
63. Ibid., p. 198. Marx does not tie in this statement with his earlier one concerning 'average value of a period of time' (p. 137). But clearly, if such averaging does take place (presumably in the longer run), then the average quantity of money required for circulation (including its average velocity) should equal the sum of the average market values and will equal the sum of real values. See p. 137.
64. Ibid., p. 195. Marx does not illustrate what he means by 'permanent changes'.
65. Ibid., p. 198.
66. In his German rendition, Marx uses both *Anhäufung* and *Akkumulation* in his discussion of the economic significance of pulling money out of circulation.
67. *Grundrisse*, p. 231.
68. Ibid., p. 232.
69. Ibid., p. 231.
70. Ibid., p. 232.
71. Ibid., p. 216.
72. Ibid., p. 225.
73. Ibid., p. 231.
74. Ibid.
75. Ibid., p. 233.
76. Ibid., pp. 231–3.
77. Ibid., p. 232.
78. Ibid., p. 234.
79. Ibid.
80. Ibid.
81. Ibid., p. 816.
82. Ibid., p. 854.
83. Ibid., p. 851.
84. 'Proudhon grasps neither how profit, nor, therefore, how interest, arises from the laws of the exchange of values. . . . The good fellow does not

understand that the whole point is that value is exchanged for labour, according to the law of values; that, hence, to abolish interest, he would have to abolish capital itself, the mode of production founded on exchange value, hence wage labour as well' (p. 844).

'The real difference between profit and interest exists as the difference between the moneyed class of capitalists and the industrial class of capitalists' (p. 852).

85. Ibid., p. 852–3
86. Ibid., p. 878. In this section of the *Grundrisse*, Marx quotes and paraphrases a number of writers on interest, profit, and money, but leaves most of them without a comment of his own unless expressing an opposing or critical viewpoint. The following two paraphrases are indicative of his pattern of reasoning:

(1) From an article in *The Economist* concerning rate of interest: 'The rate of interest depends on (a) the rate of profit; (b) the proportion in which the entire profit is divided between lender and borrower. . . . Abundance or scarcity of the precious metals, the high or low scale of general prices prevailing, determines only whether a greater or lesser amount of money will be required in effecting the exchanges between borrowers and lenders, as well as every other species of exchange . . .' (p. 862).

(2) From another article in *The Economist*: 'Interest – the consideration given for the loan of money. If the money borrowed is for the purpose of procuring capital, then the consideration given is for the use of capital (raw materials, labour, merchandise, etc.), which it obtains. If borrowed for the purpose of discharging a debt, for paying for capital previously obtained and used, then the consideration given is for the use of money itself, and in this respect interest and discount are similar. Discount is solely the remuneration for money itself, for converting money into real money; and bills are discounted for the purpose of obtaining money of a more convenient denomination. . . . The main object however in discounting depends mainly upon the supply and demand of legal tender money. . . . The rate of interest depends mainly on the demand and supply of capital, and the rate of discount entirely on the supply and demand of money' (p. 850).

87. Ibid., p. 854. Marx promises to undertake the study of money, discount, loans, and credit – on another occasion.

2 Money, Value and Price. Labour Time as the General Equivalent

Marx's subsequent lengthy elaboration concerning the issue of the replacement of metal money by chit money is introduced by yet another review of the 'contradiction' between value and price, a discourse in which he includes several references to 'universal currency'.

He defines value and price as follows:

> The *value* (the real exchange value) of all commodities (labour included) is determined by their cost of production, in other words by the labour time required to produce them. Their *price* is this exchange value of theirs, expressed in money. [1]

But Marx emphasises specifically that the value of commodities as determined by labour time is only their *average* value over a period of time (for example the price of coffee over twenty-five years), the *median price average* (Marx's terminology, emphasis added).[2] The average value – the median price average – represents 'the centre of oscillation around which the market value moves up and down . . . and market value equates itself with real value by means of constant oscillations . . .'.[3]

Price is distinguished from value:

> Price is distinguished from value . . . the two are constantly different and never balance out, or balance only coincidentally and exceptionally. The price of a commodity constantly stands above or below the value of the commodity, and the value of the commodity itself exists only in this up-and-down movement of commodity prices. Supply and demand constantly determine the prices of commodities; never balance, or only coincidentally, but the cost of production, for its part, determines the oscillations of supply and demand.[4]

Real value is different from market value:

> The *value* (the real exchange value) of all commodities (labour
> included) is determined by their cost of production, in other words
> by the labour time required to produce them. Their *price* is this
> exchange value of theirs, expressed in money. . . . *Price* therefore
> is distinguished from *value* not only as the nominal from the real.[5]

> By annulling the *nominal difference* between real value and market
> value, between exchange value and price . . . [the time-chitters]
> also remove the real difference and contradiction between price
> and value.[6]

Marx is concerned about these distinctions because – wrongly, in his
view – the socialist time-chitters believed that the replacement of
metal money (and of paper or fiat money denominated in metal
money) by labour money, denominated in labour time, would equate
the real value (the exchange value) of commodities with their nominal value (= price, that is, money value), rendering equal real value
and nominal value, value and price. He disagrees:

> the value of commodities as determined by labour time is only their
> *average value* . . . an external abstraction if it is calculated out as
> the average figure of an epoch . . . but real if it is at the same time
> recognized as the driving force and the moving principle of the
> oscillations which commodity prices run through during a given
> epoch.[7]

The time-chitters' proposal was based on an 'illusion', and their
reasoning is wrong. Average labour time being the amount of labour
time objectified [*vergegenständlicht*] in a commodity, it expresses the
real value of a commodity. In comparison, actual labour time finds its
expression in market value (= price). Therefore, the exchange of
average labour time for actual labour time amounts to non-
equivalence because the 'amount of labour time objectified in a
commodity will never command a quantity of labour equal to itself
but will command more or less.'[8] This conclusion applies to time-chits
as well: the constant depreciation of the value of commodities, over
longer periods, in relation to time-chits is due to the increasing
productivity of labour incorporated in these commodities and is
tantamount to the appreciation of time-chits, the accumulated ones

as well as the newly issued ones. In consequence, instead of being the general equivalent – which they are meant to be as the medium of circulation – the time-chits are in fact rendered inconvertible[9] because the labour of which the time-chit is representative would be exchanged sometimes against more and sometimes against less labour contained in the commodities just produced: that is, there would be no equivalence between the real value and the market (nominal) value:

> by annulling the *nominal difference* between real value and market value, between exchange value and price – that is, by expressing value in units of labour time instead of in a given objectification of labour time, say gold and silver – that in so doing they also remove the real difference and contradiction between price and value. Given this illusory assumption it is self-evident that the mere introduction of time-chits does away with all crises, all faults of bourgeois production. The money price of commodities = their real value; demand = supply; production = consumption; money is simultaneously abolished and preserved, the labour time of which the commodity is the product, which is materialized in the commodity, would need only to be measured in order to create a corresponding mirror-image in the form of a value-symbol, money, time-chits. In this way every commodity would be directly transformed into money; and gold and silver, for their part, would be demoted to the rank of all other commodities.[10]

Marx's lengthy and tedious elaboration concerning the replacement of metal money by chit money may be summed up as follows:

(1) gold and silver money, once produced, contains in itself a specific amount of labour time, as an expression of a particular level of labour productivity existing when that quantity of gold was produced; this amount of labour time defines the 'value', the real exchange value, of the particular amount of gold contained in this coin, which is its 'intrinsic' value;

(2) this money, defined in terms of the labour time necessary to produce the metal contained in it, serves as the 'general equivalent' and is convertible for commodities produced under conditions of the same level of labour-time productivity;

(3) to assure full convertibility and equivalence, over time, labour-time productivity would have to be held constant ('stationary'), then

the exchange would take place under conditions of 'equivalence': a specific amount of labour time contained in the quantity of gold incorporated into the gold coin in exchange for an equivalent amount of labour time contained in the commodity exchanged for this coin;

(4) however, the law of the rising productivity of labour time disturbs this relationship and leads to a contradiction between exchange value and price, and makes for inconvertibility between real value and market value (between exchange value and price);[11]

(5) since labour time is the value-determining element ('the value of commodities as determined by labour time is only their average value, as the average figure of an epoch . . . '[12]) and since (day-to-day) price is not equal to value, it follows that labour time cannot be 'the element in which prices are expressed, because labour time would then have to express itself simultaneously as the determining and the non-determining element, as the equivalent and the non-equivalent of itself';[13] this is so because labour time as the measure of value exists only as an ideal, whereas price as distinct form of value is necessarily money price.

(6) Price is the money value of commodities. Money has the quality of being always exchangeable for what it measures, and the quantity required for the purpose of exchange must vary, of course, according to the quantity of property to be exchanged.[14] There is a contradiction between money as measure and equivalent, on the one side, and as medium of exchange, on the other. If, in the course of the latter, a loss of metallic weight is incurred (through abrasion), circulation might be hampered if this loss is questioned.[15] In English law, coins cannot be passed as current gold sovereigns if they are deficient in weight.[16]

NOTES AND COMMENTS

1. *Grundrisse*, p. 137.
2. Ibid.
3. Ibid.
4. Ibid., p. 138.
5. Ibid., p. 137.
6. Ibid., p. 136.
7. Ibid., p. 137.
8. Ibid., p. 139.
9. Ibid. Let us recall Marx's interpretation of the term 'convertibility': an exchange only at the original, real, exchange value, based on labour time under conditions of a 'stationary labour-time productivity'(p. 139).

10. Ibid., p. 138.
11. Ibid., p. 139.
12. Ibid., p. 137.
13. Ibid., p. 140.
14. Ibid., p. 876. Marx assigns this particular view to J.G. Hubbard, *The Currency and the Country* (London, 1843), p. 33.
15. Ibid., p. 877.
16. Ibid., p. 878.

3 Money as World Money

1. PRECIOUS METALS AS MONEY. COIN AND WORLD MONEY. MONEY AND TRADE AND INTERNATIONAL TRADE.

Throughout his treatment of money and its role, Marx intersperses comments on gold and silver and their use as a money commodity, as medium of exchange, as object of accumulation, and as the ultimate means of international payment. Precious metals perform the money function particularly well because they are durable, divisible, easily transportable; also because they represent great exchange value for their size. In addition, and unlike copper (an early form of metal money), precious metals are inoxidisable and scarce.[1]

The intrinsic value of gold, its real exchange value, is the amount of labour time contained, at that particular level of labour productivity, in that quantity of gold in the gold coin. As money, gold coin reflects the labour time necessary to produce it; as the general equivalent, this coin is convertible for commodities produced under conditions of the same level of labour productivity.[2]

Marx then looks closer at scarcity, 'one of the geological properties which is common to all the precious metals':

Rarity (apart from supply and demand) is an element of value in so far as its opposite, the non-rare as such, the negation of rarity, the elemental, has no value because it does not appear as the result of production. In the original definition of value, that which is most independent of conscious, voluntary production is the most valuable, assuming the existence of demand. Common pebbles have no value, relatively speaking, because they are to be had *without production* (even if the latter consists only of searching). For something to become an object of exchange, to have exchange value, it must not be available to everyone without the mediation of exchange; it must not appear in such an elemental form as to be common property. To this extent, rarity is an element of exchange value and hence this property of the precious metal is of importance, even apart from its further relation to supply and demand.[3]

A rapidly increasing supply of gold and silver will not cause their sudden depreciation because the market for them expands rapidly even if their cost of production or their value does not proportionately increase.[4]

Contrary to the claim by many economists, the consumption of gold and silver is not inversely proportional to their costs of production (as is the consumption of other commodities), but they are 'consumed more than in proportion as wealth in general increases'.[5]

Marx attributes changes in the relative values of gold and silver to the increasingly greater scarcity of gold, on the one hand, and to the more abundant and cheaper labour in silver production, on the other. He goes through historical trends in gold/silver prices (mentioning specifically the exchange of 13 gold for one silver in Ancient Persia, of one livre of gold for 10 livres of silver at Xenophon's time and for 19 livres of silver in 422 A.D., and of one livre of gold to 14 and 15 livres of silver in the fifteenth century). He draws the following conclusion: 'The value relation between the different metals can be determined without recourse to prices – by means of a simple quantitative ratio in which one exchanges for the other'.[6]

But there is more to the value determination of gold and silver than just their cost of production:

(Gold and silver values are determined, in the first place, by their cost of production in the country of production. 'In the mining countries all prices ultimately depend on the costs of production of the precious metals; . . . the remuneration paid to the miner, . . . affords the scale, on which the remuneration of all other producers is calculated. The gold value and silver value of all commodities exempt from monopoly depends in a country without mines on the gold and silver which can be obtained by exporting the result of a given quantity of labour, the current rate of profit, and, in each individual case, the amount of wages, which have been paid, and the time for which they have been advanced.' (Senior.)[7] In other words: on the quantity of gold and silver which is directly or indirectly obtained from the mining countries in exchange for a given quantity of labour (exportable products). Money is in the first instance that which expresses the relation of equality between all exchange values: in money, they all have the same name.)[8]

Money as the commodity gold or silver, a weight-fraction of gold or silver, serves as the measure of the value of the other commodity or, speaking in general terms, of all commodities. This is so because, as the measure of value, 'the amount of gold or silver contained in a unit of money is the realization of a specific quantity of labour in general, of social labour time; [as such] it is therefore the equivalent of every other product in the proportion expressed in its exchange value.'[9]

If the quantity of gold in a coin is reduced (the coin is debased from containing one ounce of gold to consisting of two-thirds copper, and so on), then the money is depreciated and prices of other commodities rise. This is so because the *measure* (emphasis added) of prices is no longer the cost of production of one ounce of gold.[10] As *Zahlungsmittel*, the material substance of money is relevant because the exchange value of an ounce of gold is compared with that of any other commodity.[11]

However, within *circulation* (emphasis added), the material substance of money, its 'material substratum of a given quantity of gold or silver, is irrelevant . . . and can be replaced by any other symbol which expresses a given quantity of its unit. . . .'[12]

Marx juxtaposes, in their role as money, (national) coins and 'world coin' (gold and silver). As national money, coins have lost their use value as such (the value based on their metallic content); but they derive their use value from their 'quality as medium of circulation'.[13] National coin is demonetised when it is melted down, but not so gold and silver, which are a universal medium of exchange as well as a universal commodity. Melted down or valued according to its gold and silver money content, gold and silver are a 'universal money':[14]

> As medium of exchange between the nations . . . gold and silver, as . . . universal commodity, . . . are the material representative of *general* wealth. In the Mercantilist system, therefore, gold and silver count as the measure of the power of the different communities. . . . [But even] beyond Mercantilism, in periods of general crisis, gold and silver, . . . a universal equivalent for everything, also become the measure of power between nations [and] still appear in precisely this role, in 1857 as much as in 1600. In this character, gold and silver play an important role in the creation of the world market. . . . In developed trade . . . it no longer appears for the purpose of exchanging the excess production but to balance it out as part of the total process of international commodity exchange. It is coin, now, only as *world coin*. . . . Gold and silver remain the universally accepted *commodity*, the commodity as such.[15]

As world coin, money is essentially a commodity as such and not a symbol; money only as gold and silver. Only its metal content has value.[16] The more the domestic commerce is conditioned on all sides by foreign commerce, the more the value of the metal content prevails over the face value (the face which the state impresses on coin money) of the coin. Gold and silver – as world coin, as general commodity – do not need, in world trade, to return to their country of origin or point of departure.[17]

In all these reflections Marx quotes extensively from de Malynes, Misselden, Petty, Boisguillebert, and Senior, often adding short comments of his own. In one particular section he quotes Misselden: 'If less of the foreign and more of the domestic product were sold, then the difference would have to come to us in the form of gold and silver, as treasure.' Then he goes on to criticise the 'modern economists' for their making 'merry at this sort of motion', even though they still take seriously in times of crisis the possible inflow and outflow of gold and silver, 'in an artless one-sidedness of the Monetary and Mercantilist system'.[18]

Throughout his reflections on money, including gold and silver, in its function and evolution, Marx never fails to emphasise the historical evolution of these functions and the development of the monetary system, from its early beginnings to its modern, universal, scope. He names earlier forms of money (salt, hides, cattle, slaves), which are money because they have use value as objects of consumption or instruments of production.[19] Not so with the latter forms of money, which do not derive their usefulness because they are objects of consumption or instruments of production but because they have use value in serving as money and performing the money function. Precious metals have use value as objects of consumption and means of production as well as use value because of their generalised role as medium of exchange. He agrees with Adam Smith's view: that 'labour time is the original money with which all commodities are purchased',[20] but he declares that labour time cannot directly be money because it is already contained in the commodity.

With the use of the general equivalent – that is, of money – exchange is split into two separate actions: purchase and sale, giving rise to commerce as an independent function whose purpose is 'the gaining of money, of exchange values' rather than consumption or production.[21] With it, production works directly for commerce (the merchants) and only indirectly for consumption, leading to contradictions and commercial crises.

Marx's treatment of the evolution of trade and of the role of merchants is historical, but it carries over into a treatment of the effects, which ties in, nationally as well as internationally, with his views on the accumulation of capital through trade and foreign trade, and the development of capitalism.

The movement of mercantile capital, or money as it represents itself as merchant wealth, is the first form of capital: value which comes exclusively from circulation (from exchange). In this circulation there are two movements: to buy so as to sell, and to sell so as to buy; but the form M-C-C-M predominates. The merchant neither buys the commodity for his own needs (for the sake of its use value to him) nor does he sell it in order to obtain another commodity for his own needs. His direct aim is to increase value, in its direct form as money:

> Mercantile wealth is, firstly, money as medium of exchange; . . . it exchanges commodity for money and vice versa. . . . To buy cheap and sell dear is the law of trade. *Hence not the exchange of equivalents*, with which *trade, rather, would be impossible as a particular way of gaining wealth.*[22]

Use value predominates in the trade of every civilised society so long as means of subsistence and of pleasure are the chief aim.[23] Trade commences as barter, being the exchange of use values; but then through the character of economic progress, trade suppresses absolutely its character of use value, letting only that of exchangeable value remain. Trade will subjugate production more and more to exchange value; it will make subsistence more dependent on sale than on the immediate use of the product: 'It is part of the concept of value that it maintains itself and increases through exchange. But the existing value is, initially, money. Merchant wealth, as constantly engaged in exchange and exchanging for the sake of exchange value, is in fact living money.'[24] Luxury manufactures, a consequence of foreign commerce, are established by merchants who work up foreign materials, an advance over the domestic trade which arises naturally through successive improvements of the crude domestic employment in which home-grown materials are used up. Trade dominates industry in the preliminary stages of bourgeois society, but in modern society industry dominates trade.[25]

With the multiplying of needs, bartering becomes difficult: money is introduced, the common price of all things and the proper equivalent in the hands of those who have a want. Now the operation of

buying and selling is somewhat more complex than in the first stage.
From barter to sale to commerce is how trade develops:

> The merchant must intervene. What was earlier called wants is
> now represented by the consumer; industry by the manufacturer,
> money by the merchant. Trade . . . adjusts wants to needs, or
> wants to money; . . . Towards the consumer he represents the
> totality of manufacturers, to the latter the totality of consumers,
> and to both classes his credit supplies the use of money . . . *with a
> view to profit.*[26]

In the patriarchal state, utility is the true measure of values and
trade applies only to the surplus of one's production. But with
economic progress trade takes on a distributive function, of the
totality of the annually produced wealth. In performing this function,
trade suppresses the use value of the annually produced wealth and
replaces it by exchangeable value. Trade also ties in directly with the
greater utilisation of labour:

> Before the introduction of trade, the increase in the quantity of the
> product was a direct increase of wealth. Less significant at that time
> was the quantity of labour by means of which this useful thing was
> obtained. And really, the thing demanded loses none of its useful-
> ness even if no labour at all were needed to obtain it; grain and
> linen would not be less necessary to their owners . . . even if they
> fell to them from heaven. This is without doubt the true estimate of
> wealth, enjoyment and usefulness. But from the moment when
> men . . . made their subsistence dependent on the exchanges they
> could make, or on commerce, they were forced to adhere to a
> different estimation, to exchange value, the value which results not
> from the usefulness but rather from the *relation between the needs
> of the whole society and the quantity of labour which was sufficient
> to satisfy this need*, or as well the quantity of labour which might
> satisfy it in the future. In the estimation of values, which people
> endeavoured to measure with the introduction of currency,the
> concept of usefulness is quite displaced. It is *labour*, the exertion
> necessary to procure oneself the two things exchanged for one
> another, which has alone been regarded.[27]

Trade results in commercial wealth and commercial wealth is an
independent economic form, the foundation of commercial cities and

commercial peoples. Their development and independence was achieved through the carrying trade, in which they played the role of money, of mediators, between the primitive producers and the peoples on the most diverse stages of economic development.[28]

But trade between nations may lead to an unequal sharing of gains or even to fraud and exploitation:

> *Two nations may exchange according to the law of profit in such a way that both gain, but one is always defrauded [always exploits and steals from the other].*
>
> From the possibility that profit may be *less than* surplus value, hence that capital [may] exchange profitably without realizing itself in the strictest sense, it follows that not only individual capitalists, but nations may continually exchange with one another, may even continually repeat the exchange on an ever-expanding scale, without for that reason necessarily gaining in equal degrees. One of the nations may continually appropriate for itself a part of the surplus labour of the other, giving back nothing for it in the exchange, except that the measure here [is] not as in the exchange between the capitalist and worker.[29]

From crude forms of barter trade through feudalism and the emergence of the mercantile estate, the development of commerce has evolved into a system of universal relations based on personal independence, exchange, and division of labour.[30] In the course of this transformation, capital 'arises in a situation in which trade has seized possession of production itself, and where the merchant becomes producer, or the producer a mere merchant . . . and the rise of capital in its adequate form presupposes it as commercial capital, so that production is no longer for use, more or less mediated by money, but for wholesale trade.'[31] In this transformation, money becomes the embodiment of exchange value and a realised and always realisable form of capital:

> By virtue of its property as the general commodity in relation to all others, as the embodiment of exchange value of the other commodities, money at the same time becomes the realized [*verwirklichte*] and always realizable [*verwirklichbare*] form of capital; the form of capital's appearance which is always valid – a property which emerges in bullion drains; hence capital appears in history initially only in the money form; this explains, finally, the link

between money and the rate of interest, and its influence on the latter.[32]

Money flows play an important role as means of international payment. This is especially noticeable when money – in its immediate form as money, that is, value for itself, equivalent – appears as the sole absolute means of payment: as the sole counter-value, sole acceptable equivalent. This role is revealed in times of crises – harvest failures, and so forth. In this role, money pursues a moving course which directly contradicts that of all other commodities:

> Commodities are transported as means of payment etc. from the country where they are cheapest to the country where they are most expensive. Money, the opposite; in all periods where it brings out its specific inner nature, where, hence, money is called for, in antithesis to all other commodities as value for-itself, as absolute equivalent, as general form of wealth, in the specific form of gold and silver – and such moments are always more or less moments of crisis, whether a general one, or a grain crisis – then gold and silver are always transmitted from the country where they are the most expensive – i.e., where the commodity prices have fallen by the relatively greatest amount – to the country where they are cheapest, i.e., where the prices of commodities are relatively higher.[33]

Marx then quotes Fullarton's statement concerning the effect of gold flows upon the market prices of gold, particularly following a depression of exchanges, and provides a fuller explanation of this situation:

> It is a singular anomaly in the economy of the exchanges, . . . that the course of transit (of gold between two nations equally employing gold as a circulating medium) is always *from* the country where for the moment the metal is *dearest* to the country where it is *cheapest*, a rise of the market price of the metal to its highest limit in the home market, and a fall of the premium in the foreign market, being the certain results of that tendency to an efflux of gold which follows a depression of the exchanges.[34]

Marx views Fullarton's statement as follows:

– Exchange begins where communities end;
– money, the measure, the medium of exchange, and the general

equivalent is created by the exchange itself, not in internal traffic but in the trade between different communities and peoples;
- it is in external exchange that money obtains a specific significance, as medium of international payments ['*argent dans sa fonction comme étalon d'or*'][35] for the liquidation of international debts;
- in this role, money cast its spells in the sixteenth century, the infancy of the bourgeois society, holding the exclusive interest of states and the incipient political economy;
- 'The important role which money (gold and silver) still plays in international traffic has only become fully clear and been again recognised by the economists since the regular succession of money crises in 1825, 1839, 1847 and 1857.'[36]
- The money called for in this function is not a medium of circulation but capital, in the specific form of gold and silver, and not in that of any other commodity; gold and silver in their role as medium of international payments because they are 'money as value-for-itself, an independent equivalent.'[37]
- All the causes which make for the flow of bullion from one country to another manifest themselves in the state of the balance of payments, for example crop failures, war-expenditure, as continually recurring conditions which make it a necessity, not a preference, to transmit gold from one country to another;[38]
- 'Mr. Fullarton falsely treats the transmission of gold or another form of capital as a matter of preference, whereas the question is precisely those cases when gold must be transmitted in international trade, just as at the same time bills in the domestic trade must be acquitted in the legal money, and not in any substitute.'[39]
- Gold possesses in this function the property of being money, general commodity of contracts, standard of values, being immediately convertible into a medium of circulation – of being a currency.[40]

Towards the end of his reflections concerning money, in the Chapter On Money as well as in the final section of the *Grundrisse*, Marx reverts back to generalised analysis and engages in predictions *vis-à-vis* the evolution of capitalism, of trade and of society.

In the bourgeois era, society rests on exchange value and private free enterprise becomes prevalent. However, this evolution brings with itself its own contradictions, its own antitheses, on a worldwide scale:

Just as the division of labour creates agglomeration, combination, co-operation, the antithesis of private interests, class interests, competition, concentration of capital, monopoly, stock companies – so many antithetical forms of the unity which itself brings the antithesis to the fore – so does private exchange create world trade, private independence creates complete dependence on the so-called world market, and the fragmented acts of exchange create a banking and credit system whose books, at least keep a record of the balance between debt and credit in private exchange. Although the private interests within each nation divide it into as many nations as it has 'full-grown individuals', and although the interests of exporters and of importers are antithetical here, etc. etc., national trade does obtain the *semblance* of existence in the form of the rate of exchange. Nobody will take this as a ground for believing that a *reform of the money market* can abolish the *foundations* of internal or external private trade.[41]

In Marx's view, the magnitude of this evolution and the relations of production and distribution in such an evolution give rise to the scepticism about the socialists' claim that the replacement of the monetary system based on gold by one based on time-chits [*Stundenzetteln*] would abolish the existing foundations of private trade and change society. Moreover, this universal evolution will have had repercussions upon individuals, who are its principal factors. With the increase in the universal scope of this evolution, alienation sets in (for example exchange value equals the relative labour time embodied in the individual's product; but money, which is equal to the exchange value of commodities, is separated from this substance and comes to express an objective [*sachlich*] relation between persons; in consequence, the social relation between persons takes on the form of at thing – exchange value – money). This alienation takes on a universal dimension in the world market. Efforts to overcome it do not succeed, even though the responsibility exists of suspending old standpoints:

> since the general bond and all-round interdependence in production and consumption increase together with the independence and indifference of the consumers and producers to one another; since this contradiction leads to crises, etc., hence, together with the development of this alienation, and on the same basis, efforts are made to overcome it: institutions emerge whereby each individual can acquire information about the activity of all others and attempt to adjust his own accordingly, e.g., lists of current prices, rates of exchange, interconnections between those active in commerce

through the mails, telegraphs, etc. (the means of communication of course grow at the same time). (This means that, although the total supply and demand are independent of the actions of each individual, everyone attempts to inform himself about them, and this knowledge then reacts back in practice on the total supply and demand. Although on the given standpoint, alienation is not overcome by these means, nevertheless, relations and connections are introduced thereby which include the possibility of suspending the old standpoint.) (The possibility of general statistics, etc.) . . . To be further noted here only that a comprehensive view over the whole of commerce and production in so far as lists of current prices in fact provide it, furnishes indeed the best proof of the way in which their own exchange and their own production confront individuals as an *objective* relation which is *independent* of them. In the case of the *world market*, the *connection of the individual* with all, but at the same time also the *independence of this connection from the individual*, have developed to such a high level that the formation of the world market already at the same time contains the conditions for going beyond it.[42]

Marx's review and critique of Bastiat and Carey fits well into his mega-reflections: Bastiat and Carey form exceptions in an era in which the history of modern political economy had ended with Ricardo and Sismondi and the only innovative writings had had to do with circulation, but otherwise only with reproduction, greater elaboration, popularisation, and greater detail. Both Bastiat and Carey 'grasp that the antithesis to political economy – namely socialism and communism – finds its theoretical presupposition in the works of classical political economy itself, especially in Ricardo, who must be regarded as its complete and final expression.'[43]

Marx labels Carey 'the only original economist among the North Americans'.[44] He wishes to emancipate America's bourgeoisie from the state, but he ends up by calling for state intervention in seeking to protect the United States from the destructive influence of England and its striving for worldwide industrial monopoly. Carey wants world harmony, but he wishes to proceed by way of protective tariffs and the development of industrialism in the United States. Bastiat, on the contrary, is a free-trader who desires the liberation of the bourgeoisie from state supervision. In his view, world harmony can be realised by the competing national bourgeoisies practising worldwide free trade.[45]

2. GOLD EXPORTS AND CRISES

This discussion involves Marx's critical asessment of Alfred Darimon's work *De la réforme des banques* (Paris, 1856), which treated the reasons for the diminution of France's reserves and commented on the policies which the Banque de France was applying in seeking to stop the outflow of gold.

In Darimon's view, the outflow of precious metals was caused by the crop failure in France and the need to import grains. Seeking to diminish the outflow of specie by raising the discount rate and reducing the repayment period, the Banque de France was in fact hoarding its metal reserve rather than releasing it into circulation, which was the wrong thing to do because the Banque was faced with an excess demand for funds. With its insistence on maintaining the metallic standard, the Banque stood in 'basic contradiction to the requirements of circulation', even though the latter had been clearly portrayed by its portfolio.[46]

Marx's rejoinder involves two major points and several smaller ones:

(1) Darimon's view on the crop failure in France was correct, but the flight of gold from France is also explained by the following facts:

(a) the failure of the silk harvest in France and the need to import vast quantities of raw silk from China;
(b) huge speculative ventures abroad;
(c) unproductive expenditures involving borrowing on account of the Crimean War;[47]
(d) French capital investment abroad with long gestation periods, which (i) freezes exchangeable wealth in a form which creates no direct equivalent, at home and abroad; (ii) absolutely diminishes the exchangeable wealth of a nation, at home and abroad; (iii) diminishes circulation at home and leads to an unlimited increase in bank drafts; in direct consequence of which domestic prices of products, of raw materials, and of labour increase while the price per bank draft decreases and results in a 'devaluation of the country's own paper . . . and a sudden paralysis of production . . .'. [48] Marx does not go on to explain.

(2) But Darimon is a 'Proudhonist' in his critique of the Banque de France raising the discount rate and hoarding gold.[49] Marx considers

Darimon's method of analysis wrong and his conclusions false; he also distorted the Banque's portfolio figures to suit his needs:

> In his hasty effort to present in the most lurid colours his preconceived opinion that the metal basis of the bank, represented by its metallic assets, stands in contradiction to the requirements of circulation, which, in his view, are represented by the bank's portfolio, he tears two columns of figures out of their necessary context with the result that this isolation deprives the figures of all meaning or, at the most, leads them to testify against him. We have dwelt on this *fact* in some detail in order to make clear with one example what the entire worth of the statistical and positive illustrations of the Proudhonists amounts to. Economic facts do not furnish the proof of their lack of mastery of the facts, in order to be able to play with them. Their manner of playing with the facts shows, rather, the genesis of their theoretical abstractions.[50]

Marx counters Darimon's claim: the Banque de France did not increase the cost of its services because the system is based on the rule of gold and silver, but the cost went up because demand for grains exceeded supply and because grain prices went up; in consequence, there was a run on the Banque's supply of gold as the means of payment for the grain imports. Marx asks: 'And the Bank should be made an exception to these general economic laws [i.e. the disproportion of demand and supply]? *Quelle idée!*'[51]

In Marx's view, a costly consequence of the 'system as presently constituted'[52] is the need to pile up a great quantity of gold as a reserve against possible crop failure, a reserve which 'is condemned to lie fallow . . . instead of passing through the necessary transformation of production . . ., the unproductive stock of metal standing above its necessary minimum within the present system of bank organisation.'[53] He wonders whether the real issue was not 'a departure from the metal basis altogether' rather than the saving of metal by means of banknotes and other banking arrangements?[54]

Marx's conclusive statement on crop failures and gold flows sounds modern:

> The rise in the grain price is = to the fall in the price of all other commodities. . . . The rise in the grain price first of all means only that more gold and silver have to be given in exchange for a certain

quantity of grain, i.e. that the price of gold and silver has declined relative to the price of grain. Thus gold and silver participate with all other commodities in the depreciation relative to grain, and no privilege protects them from this.[55]

The depreciation of most commodities (labour included) and the resultant crisis, in the case of an important crop mishap, cannot therefore be crudely ascribed to the export of gold, because depreciation and crisis would equally take place if no gold whatever were exported and no grain imported. The crisis reduces itself simply to the law of supply and demand, which, as is known, acts far more sharply and energetically within the sphere of primary needs – seen on a national scale – than in all other spheres. Exports of gold are not the cause of the grain crisis, but the grain crisis is the cause of gold exports.[56]

3. RELATION BETWEEN MONEY METALS AND COMMODITIES. CONVERTIBILITY. DEPRECIATION.

The question of the relation between the causes making for gold outflows, money, and the two money metals, gold and silver, is certainly 'much more complex than Darimon's suggested "solution"'.[57]

First of all, gold and silver are not commodities like others: as 'general instruments of exchange'[58] they are 'privileged commodities'.[59] They are privileged commodities because of their exclusive monetary role: in moments of monetary crisis, it is gold and silver that are demanded rather than any other commodities. If part of the monetary outflow (whether this outflow is caused by domestic harvest failures, by crop failures abroad which lead to price increases of that importable, or by excessive imports due to speculation or war) involves gold and silver as capital, then 'the domestic economy incurs a real loss of production . . . because . . . a part of its invested capital or labour is not reproduced . . . and a part which has been reproduced has to be shifted to fill this gap.'[60]

Secondly, commodities are objectified [*vergegenständlichte*] labour and their corresponding value must itself appear in the form of a specific thing, a specific form of such labour, for example gold and silver. A gold or silver coin changes its value, partly relative to the value of other commodities which changes over time, partly because the coin and its metal content are the product of more or less labour time. This value changes: it sometimes equals a greater and sometimes a smaller quantity of real gold depending on whether more or fewer of the coins must be given up in exchange for other commodities, even though the denomination of the coin, as the fractional part of the weight-unit of gold, remains the same (one pound sterling).[61] Marx explains more specifically:

Gold and silver, depending on the production time they cost, would express different multiples or fractional parts of pounds, shillings, etc.: and an ounce of gold just as well be = £8 6s. 3d. as = £3, 17sh, $10\frac{1}{2}$d. These numbers would always be the expression of the proportion in which a specific quantity of labour is contained in the ounce. . . . If we compare prices in England in e.g. the fifteenth century with those of the eighteenth, then we may find that two commodities had e.g. entirely the same nominal money value e.g. 1 pound sterling. In this case the pound sterling is the standard, but expresses four or five times as much value in the first case as in the second, and we could say that, if the value of this commodity is = 1 ounce in the fifteenth century, then it was = $\frac{1}{4}$ ounce of gold in the eighteenth; because in the eighteenth, 1 ounce of gold expresses the same labour time as $\frac{1}{4}$ ounce in the fifteenth century. It could be said, therefore, that the measure, the pound, had remained the same, but in one case = four times as much gold as in the other. This is the *ideal standard*. . . . What do we do in fact when we compare £1 of the fifteenth century with £1 of the eighteenth? Both are the same mass of metal (each = 20s.), but of different value; since the metal was then worth 4 times as much as now. . . . If gold falls in value and its relative fall or rise as regards other articles is expressed in their price, then, instead of saying that an object will cost £1 of gold before, now costs 2, it could be said it still costs £1, but 1 pound is now worth 2 real *livres* of gold etc. . . . This pound changes its value, partly relative to the value of other commodities which change their value, partly in so far as it is itself the product of more or less labour time. The only firm thing about it is the name. . . . [62]

Marx then explains how the mint price of gold can rise above or fall below the bullion price: a specific sort of coin can rise above its bullion content by adding new labour to the coin.[63]

Thirdly, 'the exports of gold are not the cause of grain crisis but the grain crisis is the cause of gold exports.'[64] The crisis can be aggravated by imposing restrictions on the gold outflow (for example,

reserve requirements restrict the outflow) or by the grain-exporting
countries' insistence that the exports be paid for in gold (for example,
when the monetary drain from the grain-importing country becomes
too large).[65]

Fourthly, a domestic grain crop failure has other unfavourable
consequences concerning international finance:

- not only does the importing country suffer a loss in its real wealth
  (because the farming sector is not reproducing its capital), but it
  must also pay a higher import bill: 'the increase in imports presupposes a rise in the price';[66]
- a rise in the grain price (which Marx equates to an increase in the
  cost of the product) is tantamount to a decline in the price of all
  other commodities, leading to a situation which Marx explains as
  follows:

The surplus used to purchase grain must correspond to a deficit in
the purchase of all other products and hence already a decline in
their prices. With [the result that] the price of their production
depreciated as compared to their value, which is determined by the
normal cost of production; the same holds true, in the opposite, of
the grain price/value relation (i.e. the price rises above the value);
[original emphasis][67]

- the rise in grain prices means a relative (to the grain price)
  decrease in the price of gold and silver, a 'depreciation of gold and
  silver in terms of grain'.[68]

The propositions regarding convertibility and depreciation are a
'complex question . . . because as long as paper money retains its
denomination in gold, the convertibility of the note into gold remains
its economic law, whether this law exists *politically* or not'.[69]

The convertibility of a banknote into gold is 'only the practical
equivalence of what the face of the note expresses theoretically . . .',
of the 'equivalence of the nominal value of the banknote with its real
value expressed in gold or silver'.[70] Depreciation is the fall in real
value beneath nominal value. A £5 note is depreciated 'when it
cannot any more buy bullion of the value of £5, . . . whether or not
the note is convertible.'[71] A paper currency depreciates when (i)
uncertainty sets in (confidence in the government is badly shaken);
(ii) if too much money is issued in proportion to the needs of

circulation; (iii) when gold and silver become preferred articles of export.[72]

In their concern about economic crises, socialist monetary reformers, instead of coping with the 'underlying problem'[73] (how policy-makers should overcome the real problem of both the rise and the fall of prices), are concerned only with half the problem: how to cope with the downturn. Instead of worrying only about the appreciation of gold and silver relative to other commodities, a situation which occurs only in periods of prosperity, they should show how to prevent the depreciation of money: 'a temporary general rise in prices . . . [whereas] . . . this depreciation of metallic money . . . always precedes its appreciation . . . [therefore] . . . they ought to have formulated the problem the other way round: how to prevent the periodic depreciation of money . . . ?[74]

Marx's own solution? The abolition of prices! How? By 'doing away with exchange value':

The evil of bourgeois society is not to be remedied by 'transforming' the banks or by founding a rational 'money system' [but] by doing away with exchange value [that is with the bourgeois organisation of society].[75]

Marx then proceeds to show that convertibility depends on equivalence and gets involved in the tedious exercise of matching the pertinent terms – convertibility, appreciation, general equivalent – with their respective antitheses – non-convertibility, depreciation, non-equivalent. He pursues this path of reasoning, starting with his labour theory of value, adds value and price, and conducts the analysis in a general framework which resembles today's 'monetary economics'.

To start with, 'to be a value-symbol, money, the general equivalent, must be convertible and must be equated with a third commodity.'[76] The value (that is, the real exchange value) of all commodities (including labour) is determined by their cost of production: the labour time required to produce them.[77] The price of commodities is their exchange value expressed in money.[78] Value is real value; price is nominal value, money value.[79]

Equivalent exchange occurs when a specific amount of labour time embodied in a commodity exchanges for the same amount of labour time embodied in another commodity. But non-equivalent exchange occurs when a specified quantity of a commodity, worth so many

hours of embodied labour, can obtain in exchange for itself a greater
or lesser quantity of embodied labour time:

> If a gold sovereign were expressed in terms of a specific amount of
> labour time, this quantity of historically embodied labour time
> would become the standard of this currency. Converted into this
> amount of labour time, this standard would be stable, and an
> equivalent exchange would take place whenever the same quantity
> of gold would exchange for the same amount of labour time.
> However, an adherence to this standard can result in non-
> equivalent exchange at a time when this specified quantity of gold
> (worth so many hours of historically embodied labour) can pur-
> chase, in exchange for itself, a greater or lesser amount. This
> sovereign would appreciate when it can buy a greater amount of
> labour or depreciate when it can only buy a lesser quantity of
> labour in exchange for itself.[80]

Since convertibility is based on equivalence, an adherence to a
standard based upon a specific amount of historically embodied
labour time (that is, so many ounces of gold, which are worth so
many hours of historically embodied labour) can lead to non-
equivalent exchange at a point in time when this specified quantity of
gold can buy a greater amount of labour (than the one embodied in
this quantity of gold) in exchange for itself, or, respectively, a lesser
amount. In the former case, a currency is said to appreciate; in the
latter, to depreciate; even though the quantity of gold embodied in
the currency and the amount of historically embodied labour time in
it remains unchanged.[81]

The relation, over time, between the value of the gold sovereign,
price, stable standard of exchange, and productivity of labour (productivity of gold-producing labour) is as follows:

– the quantity of the historically embodied labour time becomes the
   standard of a currency (for example the gold sovereign); so expressed, this currency represents a stable standard, which leads to
   equivalent exchange whenever this quantity of gold is exchanged
   for the same amount of labour time;
– however, historically, the living labour becomes increasingly productive owing to the general economic law that costs of production
   constantly decline (presumably, Marx refers here to the rise in the

organic composition of capital over time as well as to the increase in the s/v over time);
- consequently, since convertibility is based on equivalence, to maintain the convertibility of a currency (of the sovereign), the productivity of the labour time necessary to produce it would have to be kept constant; if this is not done, 'the inevitable fate of this gold labour money . . . would be constant depreciation.'[82]

Changes in the value of the materials in which money represents itself (directly, as in gold, silver; or indirectly, as claims, notes, on a specific quantity of gold or silver) will bring about 'great revolutions between the different classes of a state':

> It is well known that the depreciation of gold and silver, due to the discovery of America, depreciated the labouring class and that of the landed proprietors; raised that of the capitalists (especially of the industrial capitalists). . . . In the Roman republic, the appreciation of copper turned the plebeians into the slaves of the patricians.[83] . . . This great revolution in the exchange value of the monetary substance, to the measure it proceeded, most cruelly worsened the lot of the unfortunate plebeians, who had obtained depreciated copper as a loan, and having spent or used it at the rate it then had, now owed, by the letter of their contracts, a five times greater sum than they had borrowed in reality.[84]

Marx's propositions with respect to gold as money and the relative value of gold may be summed up as follows:

(1) The increased productivity of the gold-producing labour leads to the production of more gold (coins) during the same period of labour time, whereby the real value of each gold coin goes down (the labour time contained in each is reduced);

(2) in consequence, it will take more newly minted gold (coins) to purchase commodities which contain a relatively higher proportion of labour time [even though equivalent to the labour time contained in the previously minted (old) coins];

(3) clearly, therefore, the coins in the gold standard will depreciate in terms of the other commodities, whereby the convertibility, which presumes equivalence, will be endangered;

(4) the solution to this problem of the historical tendency of gold currency to depreciate can be solved in two ways:

(a) keep constant the productivity of labour required to produce the (gold) currency; or

(b) switch to the paper currency system.

The latter, claims Marx, would be of advantage to the workers, but it would also have several drawbacks (for example, if the paper standard is composed of paper labour money – time-chits – representing the productivity of one hour's labour, the increased productivity of labour would lead to a constant appreciation of this labour money, the new chits as well as the accumulated ones, whereby non-workers would also benefit).[85]

NOTES AND COMMENTS

1. *Grundrisse*, p. 166.
2. Ibid., pp. 137–9.
3. Ibid., p. 176
4. Ibid., p. 169.
5. Ibid.
6. Ibid., p. 181
7. Marx refers here to Nassau Senior's *Three Lectures On the Cost of Obtaining Money* (London, 1830), p. 15.
8. *Grundrisse*, p. 189.
9. Ibid., p. 204-205.
10. Ibid., pp. 212–13.
11. Ibid., p. 207.
12. Ibid., p. 212.
13. Ibid., p. 226.
14. Ibid.
15. Ibid., pp. 226–7.
16. Ibid., p.228.
17. Ibid., p.229.
18. Ibid., p. 232.
19. Ibid., p. 862. Marx refers to the double standard and the need to have only one standard as the measure of value: 'Previously, in countries where gold and silver were legal standard, silver circulated almost exclusively, because from 1800 to 1850 the tendency for gold to become dearer than silver. . . . Great import of gold from California, premium on silver in Europe . . . extensive shipment of silver and replacement by gold' (p. 862).
20. Ibid., p. 167.
21. Ibid., p. 149.
22. Ibid., p. 856.
23. Ibid., p. 857.
24. Ibid., pp. 857–8.

25. Ibid., p. 858.
26. Ibid., p. 860.
27. Ibid., pp. 860–1. In this excerpt, Marx paraphrases Sismondi, *Études sur l'économie politique*, vol. II (Brussels, 1837), pp. 162, 163, 266.
28. Ibid., pp. 858–9.
29. Ibid., p. 872.
30. Ibid., p. 159.
31. Ibid., p. 859.
32. Ibid., p. 146.
33. Ibid., pp. 872–3.
34. Ibid., p. 873. From J. Fullarton, *On the Regulation of Currencies*, 2nd ed (London, 1845), p. 119.
35. Ibid., p. 873.
36. Ibid.
37. Ibid.
38. Ibid., p. 874. Marx exempts, from this consideration of gold flows arising from crises, the gold flows owing to the transmission of capital in order to place it at a greater advantage at interest and those arising from a surplus of foreign goods imported, except when these flows happen to coincide with a crisis.
39. Ibid.
40. Ibid., p. 875. In this section of the *Grundrisse* Marx quotes a number of writers on the question of gold and currency flows, even Ricardo, but he expresses no opinion of his own in favour of or in opposition to the views expressed in those quotations. Typical of such samplings with which Marx seems to be in agreement are the following:

Fullarton on Ricardo: 'Ricardo's peculiar and extreme opinion as to the limited extent of the offices performed by gold and silver in the adjustment of foreign balances. . . . Mr. Ricardo had accustomed himself so long to consider all the great fluctuations of exchange and of the price of gold as the result of the excessive issues of the Bank of England, that at one time he seemed scarcely willing to allow that such a thing could exist as an adverse balance of commercial payments . . .'(p. 875).

Fullarton on exchange rate movements: 'During the war of 1800–1814 the transactions of trade between England and continental Europe became too insignificant to affect exchanges one way or the other. It was the foreign military expenditures and the subsidies, and not the necessities of commerce, that contributed in so extraordinary a manner to derange the exchanges and enhance the price of bullion in the latter years of the war. But from 1819 to the present time, amid all the vicissitudes which the money had undergone during that eventful period, the market-price of gold has on no occasion risen above 78s. per oz., nor fallen below 77s. 6d., an extreme range of only 6 in the ounce. Nor would even that extent of fluctuation now be possible . . . since the fall to 77s. 6d. is entirely accounted for by the circumstance of the Bank having at one time thought proper to establish that rate as the limit for its purchase. . . . For many years the Bank has been in the practice of allowing 77s. 9d. for all the gold brought in for coinage' (i.e. the Bank pockets $1\frac{1}{2}$d. mintage, which the coin gives it free of charge); 'and as soon as the recoinage of sovereigns now in progress shall be completed, there will be an effectual bar, until the coin shall again become deteriorated, to any future fluctuation of the price of gold bullion in our market beyond the small fractional difference between 77s. 9d. allowed by the Bank, and the Mint-price of 77s.10 $\frac{1}{2}$d.' (p. 877).

Bosanquet, Took, on gold, currency, international balances: 'Gold can always buy . . . other commodities, whereas other commodities cannot always buy gold. The markets of the world are open to it as merchandise at less sacrifice upon an emergency that would attend an export of any other article, which might in quantity or kind be beyond the usual demand in the country to which it is sent. . . . There must be a very considerable amount of the precious metal applicable and applied as the most convenient mode of adjustment of international balances, being a commodity more generally in demand, and less liable to fluctuations in market value than any other' (p. 876).

MacLaren on money and international payments, bullion flows, capital, circulation, inflation, deflation: Marx leaves no comment whatsoever, even though MacLaren discusses very specifically and at length the relation between changing price levels because of changing quantities of money, changing flows of currency, in response to international payments in response to changing crop conditions, and so forth, and that issuing paper money in filling the gap caused by the exportation of bullion will prevent the natural fall in prices otherwise certain to ensue and held by Ricardo as an interference with the economical laws of price and from principles which would necessarily regulate a purely metallic currency (p. 880).

41. Ibid., p. 159.
42. Ibid., pp. 160–1.
43. Ibid., p. 885.
44. Ibid.
45. Ibid., p. 888.
46. Marx's definition of 'circulation' follows in the *Grundrisse*: pp. 62, 172–8.
47. Marx mentions '750 million', presumably Livres (*Grundrisse*, p. 121).
48. *Grundrisse*, pp. 122–3.
49. Ibid., p. 119.
50. Ibid.
51. Ibid., p. 120.
52. Ibid.
53. Ibid.
54. Ibid.
55. Ibid., pp. 129–130.
56. Ibid., p. 130.
57. Ibid., p. 125.
58. Ibid., p. 126.
59. Ibid.
60. Ibid., pp. 127–8. This statement reveals Marx's awareness of the decelerator effect arising from an outflow of capital (money). But this effect will

be (somewhat) offset by the rise in the price of the deficient product: 'this part, the capital part, of the monetary outflow which involves gold and silver as capital . . . does not stand in a simple arithmetical relation to the loss because the deficient product rises and must rise on the world market as a result of the decreased supply and increased demand' (p. 128). He clearly demonstrates the effect of scarcity on price in an international context.

61. Ibid., p. 799.
62. Ibid., pp. 795–7.
63. Ibid., p. 800. However, Marx then adds the following comment: 'the value of a specific sort of coin rising above its bullion content . . . has no economic interest whatsoever, and has as yet not led to any economic studies.'
64. Ibid., p. 130.
65. Ibid.
66. Ibid., p. 129.
67. Ibid. We note once again Marx's implicit acceptance of an increase in price owing to the scarcity of the product rather than on account of an increase in the cost of production.
68. Ibid., p. 130.
69. Ibid., p. 131. Marx's definition of 'convertibility': 'when the face value of a note commands a specified amount of bullion' (p. 131).
70. Ibid., pp. 131–2.
71. Ibid., p. 132.
72. Ibid. Marx does not see much difference between the 'strict' bullionists and the 'determined' anti-bullionists: the former claim that it is the Bank's obligation to convert notes into bullion that keeps the notes convertible at their face value, whereas the latter retain the denomination of the banknote and view this denomination as the note's full value against a given quantity of gold (p. 132).
73. Ibid., p. 134.
74. Ibid.
75. Ibid.
76. Ibid.
77. See Notebook I, subsection on Value and Price; *Grundrisse*, pp. 136–7.
78. Ibid., p. 137.
79. Ibid.
80. Ibid., p. 135.
81. Ibid.
82. Ibid., p. 134.
83. Ibid., p. 805.
84. Ibid., p. 807.
85. Ibid., p. 135. According to Marx, the monetary system of 'time-chits' will be of benefit not only to the workers but also to the 'chit-accumulating' non-workers. He does not specify who would be the losers, but he does point out that the workers are the losers in the gold standard system, for two reasons: first, the increasing s/v here in the production of precious metals; second, the overall depreciation of the

gold currency relative to the other commodity prices. While the first 'reason' ties in with the Marxian scheme of the economic development and its propositions with respect to the increasing exploitation of labour, the second proposition appears incompletely thought out: if a 'premium' has to be added to the gold sovereign in order to maintain constant its purchasing power relative to the commodities whose prices are increasing, then the holders of gold coins will suffer an erosion of their real purchasing power unless this premium is added – a situation Marx recognises. But he does not assess the behaviour of gold-producing capitalists and their workers.

Part II
On Capital

1 Introduction

This Chapter, a total of 538 pages in the English edition, contains The Chapter on Money as Capital (seventeen pages) and three major Sections. The former represents an attempt to explore the linkage between money (also in the form of gold and silver) and capital. Of the Sections, Section One analyses the Production Process of Capital (151 pages), Section Two describes the Circulation Process of Capital (342 pages), while Section Three, Capital as Fructiferous [*nutzbring-end*], discusses the transformation of surplus value into profit.

Marx's reflections in this Chapter are historical as well as analytical and span the evolution process of capital from its original accumulation to its universal form, the capitalist mode of production: that is, from simple circulation to developed circulation.

According to the editors, the material contained in this Chapter constitutes, with several major revisions and extensions, the essence of the three volumes of *Das Kapital*. In the English edition of the *Grundrisse*, the summary of these revisions is contained in the Foreword (pp. 56, 58–71). According to 'M.N.', the main theme of the Chapter on Capital analyses the exploitation process: that is, of accumulation and its social, political, historical, legal, and other aspects: capital as a process.

Also in the Foreword of the English edition, 'M.N.' lauds Marx for the following contributions which are contained in this Chapter:

(1) In the world of capital, inequality reigns. In opposition to the world of simple circulation, in which every individual is posited as equal and equivalent exchange is the rule, in the former the capitalist buys labour's use value in order to create exchange value, which is deemed straightforward exchange because the use value of labour to its buyer is to create exchange values, that is, commodities, products, which are to be sold; but after purchasing this labour in such a manner, capital extracts a surplus product from the workers' labour time. This surplus constitutes the source of capital accumulation and derives from the misappropriation of the workers' *Arbeitsfähigkeit* (capacity to work).[1]

(2) Surplus value does not originate in the simple exchange process (where, on the average, equal values are exchanged), but arises

71

during the production process of capital: 'all the progress of civilization . . . every increase in the powers of social production, . . . including the creation of the world market . . . enriches not the workers but, rather, capital; . . . .'[2]

(3) The distinction between the hours of necessary labour and the hours of *Mehrarbeit* makes up Marx's concept of exploitation: the worker produces values in excess of his day wage; this excess is later shared out among the industrial capitalists (profit), the bankers (interest), and the landlord (rent).[3]

(4) The distinction between profit and surplus value, 'a major breakthrough',[4] whereby Marx 'demolishes' Ricardo's theory of profit;

(5) The contradiction between the process of equivalent exchange (money circulation, in which, on the average, equal amounts of labour are exchanged; that is, the law of equivalence reigns) and the process of accumulation (the extraction, by capital, of an 'equivalent-plus, a super-equivalent'[5]), and the conclusion that the surplus value requires, upon re-entry into circulation, its 'surplus equivalent'.[6]

(6) The effects of this ingrained contradiction.

(7) The social, political, legal, and even socio-psychological aspects of the evolution of capitalism.

In the Chapter On Money, Marx spoke of international trade flows, monetary flows, and gold flows, depreciation and appreciation, international payments standards, capital accumulation on a world-wide scale and capital movements across national boundaries. In the Chapter On Capital, we should expect to find spelled out his treatment of accumulation, possibly amounting to a universal theory. In his consideration of the equalisation of national rates of profit and national rates of surplus value, he may be expected to reflect upon an international equalisation of profit rates and rates of surplus value, and possibly also of rates of exploitation. And, lastly, his treatment of the 'Economists', especially of their propositions regarding value, international values and prices, and reasons for the conduct of foreign trade, should reveal his own thoughts concerning the international economy and the theory of foreign trade.

In researching Marx's thoughts on these main issues, we shall work through this whole Chapter and then draw our specific conclusions concerning his specific views on these questions, hoping to formulate statements concerning a socialist theory of values and of foreign trade and finance.

NOTES AND COMMENTS

1. *Grundrisse*, pp. 239–43. Note the difference in the meaning of *Arbeitsfähigkeit*, the general capacity or ability to work or to perform a task, and *Arbeitskraft*, which refers to a member of the labour force or to a country's general manpower.
2. Ibid., pp. 307–8.
3. Ibid., p. 405.
4. Ibid.
5. Ibid.
6. Ibid., p. 405.

4 Money as Capital

Nature does not produce money, any more than it produces a rate of exchange or a banker. . . . To be money is not the natural attribute of gold and silver . . . but money is directly gold and silver . . . the result of social processes . . . pure exchange value.[1]

These excerpts from the lengthy introductory paragraph to the Chapter On Capital are indicative of the way Marx sets the stage for his reflections on the linkage between money and capital. He brings forth three main concepts concerning money: (1) money has three major functions; (2) money has use value as well as exchange value; (3) money is also the merely perceptible appearance of the contradictions inherent in bourgeois society. The first two concepts are generally known and find Marx's acceptance, but he is critical of those propositions which seek to remove the contradictions – as if they had been caused by money.

In Marx's view, such 'tinkering with money' reveals not only their difficulty of grasping money in its fully developed character but also represents their desire to leave everything else unchanged, in particular the developed relations of production. What must first be done is to expose the character of the evolution of the money-relation against the backdrop of the evolution of the ruling relations of production.

Marx first describes the money-relations as conceived in simple form, the form in which 'bourgeois democracy and bourgeois economists take refuge':[2] that is, the form in which all inherent contradictions of bourgeois society *appear* extinguished. In his view, this perception had developed as follows:

The money economy, the bourgeois economy, is unlike the ancient world and the Middle Ages. In it, exchange is conceived by these men as being equivalent because the individuals who act as exchangers are seen as equals: the commodities which they put up as objects of their exchange are equivalent (have the same exchange value). They recognise each other as proprietors of their exchangeable objects, and, since they do not appropriate the other's commodity by force, the exchange takes on the quality of equality, of freedom.[3]

This type of exchange manifests the social relations of equivalence: the individuals are equal and their commodities' exchange values are equivalent. But it is recognised that this equality may sometimes not be borne out: subjective errors in appraising the value; cheating; or simply a particular individual's 'natural cleverness, persuasiveness, natural superiority over the other'.[4]

Marx suggests that the right of the individual to engage in exchange 'coincides completely with the dissolution of the Roman community',[5] and that this right manifests itself as the natural freedom and equality to engage in free buying and selling, by means of money (which 'gives the equivalent its specific expression'[6]). This right renders equal the appearance of the worker and the king; it also makes money, the general form of wealth, the object of accumulation for some,[7] while others are free to enjoy their wealth: that is, to consume. In the view of these men, free will prevails: 'If one grows impoverished and the other grows wealthier, then this is of their own free will and does not in any way arise from the economic relations into which they are placed one to the other.'[8]

Marx is critical of this 'naïve perception' and attacks the socialists: adopting this simplistic view of the circulation in bourgeois society, they failed to recognise that beneath this surface of equality a process goes on in which this apparent individual liberty and equality will disappear: that is, that 'this simple form of exchange value and money latently contain the opposition between labour and capital.'[9] This is so because, whereas simple exchange pertains to 'undeveloped exchange value' in that it involves only the exchange of labour for labour, 'developed exchange value' involves capital and money as capital: 'Money as capital is an aspect of money which goes beyond its simple character as money. It can be regarded as a higher realisation;[10] as it can be said that man is a developed ape.'[11] Capital's point of departure is money and comes initially from circulation: 'Commercial capital is only circulating capital, and circulating capital is the first form of capital; in which it has yet by no means become the foundation of production. A more developed form of money capital is money interest, usury. . . .'[12]

After reviewing these early notions of money and adding his initial thoughts on the transformation of money into capital, Marx sets the stage for his own rendition of the circulation of capital. To start with, he attempts to describe the 'circulation process of capital':

This process involves the realisation[13] of capital. In this process, capital maintains its value by engaging in an exchange with living labour. In this process, surplus value is created – that is to say, capital increases: a higher value is generated because at the end of the process, 'capital contains more objectified[14] labour than the value which formed the point of departure.'[15] In the realisation process, capital has made the transition from the money form into the commodity form. In its money form, capital existed as value; in its commodity form, it exists as product. This product has a certain price, which must be realised. The realisation is possible only through the process of commodity circulation, that is, through exchange: money → capital → production → surplus value → higher value (which includes surplus value) → commodity → exchange → money plus (price).[16] This process constitutes the metamorphosis of capital: from value in its original (money) form, to capital as product and ideally as price; from its state as the composite of use values, to money which the capitalist obtains from consumers in exchange for his commodity. It is only through exchange that capital, as value plus new value, can realise itself.[17] However, since the price of capital as a product can be realised only if the commodity is exchanged for money, capital is in fact dependent on circulation: that is, it must have use value, it must be the object of a need; furthermore, it must also be exchanged for its equivalent, money.[18] The new value of capital is its exchange value, which can be realised only if it is sold: that is, if it becomes an object of consumption.[19]

With this conclusion, Marx sets the stage for his discussion of capital: production process and circulation process, which covers about 500 pages in the *Grundrisse* (pp. 250–743). His treatment of this material, even as reclassified by the editors, is cumbersome and discontinuous (for example, his attempts to calculate – and distinguish between – profit and surplus value, which is contained not only in both main Sections but also covered in an independent Section on the 'transformation of surplus value into profit'). In attempting to simplify, while also seeking to render continuous and consistent, Marx's complex treatment of capital, I have decided to present the two main sections in four Chapters. These will contain the essence of Marx's deliberations concerning capital: The Circulation Process of Capital; Simple Exchange v. Developed Exchange; The Circulation of Capital; Fixed Capital and Circulating Capital. To Marx's treatment of capital will then be added a review of his thought, as expressed in the *Grundrisse*, on value, surplus value, and profit; and on values and prices, Classical and Marxian.

NOTES AND COMMENTS

1. *Grundrisse*, pp. 239–40.
2. Ibid., p. 239.
3. Ibid., pp. 239–43.
4. Ibid., p. 241.
5. Ibid., p. 246.
6. Ibid.
7. Marx's definition of 'accumulation': withdrawal of money from circulation in its form of general wealth without withdrawing from circulation commodities of an equal price.
8. Ibid., p. 247.
9. Ibid., p. 249.
10. In the German edition, Marx uses the term *Verwirklichung*.
11. Ibid., pp. 250–1.
12 Ibid., p. 253.
13. In this particular sentence Marx uses the term *Verwertung*, which has been translated as 'realization'. The use of 'realization' as translation for both *Verwirklichung* and *Verwertung* is misleading, since the former has a metaphysical connotation (to create something that had not existed before), whereas the latter has to do with the material, with the concrete (to utilise something in a constructive sense, to generate a value out of the use of inputs and of human labour).
14. See Part I, Chapter 1, note 18.
15. *Grundrisse*, p. 402.
16. Ibid.
17. Ibid. Note the German original of 'to realize itself': *sich verwirklichen*.
18. Marx excludes 'ineffective, non-paying needs' (p. 404).
19. Ibid.

5 The Circulation Process of Capital

Marx approaches the issue of circulation (turnover) of capital from five vantage points:

A. The historical evolution of circulation: from simple ('pure') circulation to capitalist production ('developed exchange').
B. The general concept of circulation: circulation of capital and circulation of money.
C. The threefold character of circulation (circulation as a continuous process):

  1. The total process.
  2. Small-scale circulation.
  3. Large-scale circulation.

D. The overall turnover of capital:

  1. The two moments of the production process.
  2. The two moments of the circulation process.
  3. Fixed capital and circulating capital.

E. Value, surplus value, and profit.

We shall divide this lengthy treatment into six Chapters, each with its own appropriate heading.

A. THE HISTORICAL EVOLUTION OF CIRCULATION

In 'pure' circulation Marx speaks of the 'simple movement of exchange values',[1] that is, a circulation in which money is exchanged for commodities and all purchasing power has been expended on the commodities which are consumed. In pure circulation, capital cannot be realised; that is to say, this form of circulation is essentially pre-capitalistic. It ties in directly with Marx's proposition regarding equivalent exchange. Capital creation does not take place even if the money which has been withdrawn and stockpiled is brought back into pure circulation. This is because in the exchange of equivalents, the money form of wealth is exchanged for its use value present in the commodity; consequently, 'pure circulation does not carry within itself the principle of self-renewal.'[2]

Capital[3] emanates only in developed circulation. Unlike exchange value in simple circulation, in which the complete exchange value is objectified and disappears during the act of the consumption of the final good, in developed circulation capital preserves and perpetuates itself.[4] Developed circulation signifies a 'much more complex form'[5] of circulation, a movement which creates exchange value in anticipation of the accumulation of capital. This type of circulation presupposes production for exchange, which comes historically after simple exchange and began with the inter-tribal exchange of surpluses:

> Semi-barbarian or completely barbarian peoples . . . or else tribes whose production is different by nature enter into contact and exchange their superfluous products. The exchange . . . extends only the overflow and plays an accessory role to production itself. But if the trading peoples who solicit exchange appear repeatedly . . . and if an ongoing commerce develops, . . . then the surplus of production must no longer be something accidental, occasionally present, but must be constantly repeated; and in this way domestic production itself takes on a tendency towards circulation . . . [and as] the sphere of needs is expanded, . . . the organization of domestic production itself is already modified by circulation and exchange value . . . but it has not yet been completely invaded by them. This is what is called the civilizing influence of external trade.[6]

As historical proof Marx cites the effect on English wool production, and eventually on English agriculture, of the rising British imports from the Netherlands in the sixteenth century and the need to generate exports, in payment:

> Agriculture thus lost the character of labour for use value, and the exchange of its overflow . . . [was] transformed into production for exchange value. Not only was the mode of production altered thereby, but also all the old relations of population and of production, the economic relations which corresponded to it, were dissolved.[7]

In the evolutionary sense, the stages of international exchange of goods from 'barbarian' times are, in Marx's view, as follows: first, there was a circulation which presupposed a production in which only the overflow attains the character of exchange value; the next stage then envisaged production for circulation, for exchange value; finally, in the advanced state, modern production, exchange value and developed circulation are presupposed and 'it is prices which determine production on one side, and production which determines prices on the other.'[8]

B. GENERAL CONCEPT OF CIRCULATION: CIRCULATION OF MONEY AND CIRCULATION OF CAPITAL

Marx took it upon himself to clear up the 'confusion'[9] concerning money and capital, to point out the antithetical (against the propertylessness of the worker) nature of capital, and to develop the concept of capital as a process, a process beginning not with labour but with exchange value in an already developed movement of circulation.[10]

First he reviews some earlier and contemporary definitions of capital and propositions with respect to the relation between money, labour, and capital.[11] He arrives at the conclusion that these writers fail to understand that capital constitutes not a simple relation but a process, a process in the course of which labour is accumulated and objectified in a quantity of objects. He juxtaposes the sphere of monetary circulation with the world of capital. In the former, an exchange of commodities for money takes place in which the buyer gives the seller the money-equivalent (= price) of the commodity's exchange value, in return for which he obtains from the seller the commodity's use value. Equivalents are exchanged for equivalents, and equals are equals – at least so it appears, because the exchange takes place in the freely competitive marketplace. Both the producer and the consumer are deemed the same, equal.[12]

Opposite this sphere of monetary circulation is the world of capital, a world in which the laws of equivalence do not hold. This is so because

In present bourgeois society as a whole, this positing of prices and their circulation etc., appears as the surface process, beneath which, in the depths, entirely different processes go on, in which this apparent equality and liberty disappear[13] . . . and the opposite process to equivalent exchange takes place: accumulation (exploitation, non-equivalent exchange, the extraction, from labour, of an equivalent-plus) . . . .[14]

According to Marx, several crucial issues and processes are involved in this duality of opposites:

- the relation between money and capital;
- the question whether the concept of value precedes that of capital;
- the question where capital comes from initially;
- the question of the relation of capital to labour;
- the question of capital and value, of the evolution of exchange: from the process of simple exchange to the unequal exchange between capital and labour.

1. The relation between money and capital

Money as capital is a higher realisation of money:

> *Money as capital* is an aspect of money which goes beyond its simple character as money. It can be regarded as a higher realisation. . . . *Money as capital* is distinct from *money as money*. This new aspect is to be developed.[15]

2. Value and capital

What comes first, the concept of value or the concept of capital?

> The Economists . . . sometimes consider capital as the creator of values, as their source [Say's 'capital is the sum of values'],[16] while at other times they presuppose values for the formation of capital, and portray it as itself only a sum of values in a particular function.[17]

> As in theory, the concept of value precedes that of capital, but requires for its pure development a mode of production founded on capital, so the same thing takes place in practice.[18]

This determination of value then [in which the individual product has ceased to exist for the producer in general and even more for the individual worker, and where nothing exists unless it is realized through circulation], presupposes a given historic stage of the mode of social production and is itself something given with that mode, hence a historic relation. Hence, within the system of bourgeois society, capital follows immediately after money. . . . It is therefore, precisely in the development of landed property that the gradual victory and formation of capital can be studied . . . .[19]

3. Capital – initial origin?

Capital's point of departure is money, and it comes initially from circulation:

Capital comes initially from circulation, and, moreover, its point of departure is money.[20] . . . Money is the first form in which capital as such appears: M-C-C-M; that money is exchanged for commodity and commodity for money; *this movement of buying in order to sell, which makes up the formal aspect of commerce*, of capital as merchant capital, is found in the earliest conditions of economic development. . . . This motion can take place within peoples, or between peoples whose production of exchange value has by no means yet become the presupposition. The movement only seizes upon the surplus of their directly useful production, and proceeds only on its margin. . . . Commercial capital is only circulating capital, and circulating capital is the first form of capital; in which it has *as yet by no means become the foundation of production*. A more developed form is *money capital* and *money interest*, usury, whose independent appearance belongs in the same way to an earlier stage. Finally, the form C-M-M-C, in which money and circulation in general appear as mere means for the *circulating commodity* . . .; . . . within society, commercial capital as such appears only as determined by this purely consumption-directed circulation. On the other side, the *circulating commodity* . . . is similarly [the] first form of capital, which is essentially *commodity capital*.

. . . it is equally clear that the simple movement of exchange values, such as is present in pure circulation, can never realize

capital . . . . Since equivalents are exchanged for one another, the
form of wealth which is fixed as money disappears as soon as it is
exchanged for the commodity; and the use value present in the
commodity, as soon as it is exchanged for money. . . . For capital
to be created, a movement in a complex form, production which
creates exchange values which presupposes circulation as a developed moment must be posited.[21]

4. Capital and labour

Labour in its relation to capital is that of opposite extremes:

The antithetical nature of capital, and the necessity for it of the
propertyless worker, is naïvely expressed in some earlier English
economists, e.g. the Reverend Mr. J. Townsend, the father of
population theory, by the fraudulent appropriation of which
Malthus (a shameless plagiarist generally; thus e.g., his theory of
rent is borrowed from the farmer, Anderson) made himself into a
great man. Townsend says: 'It seems to be a *law of nature* that the
poor should be to a certain degree improvident, that there may be
always some to fulfil the most servile, the most sordid, and the
most ignoble offices in the community. The more delicate ones are
thereby freed from drudgery, and can pursue higher callings etc.
undisturbed' (*A Dissertation on the Poor-laws*, edition of 1817,
p. 39). 'Legal constraint to labour is attended with too much
trouble, violence, and noise, creates ill will, etc., whereas hunger is
not only a peaceable, silent, unremitted pressure, but, as the most
natural motive to industry and labour, it calls forth the most
powerful exertions' (15). (This the answer to what labour is in fact
more productive, the slave's or the free worker's. A. Smith could
not raise the question, since the mode of production of capital
presupposes free labour. On the other side, the developed relation
of capital and labour confirms A. Smith in his distinction between
productive and unproductive labours. . . . A. Smith misses the
mark only by somewhat too crudely conceiving the objectification
of labour as labour which fixates itself in a tangible [*handgreiflich*]
object).[22]

With Galiani, too, the workmen are supplied by a law of nature.
Galiani published the book in 1750. 'God makes sure that the men
who exercise occupations of primary utility are born in abundant
numbers.' . . . But he already has the correct concept of value: 'It

is only toil which gives value to things.' Of course, labour is distinct qualitatively as well, not only in so far as it [is performed] in different branches of production, but also more or less intensive etc. The way in which the equalization of these differences takes place, and all labour is reduced to unskilled simple labour, cannot of course be examined yet at this point. Suffice it that this reduction is in fact *accomplished* with the positing of products of all kinds of labour as values. As values, they are equivalents in certain proportions; the higher kinds of labour are themselves appraised in simple labour. This becomes clear at once if one considers that, e.g., Californian gold is a product of simple labour. Nevertheless, every sort of labour is paid with it. Hence, the qualitative difference is suspended, and the product of a higher sort of labour is in fact reduced to an amount of simple labour. Hence, these computations of the different qualities of labour are completely a matter of indifference here, and do not violate the principle.[23]

If the worker produces and consumes a product for which only he has use value, this act of production and consumption does not produce exchange value. Exchange value emerges when the worker's product has use value for someone else, and the worker is willing to part with his product in exchange for something for which he has use value. It is his own use value that the worker offers to the capitalist, 'as his specific, productive capacity',[24] which the capitalist solicits. The use value contained in this 'value creating, productive labour'[25] becomes a specific exchange value when 'the common element of use values – labour time – is applied to it as an external yardstick.'[26] In Marx's view, labour is 'productive' when the workers increase the capital of their master; and 'unproductive' when they render, for money, a service, a use value which does not increase the user's capital.[27]

Labour is the worker's commodity which has use value; as such a commodity, it has a price. In return for his use value (that is, the utilisation of productive labour which maintains and multiplies the producer's capital), the worker obtains from the capitalist a specific sum of exchange values, a specific sum of money, all of which happens in the market.[28]

According to Marx, there is a basic difference between selling one's labour for money and receiving, in return, a specific sum of money (of exchange values). In this exchange, two processes are involved: the former, which constitutes simple exchange and amounts to ordinary circulation; and the latter, which results in the appropriation of labour by capital, a process 'qualitatively different' from simple exchange.[29]

The former (the first) process constitutes a payment for use value, a simple exchange, in which each party obtains an equivalent: 'the one obtains money, the other a commodity whose price is exactly equal to the money paid for it.'[30] In this process the exchange value of the commodity which the capitalist buys cannot, in general terms, be determined by the manner in which the buyer uses it but rather by the 'amount of labour required to reproduce this commodity (the worker)'.[31] The wages, as the price of this commodity, 'are measured, like all other commodities, by the labour time necessary to produce the worker as such . . . '.[32] What the worker receives in return is the 'equivalent in the form of money . . . a means of subsistence, objects for the preservation of his life . . . measured by the cost of production of his labour'.[33] In exchange for his use value the worker obtains the general form of wealth, becomes co-participant in general wealth, to the limit of his equivalent.[34]

The exchange between the worker and the capitalist is a simple exchange: each obtains an equivalent: the one obtains money, the other a commodity whose *price* is exactly equal to the money paid for it; what the capitalist obtains from this simple exchange is a use value: disposition over alien labour. . . . What the capitalist does with his labour is completely irrelevant, although of course he can use it only in accord with its specific characteristics, and his disposition is restricted to a *specific* labour and is *restricted in time* (so much labour time). . . . If the capitalist were to content himself with merely the capacity of disposing, without actually making the worker work, e.g., in order to have his labour as a reserve, or to deprive his competitor of this capacity of disposing (like, e.g., theatre directors who buy singers for a season not in order to have them sing, but so that they do not sing in a competitor's theatre), then the exchange has taken place in full. . . . Since he exchanges his use value for the general form of wealth, he becomes co-participant in general wealth up to the limit of his equivalent . . . the worker receives the equivalent in the form of money, the form of general wealth; he is in this exchange an equal *vis-à-vis* the capitalist, like every other party in exchange; at least so he *seems*. In fact this equality is already disturbed because the worker's relation to the capitalist as a use value, in the form specifically

distinct from exchange value . . . is a presupposition of this seemingly simple exchange. . . . What is essential is that the purpose of
the exchange for him is the satisfaction of his need. The object of
this exchange is a direct object of need, not exchange value as
such. . . . What he obtains from the exchange is therefore not
exchange value, not wealth, but a means of subsistence, . . . the
satisfaction of his needs in general, physical, social, etc. It is a
specific equivalent in means of subsistence, in objectified labour,
measured by the cost of production of his labour. What he gives up
is his power to dispose of the latter. . . . As a rule, the maximum of
industriousness, of labour, and the minimum of consumption . . .
could lead to nothing else than that he would receive for his
maximum of labour a minimum of wages. By his exertions he
would only have diminished the general *level* of the production
costs of his own labour and therefore its general price. . . . If they
all save, then a general reduction of wages will bring them back to
earth again; for general savings would show the capitalist that their
wages are in general too high, that they receive more than its
equivalent for their commodity, the capacity of disposing of their
own labour; since it is precisely the essence of simple exchange –
and they stand in this relationship towards him – that no one
throws into circulation more than he withdraws; but also that no
one can withdraw more than he has thrown in.[35]

This – the simple – exchange appears equal, except that it does not
render the *worker* (emphasis added) wealthy, even though, in Marx's
view, the worker can under certain conditions enrich himself: he may
accumulate money and thereby pile up exchange value; or he may
practise the art of 'self-denial' – of withdrawing less from circulation
than what he put into circulation in the form of products; or, finally,
he may practise self-denial by becoming more industrious.[36]
    The latter (the second) process, the relation between capital and
labour *after* the exchange of money for the worker's use value, Marx
refers to as a form of circulation which is other than 'simple'.
Whereas in simple exchange the exchange between the worker and
the capitalist enriches neither, in the second process the issue is much
more complex because the use value which labour sells to the capitalist becomes in the hands of the latter a creative power, the force of
productive wealth, which the capitalist appropriates for himself,
whereby the worker is left unable to enrich himself.[37] In the first
process, equivalents are exchanged; in the second, developed circula-

tion, the worker is put through the form C-M-M-C of the exchange process, while the capitalist puts himself through the alternative form, M-C-C-M.

Marx is in agreement with the basic proposition of the 'Economists': that labour obtains only the equivalent for its use value, which equivalent he consumes; a situation in which no wealth is generated. But he is in total disagreement with them concerning their view about the capitalist, whom they consider not to benefit either because he incurs a sacrifice by advancing his funds, which amounts to a sacrifice of his wealth, a sacrifice which he seeks to minimise.[38] In opposition to this view, Marx submits his own interpretation of the process of wealth accumulation: capital accumulation arises from the capitalist's disposition of the worker's *Arbeitskraft* after it has been obtained at a specific cost.

As activity, labour is the living source of value, the general potentiality of wealth. By capital's appropriation of labour's use value, labour becomes objectified (whereas, on the contrary, non-objectified[39] labour amounts to non-value[40]):

Labour is the yeast thrown into [capital], which starts it fermenting. . . . The particular, the passive, substance of capital, enters into relation with the forming activity of labour . . . the subjectivity of labour, the living labour, has to be objectified in the material of capital.[41]

In this process, the concept of product attains a new interpretation: it is the result of the conversion between the passive content of capital and the activity of labour as the living source of value:

Thus, the raw material is consumed by being changed, formed by labour, and the instrument of labour is consumed by being used up in this process, worn out. On the other hand, labour is also consumed by being employed, set into motion, and a certain amount of the worker's muscular force etc. is thus expended, so that he exhausts himself. But labour is not only consumed, it is also at the same time fixed, converted from the form of activity into the form of the object: materialized; as a modification of the object, it modifies its own form and changes from activity into being. The end of the process is the *product*. . . . All three moments of the process, the material, the instrument, and labour, coincide in the neutral result – the product . . . [42] The whole process therefore appears as *productive consumption*, i.e., as consumption which terminates . . . as an *object* . . . as *product*, the result of this production process is *use value*.[43]

NOTES AND COMMENTS

1. *Grundrisse*, p. 254.
2. Ibid.
3. Marx defines the 'self-realization' of capital as the surplus value created in the act of production.
4. Ibid., p. 260.
5. Ibid., p. 255.
6. Ibid. Note Marx's claim that developed circulation commenced with foreign trade; however, he does not proceed, at this point, to suggest that capital accumulation therefore necessarily begins with foreign trade.
7. Ibid., p. 257.
8. Ibid.
9. Ibid., p. 844.
10. Ibid., p. 259.
11. Ibid., pp. 239–60.
12. Ibid., pp. 247–51.
13. Ibid., p. 247.
14. Ibid., p. 404–7.
15. Ibid., p. 251.
16. Ibid.
17. Ibid., pp. 251–2.
18. Ibid., p. 251.
19. Ibid., p. 252.
20. Ibid., p. 253.
21. Ibid., pp. 253–4.
22. Ibid., p. 845.
23. Ibid., pp. 845–6.
24. Ibid., p. 271.
25. Ibid., p. 272.
26. Ibid., p. 269.
27. Ibid., pp. 272–3. In his note on p. 305 of the *Grundrisse*, an extensive reference is provided concerning Marx's treatment of the issue of productive labour v. unproductive labour (Senior, Malthus, Adam Smith).
28. Ibid., p. 274. Marx digresses here into a discussion of the term 'market'. He speaks of the money market, which includes the money-lending market with its institutions and instruments ('interest-bearing shares, etc.') and distinguishes between the home market and the foreign market. The world market is 'not only the internal market in relation to all foreign markets existing outside it, but at the same time the internal market of all foreign markets, in turn, as components of the home market' (p. 280).

29. Ibid., p. 274.
30. Ibid., pp. 281–2.
31. Ibid., p. 282.
32. Ibid., pp. 282–3.
33. Ibid., p. 284.
34. Ibid., p. 283.
35. Ibid., pp. 281–6. Marx provides an interesting insight into his thoughts concerning the consequences of alternative actions (greater exertion v. saving) on the part of the workers: since the workers are supposed to save in order to reduce the costs of production of the capitalists, 'if the workers *generally* acted according to this demand as a *rule* . . . damage . . . to general consumption – the loss would be enormous – and hence also to production, thus also to the amount and volume of the exchange which they could make with capital, hence to themselves as workers . . .' (p. 285). But he also points to the self-contradictory behaviour of capitalists: each wants his own workers to save, but each regards the rest of the world of workers as consumers who should be enticed into consumption (p. 286).

From these observations follows Marx's rendition of a net cause – effect explanation of a crisis: the workers' attempt to save (as a group, since the individual can succeed only through will-power, greed, endurance) is self-defeating. This is so because, not consuming all of the payment for his use value in trying to save or working at maximum industriousness and living at a minimum of consumption, the worker will contribute to the diminution of the general level of production costs and therefore of his own general price. In consequence, the capitalist gets the impression that he is paying too much for the workers' use value and cuts the wage level until no saving is possible. Ultimately, in crisis, the capitalist fails and the worker receives nothing. However, Marx also notes the opposite: in an expansion, the workers can conserve their savings while their use remains of benefit to the capitalist (pp. 286–7).

How does the saved money become capital, asks Marx? It must buy (the use value of) labour. It is the essence of labour not to become capital; but labour sells its use value for the immediate satisfaction of its needs. Unlike a slave, who has exchange value, the worker has none because 'as a slave, the worker has exchange value, a value; as a free wage-worker he has no value; it is, rather, his power of disposing of his labour, effected by exchange with him, which has value' (p. 289).
36. *Grundrisse*, pp. 282–5.
37. Ibid., pp. 285–91.
38. Ibid., pp. 282–4.
39. Ibid., p. 295.
40. Ibid.
41. Ibid., p. 298.
42. Ibid., p. 299.
43. Ibid., pp. 300–1.

6 Simple Exchange v. Developed Exchange

A. CAPITAL AND VALUE: THE PROCESS OF SIMPLE EXCHANGE

The process of value creation includes preservation of the prior value, as well as its multiplication. How, asks Marx, can higher exchange value originate out of circulation itself if in simple circulation only equivalents exchange? He answers: the higher exchange value must have entered circulation as higher exchange value.[1]

To explain this transformation, Marx starts out with the simple case, where value after the production process is equal to value of capital before and where, therefore, the price of the product is equal to its costs of production (decomposed into the component parts of these costs, that is to say, the values of these component parts or, still more precisely, their prices).[2] In fact, in the simple case, 'the value of capital has preserved itself in the process of production, appearing as a sum.'[3]

But what if the value is greater than that originally present (to which, according to Marx, the 'Economists' refer as the determination of price by costs of production), for example if to the original value of capital = 100 are added 5 per cent interest and 5 per cent profit, for a total value of 110?[4] This charge, declares Marx, cannot be explained by claiming that use value is determined by exchange value (this is so because, often, commodities fall below their prices of production); or that circulation caused it; or by means of simple circulation (since in such circulation value is posited as equivalent before and after). Marx's own solution: the difference lies in that value which labour creates in the process of production and the exchange value labour gets paid by capital: *Mehrwert*.[5]

Marx goes to some lengths in providing explanations:

- if everybody sold for 10 per cent too much, nobody would make an extra 10 per cent;
- even if money sold for 10 per cent too much, it would return only 100, not 110;

– he queries how Ricardo can justify the following statement: 'foreign trade can never increase the amount of exchange value in a country'.[6] Marx explains this statement as follows: Ricardo can justify it because he takes foreign trade as simple circulation, which can never create or increase exchange value. Why not? Because if it did, the proposition that price equals costs of production would also have to read that price is always greater than the costs of production, which would make no sense. The latter can be true only in developed exchange, in which labour does not get full compensation for its value – in which, therefore, price must be higher than the costs of production.[7]

– he also questions how the capitalist would feed himself if 100 pre-production Thalers would equal 100 reproduction Thalers? Would he consume part of his capital (for example, $\frac{10}{100}$)? If so, ultimately his capital would be reduced to zero. But the capitalist is paid to put 100 Thalers into the production process, for a return. He hires labour. If labour transferred only the value which it takes out, then price would equal the cost of production and there would be no need to pay the capitalist, as no capital is involved. If, however, capitalist labour were as specific as wage labour, then the capitalist too would get a wage (an exchange value) equal to his use value, and would consume it.

– Furthermore, the capitalist must be compensated for risks of production (price fluctuations; constantly going on devaluation of capital because of increases in the force of production, which must be compensated). Also, ' . . . for the industrial capitalist, interest is among his direct expenses, his *real* cost of production', and 'the payment of interest shows that capital as such is not the mere addition of value-components.'[8] Clearly, the cost of production is not 'the sum of values which enter into production'[9] and interest is but one form of the surplus value which comes forth from production.[10]

B. CAPITAL AND VALUE: SURPLUS VALUE AND DEVELOPED EXCHANGE: THE UNEQUAL EXCHANGE BETWEEN CAPITAL AND LABOUR

An increase in the exchange value of the product would be impossible if capital paid to the worker the exact equivalent for the value which labour creates in the production process, that is, the whole surplus above the value of raw material and instruments of production.[11]

> The surplus value which capital has at the end of the production process . . . which as a higher price of the product is realized only in circulation . . . signifies, expressed in accord with the general concept of exchange value, that the labour time objectified in the product . . . is greater than that which was present in the original components of capital.[12]

> Proudhon grasps neither how profit, nor, therefore, how interest, arises from the laws of the exchange of values. . . . (The good fellow does not understand that the whole point is that value is exchanged for labour according to the law of values; that, hence, to abolish interest, he would have to abolish *capital* itself, the mode of production founded on exchange value, hence wage labour as well. Mr. Proudhon's inability to find even one difference between loan and sale: 'In effect, the hatter who sells hats . . . obtains their value in return, neither more nor less. But the lending capitalist . . . not only gets back the whole of his capital; he receives more than the capital, more than he brings into the exchange; he receives an interest above the capital' (69). Thus Mr. Proudhon's hatters reckon neither profit nor interest as part of their cost price. He does not grasp that, precisely by receiving the *value* of their hats, they obtain more than these cost them, because a part of this value is appropriated in the exchange, without equivalent, with labour. . . .)[13]

Marx's thesis on surplus value is then enunciated:

> Value for which no equivalent has been given.[14]

> Surplus value in general is value in excess of the equivalent. The equivalent, by definition, is only the identity of value with itself. Hence, surplus value can never sprout out of the equivalent; nor can it do so originally out of circulation: it has to arise from the production process of capital itself. . . . What appears as surplus value on capital's side appears identically on the worker's side as surplus labour in excess of his requirements as worker.[15]

> The great historical quality of capital is to *create* this *surplus*

labour, superfluous labour from the standpoint of mere use value, mere subsistence.[16]

In its unlimited mania for wealth, capital disciplines labour, develops general industriousness, uses labour as a commodity, replaces natural necessity with a historically created one. . . .[17]

Marx specifies that the type of labour involved is not 'any particularly qualified labour but labour in general, simple labour'.[18] In exchange for this general, simple labour, the workers obtain as price the value of their divestiture [*Entäußerung*], which is determined by the *verwirklichte Arbeit* which is contained in his commodity, a value which he must receive in order to maintain his vitality, the value which amounts to an equivalent: that price which he obtains and which leaves him in possession of the same exchange value as before.[19] Concerning special skills, Marx suggests that their values have to show themselves in the costs necessary to produce a similar labouring skill.[20]

Marx continues his reflections concerning capital and surplus value in several major Sections which follow his initial thoughts on this topic. For the sake of simplicity and clarity, despite the frequent overlaps of the items considered in these Sections, the remaining (lengthy) part of the unequal exchange between capital and labour will be divided into five additional subsections, as follows:

1. Marx's views on the propositions of the Physiocrats, of Adam Smith, and of David Ricardo concerning surplus value;
2. surplus value and the increase in the productive powers of labour;
3. surplus value, increase in labour productivity, and prices;
4. capital, surplus value, and profit;
5. devaluation of capital, overproduction, value and price.

1. Marx's views on the proposition of the Physiocrats, of Adam Smith, and of David Ricardo concerning surplus value

Physiocracy considers wealth to be the surplus above the commodities consumed in production, in particular an overabundance of agricultural products. Surplus value does not arise from labour as such but rather from the natural forces which labour uses and conducts: agriculture. Only that labour which creates surplus value is productive.

Adam Smith's proposition that the division of labour increases the natural force of labour itself implies that labour is the principal source of value. But Smith also claims that the payment for capital and the payment for land, as historical subtractions from wages justified by the law, are additional determinants. Not so, says Marx, because 'wages are the only economically justifiable, because necessary, element of production cost.'[21] Moreover, Smith confuses the determination of value by wages, on the one hand, and by the labour time objectified in the commodity, on the other.[22]

Marx's treatment of Ricardo is more complex and involves several aspects:

To start with, Marx declares that Ricardo alone understood surplus value, but he then claims that Ricardo often gets into confusion, particularly in the following two aspects concerning capital: (a) even though he understands that the creation of surplus value is the presupposition of capital, his theory of ground rent conceives the multiplication of values on a basis other than the investment of *additional* objectified labour time in the same product, which makes his theory one-sided for proposing that value go up with an increasing difficulty of production; (b) his theory of international trade is erroneous because it proposes that trade is supposed to produce only use value (which he calls 'wealth', the absolute antithesis in his thinking between value and wealth), but not exchange value.[23]

Marx's critique of these two propositions is as follows:

Apart from the growing difficulty of production, population growth, (the natural increase among workers resulting from the growth of capital) is the only avenue for the increase in values as such; but Ricardo never summarised this relation.[24] Ricardo never investigated where the distinction between the determination of value by wages and by objectified labour comes from. In his economics, money and exchange (circulation) appear as purely formal elements. In Ricardo's view, profit (and so forth) appear only as a percentage share of the product's exchange value and the creation of capital in the act of production takes the tangible form of rent, which is a crude view (and similar to that of Adam Smith; crude, that is, considering that actors, for example, are also productive workers, not in so far as they produce a play but in so far as they increase their employer's wealth).[25] This view is also simplistic since, in claiming that a day's work is always exchanged for a day's work and that an increase in values can arise, therefore, only out of an increasing difficulty of production – the use of more labour to eke out the same from a decreasing fertility of the soil – Ricardo arrives at the conclusion that profits go down because rents go up. Not so, claims Marx: since surplus value equals surplus labour and since profits and interest themselves become capital, the form of wealth based on exchange value is, contrary to Ricardo's claims, not solely concerned with use value.[26]

For Ricardo, 'wage labour and capital are conceived of as a natural, not as an historically special form [*Gesellschaftsform*] for the creation of wealth as use value'; but because he deems them 'natural', their specific form – the specific form of bourgeois wealth – is irrelevant to him. In consequence, he does not perceive this specific form of wealth as a form with exchange value as the point of departure.[27] But clearly, an increase in the exchange value of the product would be impossible if capital paid the worker the exact equivalent for the value which labour creates in the production process, that is, the whole surplus above the value of raw material and instruments of production.[28]

The remaining aspects of Marx's reflections on Ricardo in areas touching upon international trade emerge in the subsections: Surplus Value and Productive Forces; Increase in Productive Forces and Prices, and Confusion of Profit and *Mehrwert*.

Specific forms of exchange play no role in Ricardian economics, claims Marx, in his deliberations on capital and his contribution to the assessment of the role and significance of capital:

> Instead, he [Ricardo] always speaks about the distribution of the general product of labour and of the soil among the three classes, as if the form of wealth based on *exchange value* were concerned only with *use value*, and as if exchange value were merely a ceremonial form. . . . Therefore, in order to bring out the true laws of economics, he likes to refer to this relation of money as a merely formal one. . . . a weakness in his doctrine of money proper.[29]

In Marx's view, this approach leaves 'capital' insufficiently defined. In consequence, 'the exact development of the concept of capital [is] necessary, since it [is] the fundamental concept in modern economics . . . the abstract, reflected image [of capital being] the foundation of bourgeois society. . . . [therefore it is necessary] through sharp formulation . . . to bring out all the contradictions of bourgeois production. . . .[30]

To understand the concept of capital, one must understand the concept of wealth and the role of wealth as the mediator [*Vermittler*] between the extremes of exchange value and use value, bourgeois wealth representing the highest power as exchange value.[31]

Wealth presents itself more distinctly and more broadly the further it is removed from production. In this process money becomes an end rather than a means, a higher form of mediation, whereby capital as the higher form of mediation posits the lower, labour, as the mere source of surplus value; for example billbrokers and bankers *v.* manufacturers and farmers whom they posit in the role of labour (of use value, while viewing themselves as capital, the higher form, which extracts surplus value; the worst of all being that of the financier).

Capital appears as the direct unity of product and money, or, still better, of production and circulation; this unity appears at first sight to be something simple.

Ricardo reflects such simple reasoning: 'products are exchanged for one another – hence capital for capital – according to the amounts of objectified labour contained in them. A day's work is always exchanged for a day's work.'[32] But in Marx's view, this is a presupposition which entirely omits exchange itself.

However, exchange cannot be left out. The product-capital posited as product is exchange value in itself, to which exchange adds form:

The only question is now in what *proportions* this product is divided up and distributed. Whether these *proportions* are regarded as specific quotas of the presupposed exchange value, or of its content, material wealth, [is] the same thing. Moreover, since exchange as such is merely circulation – money as circulation – it is better to abstract from it altogether, and to examine only the proportions of material wealth which have been distributed within the production process or because of it to the various factors. In the *exchange* form, all value etc. is merely *nominal*; it is real only in the form of the proportion. . . . Since a full day's work is always exchanged for a full day's work, the sum of *values* remains the same – the growth in the forces of production affects only the content of wealth, not its form. An increase of values can arise, therefore, only out of an increasing difficulty in production – and this can take place only where the forces of nature no longer afford

an equal service to equal quantities of human labour, i.e. where
the fertility of the natural elements decreases – in agriculture. The
decline in profits is therefore caused by rent. Firstly the false
presupposition that a *full day's work* is always worked in all social
conditions. . . .[33]

2. Surplus value and the increase in the productive powers of labour

What happens, asks Marx, if the productive powers of labour double,
creating double the use value in the same time (feeding himself
equally well while expending 50 per cent less of his labour time)? In
answering, Marx defines 'use value' as that which the worker consumes in order to stay alive as a worker. This worker needs to work,
for example, only half a working day in order to live a whole one, and
hence be able to begin the same process again the next day.[34] The one
half day's work necessary to keep him alive, as a *living* instrument of
labour, results in his entire living day's appropriation by capital. The
latter consumes his entire day's work in the production process with
the materials of which his capital consists, giving in exchange only the
labour objectified in the workers, half a day's worth, and retaining
for himself the surplus value of his capital, a half day's objectified
labour.[35]

If the productive powers of labour double, labour creates double
the use value in the same time. Clearly, therefore, the worker's part
of the day which he needs to feed himself drops from $\frac{1}{2}$ day to $\frac{1}{4}$ day;
but he still works all day, which leaves the capitalist with an extra $\frac{1}{4}$
day for himself, adding $\frac{1}{4}$ (= 50 per cent) to the previous $\frac{1}{2}$ of surplus
value. This process goes on and on:

> [Capital], as representative of the general form of wealth – money –
> . . . is endless and limitless. . . . Capital as such creates a specific
> surplus value because it cannot create an infinite one all at once;
> but it is the constant movement to create more of the same. . . .
> Therefore, (quite apart from the factors entering in later, competi-
> tion, prices, etc.) the capitalist will make the worker work not only
> $\frac{3}{4}$ day, because the $\frac{3}{4}$ day brings him the *same surplus value*, but
> rather he will make him work the full day . . . increasing the
> surplus.[36]

To the worker, this now appears as a lengthening of time he
labours for the realisation of capital (for exchange value). The

worker knows that he is working shorter for himself and longer for the capitalist. The worker's surplus labour has increased by $\frac{1}{4}$ day; the capitalist's surplus value has increased by $\frac{1}{4}$ day. Since the productive force has doubled, clearly, surplus labour and surplus value do not increase in the same proportion even though they do increase equally. Surplus labour and surplus values are always the same increment, but their value relative to the increase in the force of production is 1/3 if the latter doubles and if labour originally worked 2/3 for his own sustenance.[37]

From these reflections, Marx concludes the following:

– The value of capital does not grow in the same proportion as the productive force increases, but in the proportion in which the increase in the productive force, the multiplier of the productive force, divides the fraction of the working day which expresses the part of the day belonging to the worker.[38]

Marx states quite clearly that value is the part that feeds the worker; the rest is clearly surplus value:

– The value [of surplus labour] can never be equal to the entire working day: that is to say, a certain part of the working day must always be exchanged for the labour objectified in the worker. Surplus value in general is only the relation of living labour to that objectified in the worker . . . Surplus value is exactly equal to relative surplus labour.[39]

Then he becomes still more specific, distinguishing between 'new value' and 'surplus value':

. . . if the working day was $\frac{1}{2}$ and the productive force doubles, then the part belonging to the worker, *necessary labour*, reduces itself to $\frac{1}{4}$ and the new value is also exactly $\frac{1}{4}$ but the total value is now $\frac{3}{4}$. While surplus value rose by $\frac{1}{4}$, i.e. in the relation of 1:4, the total surplus value $= \frac{3}{4}$.[40]

In Marx's view, the relation between an increase in the productive force, the value of capital, and the value of the worker is easily grasped: the increase in the productive force increases the value of capital and diminishes the value of the worker. This is so not because the increase in the productive force increases the quantity of products or use values created by the same labour, but because it diminishes necessary labour. As necessary labour diminishes, surplus labour is created, 'or, what amounts to the same thing, surplus value . . .'.[41] Marx is emphatic in repeating that the surplus value of capital does not increase as does the multiplier[42] of the productive force, but at a lesser rate: 'by the surplus of the fraction of the living work day which originally represents necessary labour, in excess over this same fraction divided by the multiplier of the productive force. Thus, if *necessary labour* $= \frac{1}{4}$ of the living workday and the productive force doubles, then the value of capital does not double but grows by $\frac{1}{8}$ . . . .'[43]

Every increase in the productive force of labour increases the use values for the capitalist; it also increases the productive force of capital, even though not necessarily equally in all countries:

> Thus the *absolute sum* by which capital increases its value through a given increase of the productive force depends on the *given fractional part* of the working day, on the fractional part of the working day which represents *necessary labour*, and which, therefore, expresses the original relation of necessary labour to the living work day. The increase in the productive force in a given relation can, therefore, increase the value of capital differently, e.g. in *different countries*[44] . . . in the different branches of industry . . . depending on the different relation of *necessary-labour* to the living work day in these branches. This relation would naturally be the same in all branches of business in a system of free competition, if labour were simple labour everywhere, hence *necessary labour time* the same. . . . (If it represented the same amount of objectified labour.)[45]

Marx continues his abstract analysis of the relation between the size of the surplus value of capital and increases in the productive force, but is careful to emphasise that his abstract reflections would have to be modified in view of 'additional relations'; he also places all these deliberations squarely into the theory of profit.[46] The larger is the surplus value of capital before the increase in the productive force: that is to say, the larger the amount of presupposed surplus labour, the smaller is necessarily the 'fractional part of the working day which forms the equivalent of the worker, i.e. necessary labour, an increase in the productive force will, therefore, lead to a smaller increase in surplus value.'[47] As the development of the productive force proceeds at a specific rate, the surplus value rises at a decreasing rate. It follows that the more developed capital is – that is, the more surplus value it has created – the more enormously will its productive force have to be increased in order to add (a forever decreasing) proportion to surplus value. Whereas the infinite quest for wealth causes infinite striving to increase the productive force, eventually the increase in the productive force will tend to become irrelevant to capital. This is so because

> the self-realization [*Selbstverwirklichung*] of capital becomes the more difficult the more capital has already been realized . . . not because wages have increased or the share of labour in the product but because it has *already* fallen so low, regarded in its relation to the product of labour or to the living workday.[48]

Marx is labouring very hard in seeking to provide, by way of abstract illustrations, a series of geometric progressions which will demonstrate the inverse relation between the rate of increase in the productive force and the rate of increase in surplus value. Even the editors of the *Grundrisse* admit that many of his numbers and calculations are wrong. In addition he uses, very liberally and inter-changeably, the terms 'relative value', 'new value', 'value', 'surplus time', 'surplus value', 'total surplus value', and 'value of capital', which renders the comprehension of his propositions even more difficult.[49] His proposition that the increase in the productive force of living labour increases the value of capital (as it diminishes the value of the worker) because it diminishes necessary labour is consistent with his formulations; as is his conclusion that, as necessary labour diminishes because of his increase in productivity, surplus labour and surplus value (which are equal) are increased. But, in his reckoning, the increase in the productive force of living labour does not increase the quantity of products or use values created for themselves by the same labour; that is to say, the volume of output for their own needs does not go up even though the labour force had doubled its pro-ductivity. [Neither is there a saving in labour time, because the workers are forced to continue working the same number of hours as before the increase in their productivity. The workers work fewer hours to produce whatever they need, which leaves their market in equilib-rium. But their new surplus labour, jointly with the new surplus value created by that labour, is usurped by capital, which is where the problem comes in – as Marx sees it: the producers' demand for the use values produced during the whole living-workday of labour is not sufficient to take up the new net quantity supplied to producers. Since the domestic workers' sector is in equilibrium (their new, lower income from selling their use value equals their lower expenditures from the decrease in, for example, food prices in seeking to restore their *Arbeitskraft*), the excess supply of commodities in the domestic producers' market will either have to be sold abroad or, if this is not possible, a crisis will ensue. Marx's assumption that the increase in the productive force will not increase the quantity supplied to labour may be assigned to his desire to consider solely the decreasing proportion of necessary labour to surplus labour in the process of capital accumulation, a piece of analysis which can feasibly be conducted under conditions of holding constant the share of the workers in an otherwise absolute increase in the level of the real national product, even though its money value remains unchanged.

3. Surplus value, increase in labour productivity, and prices

Marx then extends his analysis to include the effect of increases in labour productivity on prices. Two commodities are involved: wheat (first example) and gold (second example).

If the productive force in wheat production doubles, then the $\frac{1}{2}$ day objectified labour is reduced to $\frac{1}{4}$, which covers the workers' needs. In consequence, the price of labour drops from the $\frac{1}{2}$-day equivalent (13 shillings) to a $\frac{1}{4}$-day equivalent ($6\frac{1}{2}$ shillings). With this drop, the price of this fractional part of the commodity falls. But the quantity of wheat ('material production'[50]) doubles (from the previous 2 bushels to the new 4 bushels), while the 'total price' (price per bushel times quantity) remains unchanged. The total price of the material product remains at the previous 26 shillings, but the PxQ is now made up of $6\frac{1}{2}$ sh. x 4 bushels.

Marx claims here that the cost of labour had been cut in half by the doubling of the workers' productive force. However, he omits to make any reference to the capacity of the other inputs to sustain and render effective this doubling of labour's capacity (for example, will the quality-quantity of land allow this doubling of output?); moreover, Marx looks at the total product (now 4 bushels) at the price of $6\frac{1}{2}$ shillings per bushel, without specifying what the demand conditions are like for the economy as a whole: (for example, if the workers are contented to go on consuming only their previous 1 bushel of wheat, in spite of their increased productivity, then the workers' market for wheat is in equilibrium, since the workers' aggregate income is equal to their aggregate spending: 1 bushel of wheat for $6\frac{1}{2}$ sh.; however, 3 bushels of wheat remain to be sold, of which one will be consumed by the producers (their previous consumption pattern). It appears that 2 bushels will remain unsold and that 13 shillings are unaccounted for (unless we presume that a new market will open up, possibly abroad).

In addition, Marx posits that, with the value of labour dropping to $6\frac{1}{2}$ sh., the value of capital increases by $6\frac{1}{2}$ sh., to $19\frac{1}{2}$ sh. But will the producers be in equilibrium – capital worth $19\frac{1}{2}$ shillings and a quantity of wheat of 3 bushels (of which the capitalists will presumably consume 1 bushel)? Clearly, unless we assume that Marx posited that the market will clear itself at the price of $6\frac{1}{2}$ sh. per bushel, we are most likely to encounter strong pressures for the price to decrease below the postulated $6\frac{1}{2}$ sh. per bushel. Marx also fails to consider what will happen to the factor land if the productive powers of labour double: will more land have to be used, with the inevitable diminishing returns (and, in Marx's own language, an increase in the value of capital)? or will less land be required, which would then initiate a reverse movement to higher-quality land (which should decrease the cost of capital and lead to a decrease in the value of capital)? However, possibly, Marx's failure to consider these questions may imply that he was thinking in terms of constant returns (on land).[51]

What if the productive force of labour in gold doubles?

Marx declares that the 'total gold product' will increase from 26 sh. to 52 sh. (he does not specify the quantity of gold, before or after the increase in labour productivity). These 52 sh. worth of gold will now purchase the 4 bushels of wheat (the result of a doubling of the productivity of labour in wheat), the price per bushel amounting to 13 sh. The workers in gold still now earn 13 sh. (for the use value of their necessary labour), that is, $\frac{1}{4}$ day down from the $\frac{1}{2}$ day, while the share of capital will increase to 39 sh., by the addition of 13 sh. of new surplus value (note that Marx decreases the wheat share of labour from the previous 13 sh. per bushel to the new $6\frac{1}{2}$ sh. per bushel; but he retains the gold share of labour at 13 shillings' worth; this is so because he keeps the price of gold constant despite the increase in the productivity of labour in gold, whereas he decreases the price of wheat, possibly in seeking to demonstrate that in agriculture the whole benefit from an increase in labour productivity will accrue to the landowners).

Whatever may have been Marx's motivation in linking the wheat market with the gold market, a curious situation is created: the new labour cost of wheat (necessary labour) is $6\frac{1}{2}$ sh. per bushel; at this price, the workers in wheat still break even in spite of their increase in productivity; but the gold price remains at 13 sh., even after the increase in labour productivity in gold. Before the doubling of the productive force in wheat, 2 bushels were produced and sold at 13 sh. each, the value of one working day. Before the doubling of the production force in gold, 26 shillings' worth of gold were produced. In macro-terms, therefore, 26 sh. worth of gold was sufficient purchasing power to buy up 26 sh. worth of wheat (at 13 sh. per bushel). However, after the doubling of the productive force in wheat and in gold, according to Marx, 4 bushels of wheat are produced at the total price of 26 sh., but are exchanged for gold at the price of 13 sh. per bushel.

Clearly, the workers and the capitalist in the gold sector are better off than those in the wheat sector, which Marx fails to see: whereas the money earnings of the workers in wheat drop from the previous 13 sh. to the new $6\frac{1}{2}$ sh. (even though their real purchasing power is said to have remained the same, at $6\frac{1}{2}$ sh. per bushel of wheat), the gold workers' money income remains at 13 sh., with which they can now buy double the quantity of wheat (at the price of wheat to the wheat workers), a point which Marx completely neglected to consider. Moreover, in his own examples, before the doubling of the productive force in wheat only 2 bushels were produced and were sold for 26 shillings; but after the doubling of the productive force both in wheat and in gold, four units of wheat are produced for 26 shillings but are sold for 52 shillings, at double the previous revenue – an inflationary situation (but let us recall that Marx did state, in The Chapter On Money, that the increase in the forces of production will tend to depreciate continuously the purchasing power of the money metal).

Subsequent to these particular examples of the effects of increases in the productivity of labour, Marx provides additional illustrations in his quest to see himself through this problem. In so doing, he makes the following assumptions:

– that the entire living-workday is consumed in the production process, the living-workday being the 'natural amount of labour time' which the worker puts at the disposal of capital;
– that the product objectifies one working day, whatever is in it the *necessary* labour time;
– that of the objectified labour time of a whole day, the surplus value of capital has grown to 3/4 of the *necessary* objectified labour time: that is, the share of surplus value relative to the necessary labour time has increased:

– that the length of the working day has remained the same, which means that the total amount of labour remains unchanged and that there has been no absolute increase in surplus labour time; however, the relative amount of surplus labour has increased because the amount of necessary labour has decreased.

In this exercise, Marx is trying to establish how the price of the product (presupposing 'price' to be the gold and silver value of the product) – that is, the exchange value of capital – relates to the value of the product, and how the rate of profit is linked to the rate of surplus value:

> The price (presupposing this as its gold and silver value), or the exchange value of capital, has not increased with the doubling of the productive force. This [the surplus value of the capital], therefore, concerns the *rate of profit*, not the price of the product or the value of the capital. . . . But in fact the absolute values also increase in this manner, because that part of wealth which is posited as capital – as self-realising value – also increases. (*Accumulation of capitals*.)[52]

Of the examples which Marx provides as illustrations, the following will be particularly helpful in following his reasoning:

> Four hours of all-day objectified labour produce a value of 100 Thalers, which includes materials of production, instruments of production, and necessary labour:

> 50 Th. cotton + 10 Th. instruments + 40 Th. wages = 100 Thalers.

If the output is produced by the worker as the owner (in simple exchange, there is no exploitation; the worker's 'surplus value . . . is the reproduction of his own living labour capacity or of the time objectified in him'[53]), these four hours of work will produce a value of 100 Th. However, if the output is produced by capital, the hours of work will be extended to eight, resulting in a value of 140 Thalers, which includes a surplus value of 40 Thalers; the value of capital increases from the original 100 to the new 140. A new value (40 Thalers) has been created, over and beyond the replacement costs of materials and instruments of labour. As a result, the values in circulation (wages and surplus value) will have increased by a total of 80 Thalers.[54]

The following changes will ensue when the productive force of labour doubles:

If 40 Thalers represent the objectified labour time of 4 hours, then a doubling in the productive labour force will reduce the labour time to 2 hours, down to a total of 20 Thalers: that is to say, the same use value as before will be created but in half as much time. In consequence, the exchange value of labour power [*Arbeitskraft*] will have diminished by 50 per cent (that is, the price which will then be paid for the use value of this labour power) because the exchange value of the use value is measured purely by the labour time objectified in it.[55]

In simple exchange (simple exchange value), in which the worker owns the means of production, his doubling of the productive force will decrease labour (wages) from 40 Thalers to 20 Thalers, and the total value of the product is diminished by 20 Thalers, down to 80.

In developed exchange, the value remains at 140 because, with the doubling of the productive force, the share of wages decreases to 20 while the share of capital (surplus value) goes up by 20, to 60, and capital throws the same exchange value into circulation. In developed exchange the worker works two extra hours for free, which, in Marx's view, is as if the workers' absolute labour time had increased. Marx adds the following comment:[56]

> the surplus value of his capital has grown by 20 Thalers. Accordingly, only the share he gets of the 140 Thalers [is] the rate of his profit. . . . A new value has also arisen; namely the 20 additional Thalers are posited as *autonomous* value, as objectified labour which has become free, unbound from the task of serving only in exchange for earlier labour power.[57]

The value of the product remains the same, but the use value part of labour is down by 50 per cent while the surplus value part is up by 50 per cent. Twenty Thalers now produce the same value as 40 Thalers did before, whereby the exchange value of the *Arbeitskraft* is reduced by one half; capital gains a new value of 20 Thalers' worth of surplus value or surplus labour time, and it puts the same exchange value of 140 Thalers back into circulation. Quoting Ricardo, Marx seeks to show that the increase in the productive force of labour will leave capital with extra value and that these extra amounts will become capital and will increase wealth.[58]

Marx then asks what capital will do with these extra 20 Thalers? He suggests four alternatives:

(i)   he will buy extra (more productive) labour and will thereby create a larger exchange value for his product, since 20 Thalers represents more latent capital;

(ii) he will exchange the 20 Thalers for commodities other than his labour and raw material, whereby the exchange value of those commodities will go up by 20 Thalers (that is to say, the capitalist himself can consume the 20 Thalers as use values);

(iii) he may add the 20 Thalers to his capital;

(iv) he may put the 20 Thalers into general circulation, whereby the prices of the commodities bought with them will rise (because more money is put into circulation while the cost of production of gold has not fallen).[59]

What is the equivalent of these 20 Thalers which Marx terms 'the liberated part of the total exchange value',[60] and which now belongs to the capitalist? In a static state, claims Marx, this liberated exchange value by which society has become richer can only be money, in which case only the abstract form of wealth (money) has increased. But in a society in motion, this liberated part of the total exchange value (Marx does not call it 'savings') can realise itself only in *new* living labour (by putting into motion dormant labour or by creating new workers by accelerating population growth). Overall,

> or again a new circle of exchange value, of exchange value in circulation, is expanded, which can occur on the production side if the liberated exchange value opens up a *new branch* of production, i.e. a new object of exchange, objectified labour in the form of a new use value; or the same is achieved when objectified labour is put in the sphere of circulation in a new country, by an expansion of trade. The latter must then be created.[61]

It is in this context of his deliberations that Marx expresses his first summary statement of Ricardo's views on foreign trade:

> Let the presupposition be capital 1000 and workers 50. The correct deduction, which he himself [Ricardo] *also draws*: capital 500 with 25 workers can produce the same use value as before; the other 500 with the other 25 workers establish a new business and likewise produce an exchange value of 500. The profit remains the same, since it arises not from the exchange of 500 for 500, but from the proportions in which profit and wages originally divide in the 500, and since exchange deals in equivalents, which can no more in-

crease value than *external trade* can, which Ricardo explicitly demonstrates. Since the exchange of equivalents just means nothing more than that the value in the hands of A before the exchange with B still exists in his hands after the exchange with B. The total value of wealth has remained the same. Use value, however, or the *material of wealth*, has doubled.[62]

To Marx, the inference is clear: an exchange of equivalents (simple exchange, that is, if 500 are exchanged for 500) cannot increase value; neither can external trade, as Ricardo had explicitly demonstrated; even though Ricardo did show – correctly, in Marx's view – that a doubling of the productive force will permit production of the same wealth (that is, the same abundance of use values) with but one half of the previous capital and one half of the previous workers.

It appears that Marx's reasoning with respect to the disposal of the excess grain created by the increase in the productive force of workers in wheat does not lead to a consistent conclusion if at the same time an increase, at an equal rate, in the productive force of workers in gold is assumed. His attempt to match, in this type of situation, commodity circulation with the circulation of money appears to have been unsuccessful.[63]

Subsequently, Marx continues with his reflections on Ricardo's views on exchange value. On the one hand, Ricardo views wealth as depending on the quantity of commodities produced; on the other, he suggests that exchange value depends on the quantity of the productive force employed, which means that a doubling of the productive force will release one half of the previous labour and one half of the previous capital into something else, while total output (wealth) will still remain the same (this reasoning permits Ricardo to conclude that 'capital may be increased in the same manner as wealth').[64] But according to Marx, Ricardo also claims that 'historically with the progress of productive forces (and of international trade, too, he should have noted), there is growth in wealth as such', that is, in the sum of values.[65] How does Ricardo explain this, asks Marx? By suggesting that capital accumulates faster than the population, which induces wages to rise; which is then followed by an increase in the population and then by an increase in grain prices; with the resulting difficulty in the production (of grain) and hence an induced rise in the exchange value of grain. In Marx's view, this explanation by Ricardo amounts to a detour in seeking to explain a rise in exchange values.[66]

Marx is critical of Ricardo in two specific respects. First, Ricardo does not grasp the increase in exchange value which arises from increased productivity; instead, he only sees exchange value rising as a consequence of the increased difficulty of growing grain, that is, of decreased productivity. Second, his theory does not illustrate comprehensibly the growth of the population and its effect as an element in the increase in exchange values. On the one hand, he claims that capital wants more value, that is, to command more objectified labour, which is possible only if wages fall (as a consequence of an increase in the population); on the other, he also claims that the population will increase only if the value of objectified labour has increased (for example, by an increase in the demand for working days.)

What in fact is the increase in values due to, queries Marx?

The increase of values is therefore the result of the self-realisation [*Selbstverwertung*] of capital, whether this self-realisation is the result of *absolute* surplus time or of *relative*, i.e. of a real increase in absolute labour time or of an increase in relative surplus labour, i.e. of a decrease of . . . the labour time necessary to preserve the labouring capacity.[67]

In the realisation process [*Verwertungsprozeß*], the value components of capital are material, instruments of production, and living labour. Of these, the first two represent quantities of labour which are already objectified, quantities which are preserved in the present production process. But the living labour adds a new amount of labour, an addition to the already objectified labour. Living labour's quality of preserving the use value of the previous labour embodied is not paid for; what labour gets paid for is only the price of its own use value. Thus, labour creates value in addition to the values already present.[68] But this newly created value is present without an equivalent.[69] Living labour reproduces an equivalent (that part of the objectified labour time of capital which must replace the production cost of workers as workers) as well as a new creation, a new value. What labour gets paid for is the price of its use value. As use value, labour belongs to the capitalist; but labour belongs to the workers only as exchange value.[70]

4. Capital, surplus value, and profit

Profit should not be measured against total capital (raw materials +
instruments + labour) but only against labour, the objectified labour
time: 'Instead of looking at profit as if it were a profit on each of the
value components of capital equally and indifferently, must ask how
these components are made up and how much surplus labour the
wage buys in payment for objectified labour.'[71]

In simple exchange, the worker works for himself: in 9 hours, he
produces 100 Th. worth. This 100 Th. represents not capital but his
working condition. Of it, he consumes 40 for himself and 60 for
materials and instruments. If he worked an extra 3 hours (including
extra raw materials and instruments), he would produce 25 per cent
more for himself and would add that much new value. However, if
the working day is 12 hours, of which the worker works 9 hours for
himself, a surplus value of 25 per cent is created, even though the
profit is assessed (by those who confuse profit and *Mehrwert*) at 10
per cent (that is, 100 Th. + 10 per cent profit). The worker still gets
the same 40 Th., while the capitalist keeps the 10 Th. worth of
surplus value, which represents 25 per cent surplus time and produces
a surplus gain of 10 Thalers.[72]

Marx then provides several more examples which attempt to show
that the profit on the whole of capital remains at 10 per cent, even
though the new value created may be 25 per cent, 50 per cent, and
even 100 per cent above the wages fund.[73] He gets very involved with
these calculations, and proceeds to term raw materials and instruments of production 'invariable value'. But he commits many calculation errors and finally gives up: 'the devil take this wrong
arithmetic'.[74]

Then he looks at the creation of surplus value in a situation in
which he assumes that labour productivity increases. The increase in
the population increases the productive force of labour because it
makes possible a greater division and combination of labour, etc.[75]
The increase in productivity creates more surplus value by increasing
relative surplus time.[76] It creates a greater quantity of use values. The
new values result in money, more money, which will eventually
increase the amount of exchange values, even though at first the
absolute values of exchange values remains the same. How is the
amount of exchange values ultimately increased? Marx refers to
Ricardo: 'Even Ricardo admits that along with the accumulation of
capitals there is an increase in savings, hence a growth in the ex-

change values produced. The growth of savings means nothing more than the growth of independent values – of money.'[77] Overall:

> The higher productivity of labour is expressed in the fact that capital has to buy a smaller amount of necessary labour in order to create the same value and a greater quantity of use values, or that less necessary labour creates the same exchange value, realizes more material and a greater mass of use values. Thus, *if the total value of the capital remains the same*, an increase in the productive force means that the constant part of capital . . . grows relative to the variable. . . .[78]

How is the productivity of labour related to capital? Capital, like property, rests on the productivity of labour. If one can produce only enough for one, everyone is a worker, and there can be no property. Capital tends to increase the labouring population while it also tends to reduce the necessary part of that population (whereby the former serves as the primary means of achieving the latter). Clearly, therefore, property grows from the improvement in the mode of production.[79]

5. Devaluation of capital, overproduction, value and price

In the Section 'Devaluation of capital . . . overproduction', Marx contrasts the creation of surplus labour with that of surplus wealth, and of surplus labour with that of 'minus labour' (that is, relative idleness, free time, non-productive labour) and suggests that some work more than required for the satisfaction of their needs. He lauds Malthus for having recognised the necessity for lavish spending, etc.[80]

Inquiring more deeply into this situation, Marx states that capital, in its realisation, is faced with two barriers when it emerges from the production process:

(a) consumption capacity (on the assumption that the commodity has use value, that the number of consumers multiplied by the magnitude of their need for this specific product will match this use value);[81]

(b) as new value (old value plus surplus value) it requires available equivalents, in the form of money: 'There has to be an equivalent for it, even though it seems indeed as if no equivalent were available for it, since circulation was presupposed at the outset as

a constant magnitude – as having a given volume – and since, on
the other hand, capital has created a new (a higher) value.'[82] In
short, this surplus value requires a surplus equivalent.[83]

Marx queries where this additional purchasing power will come
from? Clearly, it must come in the sphere of circulation (commodity
circulation). One possibility is the constant expansion of the sphere
of circulation, 'a moving magnitude expanded by production
itself . . .'.[84] Another is the production of more gold or silver, of
more money, as the possibility of new capital. Commerce is yet
another:

The tendency to create the *world market* is directly given in the
concept of capital itself. Every limit appears as a barrier to be
overcome. As it creates more surplus labour, capital has the
tendency to create more points of exchange. . . . Clearly, the
production of surplus value due to the increase and development of
productive forces, requires the production of new consumption:
expand existing captial; create additional new needs over a larger
area; produce new needs and discover and create new use values.
Universal exchange of the products of all alien climates and lands;
science, discoveries, development of qualities as social human
being . . . all of it amounting to . . . creation of new branches of
production, i.e., of qualitatively new surplus time; . . . the creation, separate from a given production, of labour with a new
use value; the development of a constantly expanding and more
comprehensive system of different kinds of labour . . .hence the
great civilising influence of capital. . . . In accord with this
tendency, capital drives beyond national barriers and prejudice;
however, the universality towards which it irresistibly strives
encounters barriers in its own nature . . . which . . . will drive
towards its own suspension.[85]

Marx suggests at this point that 'the whole dispute is to whether
overproduction is possible and necessary in capitalist production?'[86]
In his view, Ricardo and his entire school 'never really understood
the really *modern* crises' in their childish attempts to deny that there
is general overproduction at any given moment and having in view
only the development of the forces of production and the growth of
the industrial population – supply without regard to demand – but
heedless of the barriers to consumption. Even Mill (J.S.) whose

'supply and demand are allegedly identical (because supply is allegedly measured by its own amount) is greatly confused.[87]

Marx attempts to develop his own conception of overproduction, at first not involving foreign trade: what the producing capital demands is not a specific use value but value in itself: that is, money, money as a general form of wealth. If too little money is produced (o/a of the high cost of money) then production is not identical with realisation [*Verwertung*], for which reason production cannot be transformed into money, into value; in consequence, overproduction ensues.[88] A great part of consumption (cf. Storch *v*. Say) is not for immediate use but for consumption in the production process.[89] The workers' consumption is in no way in itself a sufficient consumption for the capitalist (cf. Malthus and Sismondi).[90] In a general crisis of overproduction, the contradiction is not between the different kinds of productive capital (is not caused by capital moving from branches where it is not needed to branches where it is needed) but between 'industrial and loanable capital – between capital as directly involved in the production process and capital as money existing (relatively) outside of it . . . ;'[91] and finally, instead of proportionate production (cf. Ricardo), the limitless striving of capital for surplus labour, surplus productivity, surplus consumption, driving beyond this proportionality.[92] Production does not rest on free competition but on capital, where barriers arise in form of monopolies, natural monopolies, and so on.[93]

Then Marx brings in foreign trade: through foreign trade the barrier of the sphere of exchange is expanded, involving the entire credit system, but the imports are paid for by the surplus labour of the domestic population:

> The entire credit system, and the over-trading, over-speculation etc. connected with it, rests on the necessity of expanding and leaping over the barrier of circulation and the sphere of exchange. This appears more colossally, classically, in the relations between peoples than in relations between individuals. Thus e.g. the English forced to *lend* to foreign nations, in order to have them as customers.[94]

Marx then quotes Hodgskin on foreign trade, with particular emphasis on merchants' profits as a limitation on production and on the increasing exploitation of the labourer:

'In the present state, every accumulation of capital adds to the amount of profit demanded from the labourer, and extinguishes all that labour which would only procure the labourer his comfortable existence. . . . Profit the limitation of production.'[95]

'In a series of years the world can take no more from us than we can take from the world. Even the profits made by our merchants in their foreign trade are paid for by the consumer of the return goods here. Foreign trade mere barter, and as such exchange for convenience and enjoyment of the capitalist. But he can consume commodities to a certain degree only. He exchanges cottons etc. for the wines and silks of foreign countries. But these *represent only the surplus labour of our own population* as much as the clothes and cottons, and in this way the *destructive power of the capitalist is increased beyond all bounds*. Thus nature is outwitted.'[96]

Marx adds a statement of his own: 'Through foreign trade, the barrier of the sphere of exchange is expanded, and it is made possible for the capitalist to consume more surplus labour.'[97]

Marx then expresses his accord with the explanation of 'glut' as attributed to Malthus. First he cites Malthus:

'The very meaning of an increased demand by the labourers is, a disposition to take less themselves, and leave a larger share for their employer; and if it be said that this, by *diminishing consumption, increases glut*, I can only say that *glut then is synonymous with high profits*'.[98]

Then he provides the following comment: 'Herein the one side of the contradiction is completely expressed.'[99] The existence of this contradiction is rediscovered in Hodgskin, whom Marx cites: 'The more capital accumulates, the more the *whole amount of profit demanded does so*; so there arises an *artificial check* to production and population'.[100]

A quote from Malthus on insufficient demand serves as another reminder: 'the powers of production are only called fully into motion by unchecked demand for all that is produced . . . ',[101] which statement Marx interprets as follows: 'The demand of the labourer himself can never be adequate demand.'[102]

Overproduction cannot happen in simple exchange, since simple exchange is not concerned with exchange value but with use value:

'overproduction takes place in connection with realization [*Verwirkli-chung*], not otherwise.'[103]

But Marx disagrees with J.S. Mill and Proudhon, whose interpretation of overproduction is wrong because they are confused: they mix up price and value and bring in relations which have nothing to do with value as such.

Proudhon claims that 'the price of the product is an overcharge on top of its real value'.[104] But the capitalist's profit does not come from overcharging the worker but 'from the fact that in the whole of the product he sells a fractional part which he had not paid for, and which represents, precisely, surplus labour time.'[105] For example, if the productivity of labour doubles, the capitalist retains an extra quantity for which he does not pay in terms of necessary labour. On the assumption that the increased productivity of labour does not consume extra auxiliary materials, this increase in output costs the capitalist nothing. When higher-finish hand labour is added in manufacturing, value can be increased. This is so because the use value of the product increases in quality, while the exchange value increases by the extra labour.[106]

Marx introduces his discussion of the 'devaluation' of a product by providing his definition of value:

> The real value of a product expresses the labour time objectified in it. It contains the constant part of capital, the wage part (the part of objectified labour necessary to reproduce the living labour capacity) and the surplus value.[107]

He explains that 'surplus value' contains 'surplus labour' and that capital divides the latter into two parts: one part goes to consumption, the other becomes capital again. This 'division within capital' reflects the relation of surplus labour to necessary labour, and the magnitude of the sum to be divided into these two parts depends on the original relation of surplus labour to necessary labour: 'If the surplus value were simply consumed, then capital would not have realized itself as capital, and not produced itself as capital i.e., as value which produces value.'[108]

The definition of the 'devaluation of a product' then follows:

> His product is devalued [when] it has been sold *below* its real value, although it is sold at a *price* which still leaves him a profit . . . . When part of the objectified labour becomes valueless because it cannot sell.[109]

According to Marx, generally speaking, the determination of value includes no overcharge because the constant part of capital and the wage part must be paid for; whereas the distribution of the surplus value is subject to the relation between the capitalists and can be exchanged unequally depending on competition. He also states emphatically that in circulation workers, like other buyers, are equal partners in trade, since they have money; but not so in production, in which the master – servant relation prevails.[110] In his view, 'necessary labour time' excludes profit; however, wages (the price of necessary labour time) 'might be said to be determined by the prices of products which already include profit . . . therefore the wage must be high enough to enable the worker to buy the wheat (the cloth) regardless of what profit is included in the price of the product.'[111]

The price of the product can be lower than the value, but capital can still make a gain, which is a very important consideration in competition.[112] The determination of prices is founded on the determination of values, but new elements enter, since price, which originally appears as value expressed in money, becomes further determined as a specific magnitude, as follows:

(a) the total quantity produced becomes decisively important in the determination of price;
(b) fraud, reciprocal chicanery: one party can gain part of the surplus value which the other party loses; but this individual deception has nothing to do with the determination of value;
(c) supply and demand;
(d) competition.[113]

Since realisation means the production and the exchange of values, and since increased realisation means the production and exchange of new and larger values, it follows, in Marx's view, that the profit of capital originates not in the exchange of his commodity for the worker's money but in the exchange of his capital with living labour.[114]

Marx's reflections concerning devaluation [*Entwertung*][115] tie in with economic crises or a situation of general crisis. He calls a crisis a 'general depreciation of prices', a 'general devaluation of capital',[116] and seeks to portray, by way of numerical examples, the consequences of such a situation.

If of the value (objectified labour time) of 200 Th. (of which $\frac{2}{5}$ comprise raw materials, $\frac{1}{5}$ instruments, $\frac{1}{5}$ wages, and $\frac{1}{5}$ surplus product), which amounts to forty pounds of twist, only 180 Th. worth is sold (that is, the cost of the output to the capitalist), then the 'objectified labour in the amount of 20 Th. becomes valueless'.[117] The same happens if the capitalist gave up the value of twist of 200 Th. for the value of silver worth 180 Th.[118] Marx ponders what will then happen with the surplus of 20 Th. worth of twist, once it has got into the hands of the silver producer?

If the silver producer cannot himself sell this surplus of 20 Th. worth of twist (because, as Marx suggests,'of the overproduction of twist'[119]), then 20 Th. worth of the silver producer's capital would be set free – a relative surplus value of 20 Th. (even though the absolute value, that is, the objectified labour, to the extent that it is exchangeable, remains the same): 40 lbs. of twist for a total of 180 Th. plus 20 Th. worth of liberated capital.

Marx sees this result as identical with a situation in which the productivity of labour has increased to such an extent as to require 20 Th. less labour time for 40 lbs. of twist. In the exchange, the silver producer would exchange less labour time objectified in his silver for the labour time objectified in the twist, whereby by combined sum of the two values would decrease to 380 Th. (from the previous sum of values of 400). A general depreciation – or a destruction – of capital will have taken place, even though 'the depreciation of the twist manufacturer's 40 lbs. of output from 200 Th. to 180 Th. necessarily appears as an appreciation on the part of silver.'[120]

From this example Marx deduces the following:

(i)   The devaluation, like the *depreciation*, can be absolute and not merely relative, because value expresses not merely a relation between one commodity and another, as does price, but rather the relation between the price of the commodity and the labour objectified in it, or between one amount of objectified labour of the same quality and another.[121]

(ii) If these amounts [of objectified labour] are not equal, then *devaluation* takes place; but this devaluation is not outweighed by appreciation on the other side, for the other side expresses a fixed amount of objectified labour which remains unchanged by exchange.[122]

(iii) In general crisis, this devaluation extends to living-labour capacity itself.

(iv) [This devaluation in a crisis amounts to] a decrease of the existing value of raw materials, machinery, labour capacity; [it enables] the cotton manufacturer capital who loses on his product to buy the same value of cotton, labour, etc., at a lower price, [which] is the same for him as if the *real value* of labour etc. had decreased (as if they had been produced more cheaply owing to an increase in the productive force of labour);[123]

(v) On the other hand, a sudden general increase in the forces of production would relatively devalue all the *present values* which labour objectifies at the lower stage of productive forces, and hence would destroy the present capital as well as present labour capacity – a real decrease in production, in living labour – in order to restore the correct relation between necessary labour and surplus labour, on which, in the last analysis, everything rests.[124]

Within the production process, surplus value appears as surplus labour (a specific sum of living objectified labour), which is objectified into the surplus product and now appears as surplus capital (in contrast with the original capital).[125]

When the surplus product is realised in additional capital – that is to say, when it enters the new process of production – it then divides into: (i) means of subsistence for the workers which is exchanged for living-labour capacity (for its progressive maintenance – the labour fund; (ii) its other component parts and the material conditions for the reproduction of value, which are equal to these means of subsistence plus the surplus value.

In total, labour creates (i) a fund for the maintenance of new living-labour capacities; and (ii) the condition that this fund can be employed only if *new* surplus labour is employed with the extra part of the additional capital.[126]

Marx then explains how, in this process, additional capital is accumulated; how the surplus capital emerges from the original production process, 'for the appropriation of alien labour, of objectified alien labour'.[127] He distinguishes between 'surplus capital I' and 'surplus capital II'. The former is created by means of simple exchange between objectified labour and living-labour capacity – an exchange based on the laws of equivalence (of exchange of equivalents) as measured by the quantity of labour or labour time contained in them. Surplus capital I is the surplus capital which emerges from the original production process, the one in which no labour was expropriated, the one in which the capitalist gives up only that part of the values which he considers his own. Surplus capital II expresses the right to appropriate alien labour without an equivalent, that part of the values of surplus capital which he obtains without giving any equivalent whatsoever.[128]

The exchange between capital and labour is mediated by money, which, as payment, represents the price of the use value of labour.[129] This price,

> which begins as conventional and traditional (e.g. in old communities, when the pay of the common soldier is reduced to a minimum – determined solely by the production costs necessary to procure him) is thereafter increasingly determined economically, first by the relation of demand and supply, finally by the production costs at which the vendors themselves of these services can be produced . . . . [130]

But in forms which precede capitalist production, the individuals relate not as workers but as proprietors and members of a community who at the same time work. The aim of this work is not the creation of value but rather 'the sustenance of the individual proprietor and of his family, as well as of the total community'.[131]

After he has gained his freedom from serfdom, what the free worker sells is always nothing more than a specific – a particular – measure of *Kraftäußerung* (expending of strength, of force), his labour capacity as a totality being greater than any particular expending of this capacity. Within the relation of simple circulation, A gives B a completed use value and receives from B the latter's completed use value – an act which consumes wealth (with money acting as a mere medium of circulation), not an act which produces wealth. Marx labels this action not the transfer of money into capital but the exchange of money as revenue for a use value which will vanish when it is consumed: the 'devaluation' of values received.[132]

NOTES AND COMMENTS

1. *Grundrisse*, p. 312.
2. Ibid.
3. Ibid., p. 315.

4. Ibid., p. 324.
5. Ibid. The term *Mehrwert* appears, for the first time translated by Marx himself, as 'surplus value'.
6. Ibid., p. 316.
7. Ibid., pp. 316–17.
8. Ibid., p. 318.
9. Ibid.
10. Ibid., p. 320.
11. Ibid., p. 318.
12. Ibid., p. 321.
13. Ibid., p. 844.
14. Ibid., p. 324.
15. Ibid.
16. Ibid.
17. Ibid., p. 325.
18. Ibid., p. 324.
19. Ibid., p. 323.
20. Marx's reasoning moves along three planes: the progress of civilisation, that is, the increase in *gesellschaftliche Produktivkräfte* or of the productive powers of labour itself, which results from science, inventions, division and combination of labour, machinery, improved means of communication, and *creation of the world market* (emphasis added) (p. 308); the constantly on-going devaluation of capital resulting from this increase in the *Produktivkräfte*, which devaluation has to be compensated with profit (p. 317); and the higher stage of exchange value: developed exchange, which permits possession and preservation of general wealth which is to be taken care of with a lesser labour time of society as a whole. Throughout, capital and labour are related to each other as money and as commodity, as the general form of wealth v. the substance meant for immediate consumption.
21. *Grundrisse*, p. 330.
22. Ibid., p. 360.
23. Ibid., p. 326. Comment: If use value means simple exchange – in which, by Marx's definition, no surplus value can be created – then Ricardo's view is correct; but if international trade involves complex (that is, developed) exchange, then exchange value applies, which includes surplus value and leads to capital accumulation in the course of the evolution of trade relations, under conditions of 'unequal exchange'. However, if Marx's reference to the pursuit of unequal exchange is correct, then we are faced with several questions: (a) Is it the exchange between the countries that is unequal or is the exchange unequal because each country puts up commodities which have been produced domestically under conditions of unequal exchange (between the capitalists and the workers)? (b) What happens if one country exploits its labour in its export industry to a greater extent than does the other country in its own export industry (and how will this difference be measured)? (c) In the course of trading, can one country get directly to exploit the labour force in the trading partner's export industry and import competing industry (and, by deduction, can the stronger country's

capital exploit the weaker country's capital)? In the *Grundrisse*, no answers are found to any of these questions.

24. Ibid., p. 349.
25. Ibid., p. 329.
26. Ibid., pp. 332–5.
27. Ibid., p. 331.
28. Ibid., p. 318.
29. Ibid., p. 331.
30. Ibid.
31. Here Marx devotes much attention to the concept of 'mediator' and 'mediation' in their philosophic, social, and economic meaning, the role of the 'mediator' being that of a higher power, the power enabling the being to mediate between the extremes. Thus, Christ is the mediator between God and humanity, but more important than God; exchange value is the mediator between two extremes and is one-sided against them; capital is the mediator between production and circulation; within capital itself, one form takes up the position as use value, the other of exchange value, whereby industrial capital appears as the producer while the merchant engages in circulation, the former representing the material [*stofflich*] side while the latter represents the formal side, that is wealth as wealth; mercantile capital is the mediator between production (industrial capital) and circulation (consuming public) or between exchange value and use value, production posited as money and circulation as use value, or, alternatively, production as use value (product) and circulation as exchange value (money).

    Similarly in commerce, where the wholesaler is the mediator between the manufacturer and the retailer or between the manufacturer and the agriculturalist or between different manufacturers, but is clearly a mediator at the higher level; furthermore, commodity brokers mediate against the wholesalers, the bankers against the industrialists and the merchants, the joint-stock company against simple production, the financier as mediator between the state and bourgeois society, at the highest level (the 'wildest form of extraction of surplus value') (p. 332).
32. *Grundrisse*, p. 333.
33. Ibid.
34. Ibid., p. 304.
35. Ibid.
36. Ibid., p. 334–5.
37. Ibid.
38. Ibid., p. 337.
39. Ibid., pp. 337–8.
40. Ibid., p. 338.
41. Ibid., p. 339.
42. Ibid., p. 340. Marx's definition of the 'multiplier': the amount to which the productive force (posed as unity, as multiplicand) increases.
43. Ibid., p. 339.
44. The significance of this statement in the framework of international trade ties in with Marx's analysis of values and pricing (See Part II).
45. *Grundrisse*, p. 340.

46. Ibid., p. 341.
47. Ibid., p. 340.
48. Ibid.
49. Ibid., pp. 337–9.
50. Ibid., p. 341.
51. Ibid., pp. 341–2.
52. Ibid., p. 342–3.
53. Ibid.
54. Ibid., p. 344.
55. Ibid.
56. This reference to absolute labour time and relative labour time recalls Ricardo's distinction between intensive method and extensive method in agriculture.
57. *Grundrisse*, p. 345.
58. Ibid., p. 346.
59. Ibid.
60. Ibid.
61. Ibid., p. 348.
62. Ibid., p. 349.
63. Ibid., pp. 341–2.
64. Ibid., p. 350. Let us recall that 'wealth' to Ricardo means an abundance of use values. Let us also note that Marx distinguishes four components of capital: two are part of the living-workday: wages and profit, that is, necessary labour and surplus labour; the remaining two are materials of labour and instruments of labour. The latter already contain a fixed quantity of use value [*vergegenständlichte Arbeit*], which is converted into exchange value during the process of exchange (p. 354).
65. *Grundrisse*, p. 350.
66. Ibid., pp. 350–1.
67. Ibid., p. 359. Purely natural material in which no human labour is objectified has no value. If the productive force of labour doubles, a newly created value is present without an equivalent. Surplus value is money, money which in itself is already capital; as such, it constitutes a claim on *das werdende Arbeitsvermögen*.

    Marx produces numerous examples in seeking to demonstrate the effects of an increase in the productive force of labour. But he commits many errors (as acknowledged by the editors) and at times uses 'interest' instead of 'surplus value' (pp. 364–8).
68. Ibid., p. 365.
69. Ibid., p. 368.
70. Marx's reflections concerning capital are continued in Notebook IV (mid-December 1857–22 January 1858), which contains the beginnings of the circulation process of capital, his propositions with respect to the original accumulation of capital, and his assessment of the 'confusion' between surplus value and profit. In it, the following specific items seem of particular significance in his treatment: overproduction and workers' demand; commodity price and labour time; determination of values and prices; the general rate of profit; devaluation during crises; barriers to capitalist production.

71. Ibid., p. 374.
72. Ibid., p. 376.
73. Marx's definition of the wages fund: 'The wages fund is formed by the variable part of capital; it is the objectified labour spent to buy living labour' (p. 377).
74. Ibid.
75. Ibid., p. 400.
76. This is so because labour, now more productive, needs less time to produce the means of its own sustenance.
77. Ibid., p. 387.
78. Ibid., p. 389.
79. Ibid., pp. 395–401.
80. Ibid., p. 401.
81. This barrier ties in with Marx's other proposition: that during its *Verwertungsprozeß*, capital is in fact 'devalued' [*entwertet*], that is, suffers a reduction in its exchange value because 'by increasing the force of production, it decreases the relative, the necessary, labour time and therefore reduces the costs of its own production' (ibid).
82. *Grundrisse*, p. 405.
83. Ibid.
84. Ibid., p. 407.
85. Ibid., pp. 408–10.
86. Ibid., p. 411.
87. Ibid.
88. Ibid., p. 412.
89. Ibid., pp. 412–13.
90. Ibid., p. 413.
91. Ibid.
92. Ibid.
93. Ibid., p. 414.
94. Ibid., p. 416.
95. Ibid., p. 417. Quoted from Hodgskin, *Popular Political Economy*, pp. 245–6.
96. Ibid. Quoted from Hodgskin, *The Source and Remedy of the National Difficulties*, pp. 17–18.
97. Ibid.
98. Ibid. Quoted from *Enquiry*, 1821, p. 12.
99. Ibid.
100. Ibid. Quoted from Hodgskin, *Notebook*, p. 46.
101. Ibid., p. 424. Quoted from Malthus, *Principles of Political Economy*, pp. 378–82.
102. Ibid., p. 420.
103. Ibid., p. 424.
104. Ibid., p. 426.
105. Ibid., p. 427.
106. Ibid., pp. 415–20.
107. Ibid., p. 430.
108. Ibid., p. 444.
109. Ibid., pp. 444–45.

110. Ibid., pp. 411–15.
111. Ibid., p. 425. Marx states specifically that the prices of consumption goods include surplus labour time, which suggests that they include at least some profit.
112. Ibid., p. 432.
113. Ibid., pp. 432–5.
114. Ibid., p. 439.
115. In German, *Entwertung* and *Abwertung* mean two different things: the latter means 'devaluation of a currency', while the former stands for 'debasing', 'demonetizing', 'rendering valueless', 'rendering invalid', which, it appears, is the meaning Marx assigns to this term. In German, the opposite of *Abwertung* is *Aufwertung*, a clear antonym. But the opposite of *Entwertung* is *Verwertung*, which means 'creating value' or 'adding to the value of a thing', 'rendering useful or valuable'. Its standard (Marxian) translation is 'realization', which does not convey this meaning.
116. *Grundrisse*, p. 446.
117. Ibid., p. 445.
118. Since the surplus product = 40 Th., the remaining 20 Th. are only $\frac{1}{2}$ of the surplus value, which Marx divides into 10 Th. for the capitalist's consumption and 10 Th. for the capitalist's new production.
119. *Grundrisse*, p. 445.
120. Ibid., p. 446.
121. Ibid.
122. Ibid.
123. Ibid.
124. Ibid. In French, *Verwertung* means *valorisation*, and *verwertet* means *c'est valorisé*, that is, 'has attained value', which is preferable to the English (Marxian) translation, 'has realized itself'. Marx's own terminology is confusing. He posits that in the production process capital 'has realized itself', by which he means 'has created value'; but the capital then becomes 'devalued' [*entwertet*] when it makes the transition from money to the form of a particular commodity; it then 'realizes itself', with its new value, when the product is thrown into circulation and the value of 100 becomes that of 110; finally, it is transferred back into the money form, the general measure of commodities, which form includes the new value which the capital has created (pp. 446–8).
125. Marx adduces to capital several interesting characteristics. In its elemental form (particular real form), capital belongs to the individual capitalist. In its general form, it accumulates in banks or is distributed by them, in accordance with the needs of production ('as Ricardo says, so admirably distributes itself in accordance with the needs of production . . .' (p. 449). Through loans, etc., it forms a level between different countries: 'If it is therefore e.g. a law of capital in general that, in order to realize itself, it must posit doubly, and must realize itself in this double form, then e.g. the capital of a particular nation which represents capital *par excellence* in antithesis to another will have to lend itself out to a third nation in order to be able to realize itself' (p. 449).

Let us briefly recall the French equivalents of basic Marxian terms: *Mehrwert = survalue*; *Mehrprodukt = surproduit*; *Mehrarbeit = surtravail*; *zusätzliches Kapital* ('surplus capital') = *capital additionnel*.

126. Ibid., p. 455.
127. Ibid., p. 456.
128. Ibid., pp. 457–8.
129. Ibid., p. 467.
130. Ibid., pp. 467–8.
131. Ibid., pp. 471–2.
132. Ibid., pp. 465–6.

7 The Circulation of Capital

A. THE THREEFOLD CHARACTER OF CIRCULATION (CIRCULATION AS A TOTAL PROCESS)

The total process of circulation involves the course of capital through its different moments. The total process is posited as a flow, as a double movement:

> Double movement from the circulation of capital *as such* itself. In the first phase, it ejects itself out of the movement of capital as use value, as commodity, and exchanges itself for money. The commodity . . . in its presence as use value, its being for consumption. . . . Capital creates articles of consumption, but ejects them from itself in this form, ejects them from its circulation. . . . The commodity which is ejected as such from the circulation of capital loses its character as value and fulfils the role of use value for consumption, as distinct from fulfilling it for production. But in the second phase of circulation, capital exchanges money for commodity. . . . While it presupposes consumption in the first phase, in the second it presupposes production, production for production; for value in the form of the commodity is here taken into the circulation of capital from the outside . . . as use value for capital itself, use value for its production process.[1]

Regarded as a whole, circulation appears threefold:[2]

1. The total process: the course of capital through its different moments;
2. Small-scale circulation: the circulation process between part of capital and labour capacity;
3. Large-scale circulation: the realisation of the price of the commodity, which involves the entire value of the product.

1. The total process

Posited as a flow, the total process is seen as circulating. However, the continuity of the circulation is subject to interruptions because the composite flow comprises different capitals, each fixated in a different relation:

> In so far as the continuity is virtually interrupted, and many resist the passage into the next phase, capital here likewise appears as fixated in different relations, and the various modes of this fixation constitute different capitals, commodity capital, money capital, capital as conditions of production.[3]

2. Small-scale circulation

Small-scale circulation involves that part of capital which circulates between capital and labour capacity; the process between capital and labour capacity generally, which accompanies the production process and enters into circulation: the *approvisionnement*. This mode of circulation is continuous and proceeds simultaneously with the production process:[4]

> It is that part of capital which is paid out as wages, exchanged for labouring capacity. . . . The capitalist does not exchange capital directly for labour or labour time; but rather time contained, worked up in commodities, worked up in living labour capacity. The living labour time he gets in exchange is not the exchange value, but the use value of labour capacity. . . . But the use value of the value the capitalist has acquired through exchange is itself . . . more labour time than is objectified in labour capacity, i.e. more labour time than the reproduction of the living worker costs. Hence, by virtue of having acquired labour capacity in exchange as an equivalent, capital has acquired labour time – to the extent that it exceeds the labour time contained in labour capacity – in exchange *without equivalent*; it has appropriated alien labour time *without exchange* . . . dispossession [*Entäusserung*] of his labour.[5]

In small-scale circulation, capital advances the worker the wages which the latter exchanges for products necessary for his consumption, which money enables the worker to exchange his labour for alien labour: 'Capital can give him claims on alien labour, in the form of money, only because it has appropriated his own labour.'[6]

Small-scale circulation involves that part of the capital value which circulates as wages and never enters the production process as the product of the previous production process:

> In the small-scale circulation capital . . . the capital never leaves the circulation process and never enters into the production process of capital as use value, as the product of the previous production process, but as *value*, in that necessary labour is the reproduction of wages.[7]

Fixed capital is the inverse of capital circulating as wages: 'It remains as use value in the production process (never[8] goes back into circulation; it enters circulation only as part of the value of the finished product).'[9]

Small-scale circulation has two aspects: (a) in respect to its form (as contract, exchange, type of intercourse); and (b) with regard to its use value: 'its material character as a consumable product entering directly into individual consumption'.[10]

In small-scale circulation, the circulating capital appears in the form of what is specified for the workers' individual consumption; generally for direct consumption and therefore in the form of finished products.[11] In consequence, in reference to the natural conditions of the workers' survival, capital in small-scale circulation is meant to serve as use value, that which enters directly into the workers' individual consumption. Marx terms this consumption 'productive consumption' because 'this, his reproduction, is itself a condition for capital, . . . capital therefore calls this consumption *productive consumption* – productive not in so far as it reproduces the individual, but rather individuals as labour capacities'.[12]

Marx views this part of capital as constantly circulating, as *approvisionnement*: capital which is constantly consumed, with the purpose of constantly to reproduce.

What is the relation between money and circulation capital (in small-scale circulation), asks Marx? There is a striking difference between capital and money, the circulation of capital and the circulation of money. Capital pays wages, that is weekly; the worker takes his wages to the grocer, and so on; the latter directly or indirectly deposits them with the banker; the following week the manufacturer takes them from the banker again, in order to distribute them among the workers, and so on: 'The same sum of money constantly circulates new portions of capital . . . and the sum grows with the number of workers.'[13]

But the sum of money itself does not determine the portions of capital which are thus circulated:[14]

> If the money value of wages rises, then the circulating medium will increase, but the mass of the medium does not determine the rise. If the production costs of money did not fall, then no increase of money would exercise an influence on the portion of it entering into this circulation.[15]

3. Large-scale circulation

Large-scale circulation appears as the movement of capital outside the production phase; it spans the entire period from the moment when capital exits from the production process until it enters it again.[16] Unlike the labour time, which appears in the production phase, the time expended in large-scale circulation constitutes 'circulation time'. The circulation process of capital is always posited in the form of an exchange of equivalents. This is so because:

> values which become exchanged are always objectified labour time, an objectively available, *reciprocally* presupposed quantity of labour (present in a use value). Value as such is always an effect, never a cause. It expresses that amount of labour by which an object is produced, hence – presupposing the same stage of the productive forces – the amount of labour by which it can be reproduced.[17]

Marx recognises that part of circulating capital enters into large-scale circulation, which involves the entire value of the product, the realisation of the price of the commodity; and that the other part, 'which continuously accompanies the process of production itself, the circulation of that part which is transformed into wages . . .' naturally depends on whether the labour is used for the production of fixed capital or of circulating capital, that is, whether these wages themselves are replaced by a use value entering into circulation or not.[18]

Marx's desire to be specific about the distinction between small-scale circulation and large-scale circulation seems to have arisen in response to his concern with the question of whether accumulation had emerged prior to labour or whether it was a result of labour, an issue discussed intensively during his time.[19] In his view, the 'Economists' were making a great show of the observation that the side of capital must possess raw materials, instruments of labour, and the necessaries of life so that the workers can live during the production process, from which observation was derived the view that accumulation must have arisen prior to labour and not sprung out of it, and that the capitalists' mode of appropriation had developed out of the simple and 'just' laws of equivalent exchange, that is, of the relations of production which manifest the following characteristics:

- use value predominates;
- exchange value and its production presuppose the predominance of the use-value form;
- production is for direct consumption;
- labour itself is presupposed as craftsmanlike, having specific skills, and as property (not merely as source of property);
- payments in kind and services in kind predominate over payments in money and money services.[20]

Marx's response to all this: even though the conceptual specification of capital encounters difficulties (for example living capital, dead capital, capital lent out, money capital, and so on), 'it is clear that the true nature of capital emerges only at the end of the second cycle, in which production appears as the conclusion and the point of departure and return.'[21]

B. THE TURNOVER OF CAPITAL[22]

1. The production process and the circulation process

In the 'turnover of capital', which Marx also calls 'capital in process', 'working capital', two principal processes are involved: the production process and the circulation process.

Together these two processes constitute one complete turnover of capital. Marx first classifies the process of the complete turnover of capital as a duality, whose two principal phases conceptually begin with the transformation of money into relations of production [*Produktionsverhältnisse*]. In the complete turnover, four stages (moments) are involved:

(1) The real production process and its duration.
(2) The transformation of the product into money and the duration of this process.
(3) The transformation of the money in proper proportions into raw materials, means of labour, and labour: that is, into the elements of productive capital.
(4) The exchange of a part of the capital for living-labour capacity, which phase is regarded as a particular moment because the labour market is ruled by laws other than those ruling the product market – population being the main thing, not in absolute but in relative terms; the moment of the capitalist's purchase of the commodity labour capacity and his appropriation of the productive power of labour beyond the wages he pays for labour's use value.[23]

With 'capital in the process of becoming', Marx redesigns at this stage the four moments and assigns each its distinct character:[24]

First moment: Creation of surplus value, or immediate production process; its result: the product.

Second moment: Bringing the product to the market, or the transformation of the product into a commodity.

Third moment: (α) Entry of the commodity into ordinary circulation, or circulation of the commodity; its result: transformation into money, the first moment of ordinary circulation. (β) Retransformation of money into relation of production [*Produktionsverhältnisse*], or monetary circulation: in ordinary circulation, the circulation of commodities and the circulation of money always appear distributed among two different subjects. Capital circulates first as a commodity, then as money, and vice versa.

Fourth moment: Renewal of the production process, which appears here as reproduction of the original capital, and production process of surplus capital.[25]

Marx starts his deliberations with the statement that 'the value which capital posits in one cycle, one revolution, one turnover, is equal to the value posited in the new production process, that is, equal to the value reproduced plus the new value.'[26]

When is one complete turnover completed? There are two possibilities, suggests Marx: at the point at which the commodity is transformed into money; or at the point where the money is transformed back into relations of production – the result being absolutely equal to the value posited in the production process:[27]

The total production process of capital includes both the circulation process proper and the actual production process. These form the two great sections of its movement, which appears as the totality of these two processes. On one side, labour time, on the other, circulation time . . . as unity of production and circulation. This unity itself is motion, process.[28]

Circulation belongs within the concept of capital . . . . Capital, in its reality, therefore appears as a series of turnovers in a given *period*. It is no longer merely *one turnover*, one circulation; but rather the positing of . . . the whole process.[29]

Harvests are mostly *annual*; it follows that the *year* (except that it is figured differently for various productions) has been adopted as the general period of time by which the sum of the turnovers of capital is calculated and measured; just as the *natural working day* provided such a natural unit as measure of labour time. In the calculation of profit, and even more of interest, we consequently see the unity of circulation time and production time – capital – posited as such, and as its own measure. Capital itself is *in process* – hence as accomplishing one turnover – is regarded as *working capital*, and the fruits, which it is supposed to yield, are calculated according to its working time – the total circulation of one turnover.[30]

Marx terms the capital involved in the whole of circulation (involving all phases of this movement) 'circulating capital';[31] but he emphasises that in each phase the capital pertaining to each 'is restricted to a particular form, non-circulating capital'.[32]

The economic circulation of the product begins when the product is brought to the market, that is, becomes a commodity, the second phase.[33]

2. Circulation time and circulation costs

One turnover of capital is equal to the production time and the circulation time. When circulation costs are presumed to equal zero, then the result of one turnover of capital (that is, the single course of capital through its different moments) equals the value posited in the circulation process.[34] But if circulation costs which cost objectified labour are incurred, then these circulation costs are subtracted from the sum of values:

Circulation – since it consists of a series of exchange operations with equivalents – cannot increase the value of circulating commodities. Therefore, if labour time is required to undertake this operation, i.e. if values have to be consumed, for all consumption of values reduces itself to the consumption of labour time or of objectified labour time, products; i.e. if circulation entails costs and if circulation time costs labour time, then this is a deduction from, a relative suspension of the circulating values; their devaluation by the amount of the circulation costs.[35]

Marx backs up this proposition by referring to the exchange between a fisher and a hunter: the time which both lose in exchanging would create neither fish nor game. If they commission a third person, they would lose no labour time directly but would have to cede a proportional share of their product. But if they worked as joint proprietors (for their mutual consumption), no exchange would take place and there would be no costs of exchange.[36]

(1) Zero circulation time; velocity of circulation time

The process of capital as value begins with money and ends in money. The latter quantity is larger than the former, and the difference is only quantitative.[37] Circulation time is different from production time, and the renewal of the production process (the retransformation of money into capital as such) depends on the time capital requires to complete its circulation: that is, on circulation time. The total value is created by capital and includes reproduced value and new value. This value is realised in circulation but is determined exclusively in the production process. But the more rapid the circulation (the shorter the circulation time) in one complete turnover of capital, the more often the same capital can repeat the production process, the greater the sum of values created:

> The sum of values created by the capital in a specific cycle of turnovers of capital, is *directly proportional to the labour time and inversely proportional to the circulation time*. In a given cycle, the total value (consequently also the sum of newly posited surplus values) is equal to the labour time multiplied by the number of turnovers of the capital.[38]

Circulation time is the time during which capital is separated from the process in which it absorbs labour; it is not value-creating, not a value-creating element but only the transposition of previously created value from one form to another. Circulation means a series of exchanges. No matter how many exchanges may be involved and how much time the completion of these operations may cost, circulation is merely the exchange of equivalents. This positing of values as equivalents 'naturally cannot posit them as non-equivalents'.[39]

Circulation time appears as time during which the ability of capital to reproduce itself, and hence to reproduce surplus value, is suspended.[40] Circulation time is, therefore, not the time during which capital creates value, but rather during which it realises the value created in the production process. Circulation does not increase the quantity of the product but transposes the product into another form, the commodity.[41]

The productivity of capital is at a maximum when circulation time equals zero. In consequence 'the necessary tendency of capital is circulation without circulation time, and this tendency is the fundamental determinant of credit and of capital's credit contrivances.'[42]

The velocity of circulation time is the time in which circulation is accomplished. It is a determinant of how many products can be produced in a given period of time, how often it can reproduce and multiply its value.

What is the relation between the speed of circulation and value?

While circulation does not itself produce a moment of *value-determination*, for that lies exclusively in labour, its speed does determine the speed with which the production process is repeated, values are created – thus if not values, at least to a certain extent the mass of values.[43]

(2) Circulation costs: In its totality, moment (2), the bringing of the product to the market, involves two elements as direct moments of production, of transportation, and of communication: (a) time: how long capital will need to realise itself after the production process, that is, the exchange of capital for money; (b) space: the return is delayed by the greater distance of the market in space.

Both of these elements involve costs. However, the costs of circulation are not direct moments of production; they arise from circulation as an 'economic act',[44] interest and credit being specific examples.

Circulation costs are an aspect of the whole transformation process.[45] Only in the market is the product a commodity. Circulation is an essential process of capital since the production process cannot be begun anew before the transformation of the commodity into money.[46] The costs of circulation in the transition from product to money can be = 0. But, suggests Marx, it is

> only in connection with interest and particularly with credit [that] we can speak of the *costs of circulation* arising from circulation as an economic act – as a relation of production, not as a direct moment of production, as was the case with the *means of transport and communication*. . . . However, as far as circulation itself creates costs, itself requires surplus labour, it appears itself included within the production process.[47]

Marx provides a more explicit explanation:

> Circulation can *create value* only in so far as it requires fresh employment – of *alien labour* – in addition to that directly consumed in the production process. This is then the same as if more *necessary labour* were used in the direct production process . . . only the actual *circulation costs* increase the *value* of the product, but decrease the surplus value. The costs of circulation generally . . . are to be regarded as deduction from *surplus value*, i.e. as an increase of necessary labour in relation to surplus labour.[48]

In Marx's view, the spatial aspect involves a universal dimension. Since capital posits the universal development of the productive forces (including the development of science), the result is the universality of intercourse, which has the world market as its basis, and hence the universality of the individual:

> The more developed the capital, therefore the more extensive the market over which it circulates, which forms the spatial orbit of its circulation, the more does it strive simultaneously for an even greater extension of the market and for the greater annihilation of space by time.[49]

But space itself involves circulation costs and, if circulation costs labour time, it represents a deduction from surplus value.

(a) *Faux frais de production*: A machine which saves circulation time but itself costs labour and is the product of labour represents for capital *faux frais de production*.[50] Do these costs, which are incurred after the completion of the production process, add to the value of the output? In answering, Marx states categorically that 'circulation costs as such can . . . never increase the value.'[51] These costs belong to the *faux frais de production*, which in turn belong to the inherent costs of production resting on capital:

> The merchant's trade and still more the money trade proper – in so far as they do nothing but carry on the operations of circulation as such, e.g., the determination of prices (measurement of values and their calculation), these exchange operations generally, as a function which has gained independence through the division of labour, in so far as they represent this function of the total process of capital – represent merely the *faux frais de production* of capital. In so far as they reduce these *faux frais*, they add to production, not by creating value, but by reducing the negation of created values. If they operate purely as such a function, then they would always only represent a minimum of *faux frais de production*. If they enable the producers to create more values than they could without this division of labour, and, more precisely, so much more that a surplus remains after the payment of this function, then they have in fact increased production. Values are then increased, however, not because the operations of circulation have created value, but because they have absorbed less values than they would have done otherwise.[52]

To Marx, the costs of circulation include the following:

- the costs of movement;
- the costs of bringing the product to the market (insurance, and so on); but he does not specify whether transport costs belong to this category or to the previous one;
- the labour time required to effect the transfer from one process to another (Marx names here specifically the accounting operations and the time they costs, 'the foundation of a special, technical money trade'; but he does state that he would consider later whether these costs are to be regarded a deduction from the surplus value of the product);
- the cost of money (as it involves labour time), which adds to the cost of exchange;
- the cost of the circulation of capital;
- the costs of intermediaries (merchants, arbitrageurs).[53]

Marx is not concerned here with the technological process of transforming raw materials into commodities; neither does he inquire into
the physical conditions of bringing the finished product into the
second (the circulation) process. Instead, he emphasises that the
costs of circulation as such, 'the costs arising from the motion through
the different economic moments as such . . . do not add anything to
the value of the product, are not value-positing costs, regardless of
how much labour they may involve. They are merely *deductions from
the created* value.'[54] . . . Two individuals engaged in a reciprocal
division of labour and exchange, a situation of barter, add nothing to
the products' exchange values.[55]

(b) Transportation costs: But Marx does seem particularly concerned about transportation costs, which issue he discusses at some
length. In his view, transportation costs (the bringing of the product
to the market) are part of the production process itself, since the
product becomes a commodity only when it reaches the market:

> We have seen that transport (and hence the means of communica-
> tion) do not determine circulation in so far as they concern the
> bringing of the product to the market or its transformation into
> commodity. For in this respect they are themselves included as part
> of the production phase. But they determine circulation in so far as
> they determine (1) the return; (2) the retransformation of the
> capital from the money form into that of the conditions of pro-
> duction. The more rapid and uninterrupted the supply of material
> and *matières instrumentales*, the smaller a supply does the capitalist
> need to buy. He can therefore all the more often turn over or
> reproduce the same circulating capital in this form, instead of
> having it lie around as dormant capital. . . . All this shows how
> with the development of production there is a relative decline in
> accumulation in the sense of hoarding; increases only in the form
> of fixed capital, while however continuous simultaneous labour
> (production) increases in regularity, in intensity, and in scope. The
> speed of the means of transport, together with their all-sidedness,
> increasingly transforms (with the exception of agriculture) the
> necessity of antecedent labour, as far as circulating capital is
> concerned, into that of simultaneous, mutually dependent, dif-
> ferentiated production.[56]

However, in so far as the return on capital – that is, circulation time –

must grow with the distance of the market from the point of production, the means of transportation becomes relevant: the abbreviation of circulation time by means of transport 'appears as belonging directly to the examination of the circulation of capital. But, this actually belongs to the doctrine of the market, which itself belongs to the section on capital.'[57]

If transportation costs arc incurred, where are they included? If the production process is to include getting the good to the market (Marx names China, as an example of a distant country), then the transportation costs would have to be included in the realisation costs [*Verwirklichungskosten, Realisierungskosten*]. This means that total costs of production would include the labour time objectified in the direct production process and the labour time contained in transportation.[58]

But if transportation costs are thus incurred and included, can a surplus value be extracted from such costs? Do transportation costs involve surplus labour? Marx suggests that the product must pay its own exchange value (that is, the labour objectified in itself) as well as the surplus time employed on its transport. However, 'whether he can or cannot extract the surplus value depends on the wealth of the country into which he brings the product and on its needs, on the use value of the product for this land.'[59] He concludes that if the issue is the same as in direct production when the workers are not paid for a part of the transportation time, then surplus value is extracted. However, he adds that neither should the worker bc cmployed longer than the time that is required for transporting the product: if the capitalist did so, he would throw away labour instead of realising [*verwerten*] it.[60]

The means of transport and communication constitute the physical conditions of exchange. Their creation by capital is an 'extraordinary necessity' as it annihilates space by time.[61] They are directly linked with mass production, distant markets, and must be produced by cheap means. Sea routes as well as highways are of key significance: 'The improvement of the means of transport and communication likewise falls into the category of the development of productive forces generally.'[62] The construction of highways falls upon the government, the community, since they do not cover their production costs.[63] If an individual is to build a highway, the work must provide a profit.[64] Since highways do not cover their production costs, they do not constitute a source of a country's wealth but are 'pure reductions from production and are deducted from the common surplus product of the country'.[65] This is so because the labour needed to build highways must come from the labour other than that required for the reproduction of the labour capacity, the direct labour needed for the subsistence of labour. This 'surplus' labour, suggests Marx, must be paid for from surplus tax revenue raised for this purpose or in the form of indirect taxes.[66] The quantity of labour needed to build would depend on the amount of labour capacity (that is, the concentration capacity: the mass of individuals capable of labour plus the unification of their forces) and the level of development of the productive force of labour (the mass of use values which it can create in a given span of time).[67]

If the value of the road cannot be realised (if the capitalist cannot *verwerten* it) it will still be built and will be paid for, communally: 'it is built only because it is a necessary use value for the commune, because the commune requires it at any price.'[68]

Generally, the capitalist will not build a road, except for profit, but he will in particular if the following conditions prevail:

– capital must be plentifully available (for example slow turnover because of slow realisation);
– must bring adequate interest (or even more than interest);
– the road must be worthwhile enough to productive capital (industry) to pay a user's price which, given adequate traffic volume, will permit the road to pay for itself (that is to say, the price demanded from the users is worth that much exchange value for the producers, or supplies a productive force for which they can pay that much).[69]

However, capital will shift the burden on to the shoulders of the state or will often secure this payment by 'means of protective tariffs, monopoly, State coercion . . .', unless, 'for capital, if it is to undertake building the road, it must be presupposed that not only the necessary labour time but also the surplus labour time worked by the worker can be paid for – this is where the profit comes from.'[70]

In this context, Marx adds an interesting reflection on the powers of the state *v.* the self-interest of the capitalists:

Where the State traditionally still takes up a position superior to capital, it still possesses the authority and the will to force the society of capitalists to put a part of their *revenue*, not of their capital, into such generally useful works, which appear at the same time as *general* conditions of production.[71]

Incidentally, the State itself and everything connected with it belongs to these deductions from *revenue*, belongs so to speak to the *consumption costs* for the individual, the production costs for society. A road itself may so increase the force of production that it creates new traffic which then makes the road profitable. These are works and investment which may be necessary without being productive in the capitalist sense, i.e., without the realisation of the *surplus labour*, through exchange, as *surplus value*.[72]

Marx sums up his inquiry into the nature of costs involving space as follows:

> Economically considered, the spatial condition, the bringing of the product to the market, belongs to the production process itself. The movement through which it gets there still belongs to the cost of making it. The spatial moment is connected with the expansion of the market.[73]

(c) Money costs: As regards the other major group of concerns involving circulation costs, money costs, Marx suggests that the costs of circulation proper achieve a significant independent development in the money trade. These costs are not reducible to productive labour time.[74] As an example, he illustrates the role of a middleman hired as an intermediary by fifty exchangers, the contract running for one year. The intermediary spends an entire year in circulation, for pay. If his pay covers only his necessities of life (which means that his pay is equal to or less than a full year's labour), then the exchangers would be better off (their surplus value would be reduced by a smaller amount) than they would if he received the equivalent of his entire, objectified, labour time. But one way or the other, the middleman's contribution would have added nothing to the value of the commodity. All that would happen is that he would receive part of the surplus.[75]

In Marx's view, money also constitutes a potential cost. To the extent that money consists of precious metals or of paper, it creates an expense, as it costs labour time. But it adds no value to the exchanged objects: it does not increase their exchange value; rather, the costs of money are a deduction from these values:

The preciousness of the instrument of circulation, of the instrument of exchange, expresses only the *costs of exchange*. Instead of adding to value, they subtract from it. Gold money and silver money e.g., are themselves values, *like others* (not in the sense of money), in so far as labour is objectified in them. But that these values serve as a *medium of circulation* is a deduction from disposable wealth.[76] The same relation holds for the production costs of the circulation of capital. This adds nothing to the values.[77]

Finally, Marx ties in 'brevity' (efficiency?) of circulation time with the determination of surplus value, through the 'coefficient of the production process': surplus value is determined not simply by the surplus labour appropriated by capital in the production process, but by the coefficient of the production process: that is to say, 'the number which expresses how often the production process is repeated over a given period of time. In turn, this coefficient is determined by the circulation time required by the capital for one turnover.'[78]

NOTES AND COMMENTS

1. *Grundrisse*, p. 730.
2. Ibid., p. 678.
3. Ibid.
4. Ibid., pp. 673–8.
5. Ibid., p. 674.
6. Ibid., p. 700.
7. Ibid., p. 673.
8. There are exceptions: a part of the seed in agriculture does enter into *circulation* as use value because it multiplies itself (p. 716).
9. *Grundrisse*, p. 681.
10. Ibid., p. 678.
11. Ibid., p. 675.
12. Ibid., p. 676.
13. Ibid., p. 677.
14. Marx terms money and money circulation 'simple circulation'.
15. *Grundrisse*, p. 677.
16. Unlike the labour time which appears in the production phase, Marx labels the time expended in large-scale circulation 'circulation time'.
17. *Grundrisse*, p. 673.
18. Ibid., p. 721.
19. This discussion is contained in Notebook V, written between 22 January and the beginning of February 1858 in response to Marx's concern with

the question of whether accumulation had arisen prior to labour or whether it is the result of labour.

20. *Grundrisse*, pp. 502–4.
21. Ibid., p. 514.
22. The discussion of 'the turnover of capital' is contained on pp. 520–60 and 618–40 of the *Grundrisse*. Marx defines circulation as follows: the transformation into money as soon as the product has achieved its final form for consumption and has been brought to its point of destination.
23. At this particular time, Marx emphasises that he is concerned chiefly with a situation of 'capital which has become', in particular with moment II; suggesting that moment III 'can be considered only when the theme is not capital generally but many capitals; whereas moment IV belongs to the section on wages, etc.' (p. 619).
24. *Grundrisse*, p. 619.
25. Ibid. The numerical notation follows Marx's original.
26. Ibid., p. 624.
27. Ibid.
28. Ibid., p. 620.
29. Ibid., p. 638–9.
30. Ibid., p. 640.
31. Ibid., p. 630.
32. Ibid., p. 620.
33. Ibid., p. 624.
34. Ibid., p. 626.
35. Ibid., p. 632.
36. Ibid., p. 633.
37. Ibid., p. 626.
38. Ibid., p. 627.
39. Ibid., p. 663.
40. Ibid., p. 658.
41. Ibid., p. 659.
42. Ibid.
43. Ibid., 538.
44. Ibid., p. 524.
45. Marx terms the transformation process a 'qualitative process of value' (p. 524). The sum of values produced in a given epoch is 'the total *Verwertung* of capital' (p. 544).
46. Ibid., p. 535.
47. Ibid., p. 524.
48. Ibid., p. 548.
49. Ibid., p. 539.
50. Ibid., p. 633.
51. Ibid., p. 671.
52. Ibid., p. 633.
53. Ibid., pp. 615–21.
54. Ibid., p. 624.
55. Ibid., p. 625.
56. Ibid., p. 825–6.
57. Ibid., p. 672.

58. Ibid., p. 522.
59. Ibid.
60. Ibid.
61. Ibid., p. 525.
62. Ibid., p. 523.
63. Ibid., p. 525.
64. How does Marx see the building of roads?
    'If it can be built at all, it proves that the society possesses the labour
    time (living labour and objectified labour) required for construction.
    Why then, as soon as production is based on exchange value and division
    of labour appears does road building not become the business of indi-
    viduals? (and it does not so become where it is conducted through taxes
    by the state). First of all: the society, the united individuals, may possess
    the surplus time to build the road, but only in concentration. Concentra-
    tion is always the addition of the part of labour capacity which each
    individual can employ on road building, apart from his particular work;
    but it is *not only* addition. The unification of their forces increases their
    force of production; but this is by no means the same as saying that all of
    them added together numerically would possess the same labour ca-
    pacity if they did not *work together*, hence if to the sum of their labour
    capacities were not added the surplus existing only in and through their
    united, combined labour. . . . Capital effects the same concentration in
    another way, through the manner of its exchange with free labour.
    Secondly: On one side, the population may be developed far enough,
    and the support which it finds in the employment of machinery etc. may
    be far enough advanced on the other side, so that the power arising only
    from the material, *massive concentration* of labour – and in antiquity it is
    always this *massive* effort of forcibly concentrated labour – may be
    superfluous, and a *relatively* smaller *mass of living labour* may be
    required. A special class of road-workers may form, employed by the
    state, of a part of the occasionally unemployed population is used for
    it . . .' (pp. 528–9).
65. Ibid., p. 525.
66. Ibid., p. 528.
67. Ibid., p. 526.
68. Ibid.
69. Ibid., p. 529.
70. Ibid., p. 532.
71. Ibid., p. 531.
72. Ibid.
73. Ibid., p. 534.
74. Ibid., p. 625.
75. Ibid.
76. Marx seems to suggest here that the more expensive the medium of
    exchange (the more labour goes into creating it), the more the dispos-
    able wealth of the economy is diminished.
77. *Grundrisse*, p. 625.
78. Ibid., p. 627.

8 Fixed Capital and Circulating Capital

Is money fixed capital or circulating capital?

> In so far as it always serves merely as an instrument of circulation, which is itself a moment of the total reproduction process, it is *fixed capital* – as an instrument of circulation. But its use value itself is only to circulate and never to be absorbed either into the production process proper nor into individual consumption. It is the part of capital constantly fixed in the circulation phase, and in this respect it is the most perfect form of circulating capital; in the other respect, because it is fixed as an instrument, it is fixed capital.[1]

A. PROBLEMS OF DEFINITION

The total turnover of capital, especially the time dimension involved in moments (1), the production phase, and (2), the circulation phase, reveals one of the most controversial subjects of debate before Marx as well as during his time: the definitions of and the distinction between 'fixed capital' and 'circulating capital'. Marx himself expressed great interest in this issue, as evidenced by his repeated deliberations, throughout the Chapter On Capital, concerning this debate, which revealed the existence of 'much miscomprehension e.g. Proudhon and his gang . . . regarding the definition of these two forms of capital, also because of the different kinds of return to either . . . the difference between selling and renting, annuity, interest and profit; . . . .'[2] Marx undertook to clarify these distinctions and to rectify these misconceptions.[3]

In the total labour process the original division of capital comprised means of labour, materials of labour, and living labour. Capital is divided into these three elements in accordance with its material composition, and the labour process is 'the merging of these three elements into each other'.[4] In the original division within the production process, means of labour appear as fixed capital, while

145

materials of labour and product of labour appear as circulating capital.[5]

Total capital is thus divided into fixed capital and circulating[6] capital, the latter issuing from the former:

> The capital is annually reproduced in different and changing portions as raw material, as product, and as means of production; in a word, as fixed capital and as circulating capital. The minimum supposed reproduction required is that part of circulating capital which will exchange for labouring capacity, the means of production, and for the maintenance and the consumption of the machinery and of the instruments.[7]

Whereas circulating capital never enters into the production process, fixed capital is 'fixated in the production process and consumed within'.[8] Fixed capital is 'the capital which consumes itself in the production process – the means of production in the strictest sense. Its value is that which eats itself up in the production process.'[9]

Fixed capital returns its value in successive parts, whereas each part of circulating capital is exchanged in its entirety. In the former, the existence of the value coincides with that of the use value.[10] Fixed capital, the 'inverse'[11] of small-scale circulation, remains in the production process and enters circulation only as part of the value of the finished product. With fixed capital, circulation is determined by the time in which it is consumed as use value within the act of production; with circulating capital, reproduction is determined by circulation time. It follows that the turnover time of a total capital is divided into circulating capital and fixed capital:[12]

$$S = c + f, \text{ where } f = \frac{1}{x} S, c = \frac{1}{y} S, \text{ and therefore } S = \frac{S}{x} + \frac{S}{y}.$$

Thus, in the case of fixed capital, the turnover of capital is reduced because the fixed capital is consumed slowly within the production process, the length of the duration time required for its reproduction. In the case of circulating capital, the decreased turnover arises from the prolongation of circulation time, specifically from the circulation time of the second half of circulation process time (the retransformation into money, which phase Marx labels 'the second half of the circulation process proper'[13]). Another cause for a decreased turnover arises from a longer time capital requires to emerge as a product from the production process.

By its form fixed capital is use value, but by its content it is exchange value. The value of fixed capital is transposed directly or indirectly, in successive bits, into the value of the product over the course of the years required to reproduce this fixed capital. This means that fixed capital returns as value only successively, 'enters into the price of the product only in successive bits'.[14] Fixed capital is transposed as value into newly extracted raw materials or into manufactured raw materials: that is, used up as use value in the production process:

> Use value for capital as such is only value itself. Circulating capital realizes itself as value for capital as such only when it is sold. . . . Fixed capital, by contrast, realizes itself as value only as long as it remains in the capitalist's hands as a use value, or, expressed as an objective relation, as long as it remains in the production process, which may be regarded as the inner organic movement of capital. . . . Hence, since *fixed capital*, once it has entered the production process, remains in it, it also passes away in it, is consumed in it. . . .[15]

Fixed capital is a produced production force, is productive capital, both by its quantity and its quality. It is capital which has lost its fluidity and has become identified with a specific use value.[16] It itself represents a given quantity of objectified labour time and has value only in so far as it itself is produced. It increases the mass of use value created in a given time; but it can impart value only if it is itself produced, if it represents a given quantity of objectified labour time.[17]

Since it does not serve as an immediate object of personal consumption, fixed capital does not circulate as *use* value and never enters circulation as *use* value: 'it is not a direct use value for consumption; . . . it is not once exchanged as product for money.'[18]

Fixed capital can enter into circulation as value only to the extent that it passes away as use value in the production process: 'its circulation as value corresponds to its consumption in the production process as use value.'[19] When fixed capital is dissolved into value, it is absorbed into circulation, whereby its use value has passed away and must be replaced by a new use value of the same kind. Its reproduction time is determined by the time in which it is used up, consumed, within the production process.[20]

The time in which fixed capital is consumed and in which it must be reproduced in its form as use value depends on its relative durability:

'The necessary reproduction time of fixed capital, together with the proportion of the total capital consisting of it, modify the turnover time of total capital, and thereby its realisation.'[21]

The durability of fixed capital influences realisation, specifically 'the greater durability of capital (diminution of its necessary reproduction time) and the proportion of fixed capital to total capital.'[22]

To the extent that the instrument of production is itself a value, objectified labour, it does not contribute as a productive force. If a machine which cost 100 working days to make replaced only 100 working days, then it would in no way increase the productive power of labour and in no way decrease the cost of the product. The more durable the machine, the more often can the same quantity of product be created with it, or the more often can the circulating capital be renewed, its reproduction be repeated, and the smaller is the value-share (that required to replace the depreciation, the wear and tear of the machine); i.e., the more is the price of the product and its unit production cost decreased.[23]

The realisation [*Verwertung*] of capital is influenced by two factors:

(a) the greater durability of capital and the proportion of fixed capital to the total capital;
(b) a slower turnover due to a greater distance in space of the market from which the capital returns as money, so that a longer time is required to complete the path of circulation (for example, capital working in England for the East India market returns more slowly than that working for nearer foreign markets or for the domestic market), or to the production phase itself being interrupted by natural conditions, as in agriculture.[24]

In his attempt to single out the major characteristics of fixed capital, Marx admits that the definition of fixed capital is by no means clear-cut, suggesting that definitional difficulties arose from the introduction over time of fixed capital directly into the production process and indirectly into the circulation process, and from the fact that originally some forms of fixed capital had figured as circulating capital and had become fixed capital only with the evolution of the capitalist mode of production (for example machines to a machine-maker are a circulating product but are fixed capital to the product manufacturer; houses, to the building trade, are circulating capital, but are fixed capital for those who buy them or rent them, for production).

However, there are aspects which are peculiar to fixed capital:

(a) the return of its value in successive parts;
(b) turnover time, which consideration becomes important when the fixed capital appears not as a mere instrument of production within the production process, 'but rather as an independent form of capital, e.g., bridges, railways, canals, roads, land improvements, etc. . . . . which aspects [declares Marx] we will enter when we study interest.';[25]
(c) factors which make for a reduction in the cost of machinery or which cost capital nothing:

> An increase of the force of production which costs capital nothing, is the division of labour and the combination of labour within the production process (large-scale production); another productive force which costs nothing (except schoolmasters, scholars) is scientific power. The growth of the population is a productive force which costs nothing: therefore all the social powers developing with the growth of the population and with the historic development of society costs capital nothing. It follows that every reduction in the cost of machinery is a gain for capital: a machinery which costs nothing has maximum value for capital. Fixed capital is employed only to the extent that its value is smaller than the value it posits.[26]

(d) in addition, in specific cases, fixed capital can also *circulate* as use value: it can be bought and paid for directly for its use value, for example means of communication, of transport, of bringing products to the market.[27]

However, in none of these cases does the fixed capital leave the production process, for instance, railways, even though, to others, railways serve as a means of consumption, for example holiday travel.[28]

Marx emphasises that this type of fixed capital is different from the machinery used up in the production process, different because a study of fixed capital which *can* circulate as *use* value gives rise to several specific considerations:

(i) unlike machine-form fixed capital, which is used up within its *own* production process, this form of fixed capital is used up simultaneously by various capitals; this form of fixed capital is not locked into a particular branch of production but serves as an 'inter-connecting artery'[29] in a mass of particular production processes;

(ii) this type of fixed capital is produced by a particular branch of production but is sold to many producers who consume it directly, in the same common form, as a general commodity; it is sold as a general commodity it has *use* value for direct consumption.[30]

(iii) This type of fixed capital is unlike machinery. Machinery is an agent of production in a particular production process and appears as a presupposition of the production process, not as a result. In the simple circulation of capital, the value of machinery, of fixed capital, includes no surplus value for its user since only its own value has to be replaced (which is consistent with Marx's view on simple circulation). But this type of fixed capital, for example railways, itself circulates as use value, is used and directly paid for by the capitalist – the general social production process. Its value includes the surplus value and, therefore, the interest and the profit, if any: that is to say, the determination of its value goes beyond the simple circulation of capital because 'it is simultaneously an instrument of production and is realised by [its] seller as product, as capital.'[31]

As means of production, this fixed capital is the product of capital and as such it contains objectified surplus time. While its use value can be sold into circulation, it cannot be sold while serving as an instrument of production. It therefore shares with machinery 'the quality that its value returns only successively; but it also has an aspect unique to itself: this return of value includes the return of its surplus value, of the surplus labour objectified in it.'[32]

(iv) In some cases the question has arisen whether fixed capital may be included in '*matières instrumentales*' (coal, oil, wood, grease). Marx argues that these materials are completely used up in the production process. But they are brought into the production process ('when they lose their property of being potentially circulating capital')[33] even though some of these materials have a value outside production and can be consumed in other ways.

B. FIXED CAPITAL AND CIRCULATING CAPITAL: ADDITIONAL MARXIAN PERSPECTIVE

After his treatment of the definitional problems, Marx goes on to review the less controversial aspects of fixed capital and circulating capital and then poses several incisive questions.

Fixed capital and raw materials: Fixed capital cannot work without raw materials. The employment of fixed capital on a larger scale presupposes the expansion of the part of circulating capital consisting of raw materials, hence of the growth of capital generally.[34] But the expansion of fixed capital presupposes the relative decrease of the portion of capital exchanged for living labour.[35]

Fixed capital and social productivity of labour: Fixed capital embodies the social productivity of labour as a property inherent in capital. This productivity includes scientific power, the combination of social powers within the production process, and the skill transposed from direct labour into the machine (that is, the 'dead productive force'[36]). The wealth-generating capacity (the ability to wait until large-scale means of generating wealth are created) is tied to an increasing size and capacity of machines; to science; to the replacement of human labour by machines; to inventions; but this capacity sets labour free (renders labour superfluous).[37]

Significance of 'larger capital':   Since larger capital consists of more fixed capital, it has slower turnover, but larger capital does not create more surplus value than a smaller one with a relatively more rapid turnover. Nevertheless the larger capital has to search out more distant markets, which occurs as soon as the present, physical, market ceases being 'an economic market'[38], that is, as the economic market becomes more and more distant from the place of production. Trade brings in different countries into intercourse: it discovers new markets. This evolution Marx labels 'something entirely different from the mere cost of circulation required to carry out a given mass of exchange operations; it is the positing not of the operations of exchange but of the exchange itself. Creation of markets.'[39]

Capital, production interruptions, and market distance: Production interruptions and market distance (which has bearing on circulation time)[40] are of importance in the creation of value (and of surplus value) within a given period of time:

> Since capitals are (1) divided into fixed and circulating capital in unequal portions; (2) [have] an interrupted or uninterrupted production phase and return from more distant or nearer markets, hence, unequal circulation time; it follows that the determination of the surplus value created in a given time, e.g. annually, must be unequal because the number of reproduction processes in the given period is unequal. The amount of value created appears determined not simply by the labour employed during the immediate production process, but by the degree to which this exploitation of labour can be repeated within a given period of time.[41]

Marx agrees with J.S. Mill's proposition concerning the existence of fixated capital as tied down, non-disposable capital stuck in one phase of the total circulation process: a great part of the capital of the nation which always lies idle, a situation which, in Marx's view, may lead to serious consequences. Fixed capital is a use value fixated in this form:

> A use value snatched away from consumption as well as from circulation. The transformation of circulating capital into fixed capital presupposes relative surplus capital, since it is capital employed not for direct production but rather for new means of production.[42]

> For circulating capital, an interruption, if it does not last so long as to ruin its use value, is only an interruption in the creation of surplus value. But with fixed capital, the interruption, in so far as in the meantime its use value is necessarily destroyed relatively unproductively, i.e., without replacing itself as value, is the destruction of the original value itself.[43]

It is extremely important to grasp these aspects of circulating and fixated capital as *specific characteristic forms* of capital generally, since a great many phenomena of the bourgeois economy – the period of the economic cycle, which is essentially different from the single turnover period of capital; the effect of new demand; even the effect of new gold- and silver-producing countries on general production – [would otherwise] be incomprehensible. It is futile to speak of the stimulus given by Australian gold or a newly discovered market. If it were not in the nature of capital to be never completely occupied, i.e., partially *fixated*, devalued, unproductive, then no stimuli could drive it to greater production. At the same time, [note] the senseless contradictions into which the economists stray – even Ricardo – when they presuppose that capital is always fully occupied; hence explain an increase in production by referring exclusively to the creation of new capital. Every increase would then presuppose an earlier increase in the growth of the productive forces.[44]

In this context, Marx makes an interesting reference to the existence of 'dormant capital' and 'money that lies fallow' and their effects:

The concept of *dormant capital*, capital lying fallow, can refer only to its barren existence in one of these aspects, i.e. in one of the phases of the whole of circulation, and it is a condition of capital that part of it always lies fallow. . . . Money itself, to the extent that it forms a particular part of the nation's capital, but always remains in the form of medium of circulation, i.e. never goes through the other phases, . . . can likewise lie fallow, be fixated in the form of money of value withdrawn from circulation. During crises – after the moment of panic – during the standstill of industry, money is immobilised in the hands of bankers, billbrokers, etc. . . . [crying] out for a field of employment where it may be realised as capital.[45]

In what sense does fixed capital create value? In so far as it increases relative surplus time, or decreases necessary labour time:

Fixed capital creates value not in so far as it has value – for the latter is simply replaced – but rather only in so far as it increases relative surplus time, or decreases necessary labour time. In the same proportion then, as that in which its scope grows, the mass of products must increase, and the living labour employed relatively decrease.[46]

But surplus labour can be increased only relatively, by means of greater productive power of labour (productive power resting on division and combination of labour), which will decrease the labour power employed (relative to the capital which sets it in motion), i.e. same labour could be hired at half the previous wages, increasing surplus value.[47]

The tendency of capital is to link up absolute with relative surplus value, by stretching the working day while reducing the necessary labour to a minimum, by developing the intensity of the productive power of labour and the greatest possible diversification of the use value of labour (of the branches of production). The increase in the productive force of labour arising of itself (large-scale production, division and combination of labour, saving on certain expenses when labour is done in common, i.e. large buildings) capital does not pay for. To make harvests more productive, it is not even necessary for the number of instruments to have grown, but rather merely for them to be concentrated and for the work, previously done fragmentarily by hundreds, to be done communally. However, what is required for all forms of surplus labour is growth of population . . . the basic source of wealth.[48]

What is the relation between production, capital, and exchange?

With capital, production itself is on all sides subordinate to exchange. These exchange operations, circulation as such, produce no surplus value, but are conditions for its realisation. They are conditions of the production of capital itself. . . . The transformation into money is necessary for the reproduction of capital as such, and its reproduction is necessarily the production of surplus value.[49]

Can use value itself place limits upon the reproduction phase? In Marx's view, it can:

Use value itself places limits upon the reproduction phase. Wheat must be reproduced in a year. Perishable things like milk etc. must be reproduced more often. Meat on the hoof does not need to be reproduced quite so often, since the animal is alive and hence resists time; but slaughtered meat on the market has to be reproduced in the form of money in the very short term or it rots. The reproduction of value and of use value partly coincide, partly not.[50]

Can any fixed capital be faux frais de production? It can:

All unnecessary fixed capital appears as *faux frais de production*, like all unnecessary circulation costs. If capital could possess the machinery without employing labour for the purpose, then it would raise the productive power of labour and diminish necessary labour without having to buy labour.[51]

How is the mode of production of capital linked with modes of production antedating capital? Marx admits that the mode of production of capital may develop in one sector while in other sectors modes of production antedating capital may still be dominant. But he predicts that the former mode will conquer all other modes in the course of development and through competition on a worldwide scale:

When an industrial people producing on the foundation of capital, such as the English, e.g., exchange with the Chinese, and absorb value in the form of money and commodity from out of their production process, or rather absorb value by drawing the latter within the sphere of the circulation of their capital, then one sees right away that the Chinese do not therefore need to produce as capitalists. Within a single society, such as the English, the mode of production of capital develops in one branch of industry, while in another, e.g. agriculture, modes of production predominate which more or less antedate capital. Nevertheless, it is (1) its necessary tendency to conquer the mode of production in all respects, to bring them under the rule of capital. Within a given national society this already necessarily arises from the transformation, by this means, of all labour into wage labour; (2) as to external markets, capital imposes this propagation of its mode of production through international competition. Competition is the mode generally in which capital secures the victory of its mode of production.[52]

Finally, what is 'immovable capital'? In Marx's view, it is the most tangible form of fixed capital:

every form in which the product of industry is welded fast to the surface of the earth. . . . The immovable use value, such as house, railway, etc., is therefore the most tangible form of fixed capital. It can circulate as title but not as use value (it cannot circulate in the physical sense).[53]

C. LABOUR AND CAPITAL (FIXED CAPITAL)

All powers of labour are transposed into powers of capital, fixed capital as well as circulating capital, even though capital itself is objectified labour time. Fixed capital is a product of labour:

> all powers of labour are transposed into powers of capital; the productive power of labour into fixed capital (posited as external to labour and as existing independently [*sachlich*, i.e. as object] of it; and, in circulating capital, the fact that the worker himself has created the conditions for the repetition of his labour, and that the exchange of this, his labour, is mediated by the co-existing labour of others, appears in such a way that capital gives him an advance. . . . Capital in the form of circulating capital posits itself as mediator between the different workers.[54]

Fixed capital is itself a product of labour, and of alien labour merely appropriated by capital.[55]

Fixed capital produces value, that is, increases the value of the product in only two respects: (a) in so far as it has value, that is, is itself the product of labour, a certain quantity of labour in objectified form; (b) in so far as it increases the relation of surplus labour to necessary labour, by enabling labour, through an increase in its productive powers, 'to create a greater mass of the products required for the maintenance of living labour capacity in a shorter time'.[56]

The increase in the productive powers of labour tends to decrease, to a minimum, the amount of labour required for production:

> Through this process, the amount of labour necessary for the production of a given object is indeed decreased to a minimum, but only in order to realize a maximum of labour in the maximum number of such objects. The first aspect is important, because capital here – quite unintentionally – decreases human labour, expenditure of energy, to a minimum . . . the condition of its emancipation.[57]

But in opposition to Lauderdale (who wants to make fixed capital into an independent source of value – 'how can he? if capital is such a source only in so far as it itself is objectified labour time and itself posits surplus labour time?'[58]) and the 'Economists' (in whose imagination 'capital leaps to the aid of the individual worker'[59]) Marx argues that capital can be effective only with masses or workers and that the employment of machinery 'historically presupposes superfluous hands': 'It enters not in order to replace labour power where this is lacking, but rather in order to decrease massively available labour power to its necessary measure.'[60]

Through the division of labour, the workers' operations are transformed into increasingly mechanical ones and gradually the workers are replaced by a mechanism: 'capital absorbs labour into itself'.[61]

In this evolution, at the beginning the division within the production process was into means of labour, materials of labour, and the final product of labour; at the end, it appears as two kinds of capital, in certain proportions: circulating capital (means of labour and materials of labour) and fixed capital.

The presupposition of the production resting on value is

> the mass of direct labour time, the quantity of labour employed, as the determinant factor in the production of wealth. But with the development of large industry, the creation of real wealth comes to depend less on labour time and on the amount of labour employed than on the power of the agencies set in motion during labour time; the effectiveness of these agencies is out of all proportion to the direct labour time spent on their production, but depends on the general state of science and on the progress of technology, or the application of this science to production.[62]

In the course of this development (of science and of large industry),

> real wealth manifests itself . . . in the monstrous disproportion between the labour time applied, and its product, as well as in the qualitative imbalance between labour, reduced to a pure abstraction, and the power of the production process it superintends. Labour no longer appears so much to be included within the production process; rather, the human being comes to relate more as watchman and regulator to the production process itself. The worker . . . steps to the side of the production process instead of being its chief actor.[63]

The consequence of all this is that eventually production based on exchange value will break down:

As soon as labour in the direct form has ceased to be the great well-spring of wealth, labour time ceases and must cease to be its measure, and hence exchange value must cease to be the measure of use value. The *surplus labour of the mass* has ceased to be the condition for the development of general wealth, just as the *non-labour of the few*, for the development of the general powers of the human head. With that, production based on exchange value breaks down, and the direct, material production process is stripped of the form of penury and antithesis.[64]

Marx ties in the reduction in necessary labour time in his interpretation of the capitalist's quest for increasing surplus time, with his propositions concerning the evolution of capital towards the true wealth of the nation, an evolution in the course of which the decrease of necessary labour time will lead to the free development of the individual (of 'individualities'[65]): their artistic, scientific, and so forth, development in the time set free, time created by the increasing capital means. He labels capital a 'moving contradiction'[66]: on the one hand, it pushes to decrease labour time to a minimum; on the other, it posits labour time as sole measure of and source of wealth. This means that it diminishes the necessary form of labour while seeking to increase it in the superfluous form. On the one hand, it applies all powers of science, of nature, of social combination and social intercourse in order to make wealth creation relatively independent of labour time employed on it. On the other, it desires to use labour time as the measuring rod for the giant social powers thereby created while confining these forces within limits required to maintain the already created value as value. To capital, forces of production and social relations are the means which it uses to produce on a limited foundation. But true wealth will be possible only once this limited foundation has been blown 'sky-high'.[67] As a confirmation of his view, he quotes from a pamphlet (by anonymous), *The Source and Remedy of National Difficulties* (1821), p. 6:

'Truly wealthy is a nation when the working day is 6 rather than 12 hours. Wealth is not command over surplus labour time' (real wealth) 'but *disposable time* outside that needed in direct production, for *every individual* and the whole society.'[68]

1. The Productivity of Labour

The production of the means of production can be undertaken only once a certain degree of productivity has been reached in the degree of development of wealth, since a part of the wealth must be withdrawn from immediate consumption and from production for immediate consumption, including labour. Thus, the production of the means of production requires a certain level of productivity and of relative overabundance. As production aimed at the satisfaction of immediate needs becomes more productive, a greater part of production can be directed towards the production of the means of production.[69]

In Marx's view, it is essential to recognise that (i) the magnitude of the relative surplus labour time depends on the productivity of necessary labour, and (ii) the magnitude of the labour time (living and objectified) employed on the production of fixed capital depends on the productivity of the labour time spent in the direct production of products; of which surplus population and surplus production are a precondition. There is a proportion between building more railways, canals, telegraphs, and so forth, and building the machinery directly active in the direct production process. A disproportion, due to the constant underproduction and overproduction of modern industry, causes constant fluctuations and convulsions when sometimes too little and at other times too much circulating capital is transferred into fixed capital.[70]

In Marx's view, two additional dimensions of fixed capital must also be pointed out: first, the production of fixed capital is directed immediately not towards the production of direct use values but towards the production of the means of value creation; in this particular sense, fixed capital, with its position in total production, is the measuring rod of the development of wealth founded on the mode of production of capital; second, the durability of fixed capital as means of production is not only a requisite physical quality but also a required quality of its use value; this is so because the more often it has to be replaced, the costlier it is and because its duration is an increase in its productive force.[71]

Since there are different ways in which machinery diminishes labour, Marx reflects on the effect on value of the replacement of labour capacity by machinery. What is the purpose, he asks, of taking away part of the capital from its variable and self-multiplying portion (that which exchanges for living labour) and adding it to the constant part, the part whose value is merely reproduced or maintained in the product? The purpose is to make more productive the remaining portion of variable capital which exchanges for living labour. In this type of situation he distinguishes between three cases. In the first, 'the value of the machinery is equal to the value of the labour capacity it replaces. In this case the newly produced value would be diminished not increased, if the surplus labour time of the remaining part of labour capacity did not grow at the same rate as its amount is diminished',[72] for example if one half of the workers is dismissed, the surplus labour time of the remaining half would have to double for value to remain the same. In the second case, the surplus labour time of the remaining part of labour capacity grows at the same rate as the amount of labour capacity is diminished; clearly, this alternative is of no interest to capital because 'what it would gain in surplus labour time on one side, it would lose on the part of capital which would enter production as objectified labour, i.e., as invariable value.'[73] In the third case, the surplus labour time of the remaining part of labour capacity is expected to grow at a greater rate than the rate of the reduction of labour capacity. This case is of interest to the capitalist, but he must bear in mind three possible effects:

> This can happen either because the entire expenditure incurred for the previous instrument of production must be deducted. In this case the *total sum of the capital laid out diminishes*, and, although the relation of the total sum of employed labour relative to the constant part of the capital has diminished, the surplus labour time has remained the same, and has hence grown not only relative to the capital laid out for labour, for necessary labour time, but also relative to the total capital, to the total value of capital, because the latter has diminished. Or, the value for machinery may be as great as that previously laid out for living labour, which has now become superfluous; but the rate of surplus labour of the remaining capital has increased so that the 50 workers supply not only as much surplus labour as the 100 did before, but a greater amount. Say, e.g. instead of 4 hours each, $4\frac{1}{2}$ hours. But in this case a greater part of the capital is required for raw materials etc., in short, a greater total capital is required. If a capitalist who previously employed 100 workers for £2 400 annually, lets 50 go, and puts a machine costing £1 200 in their place, then this machine – although it costs him as much as 50 workers did before – is the product of fewer workers, because he pays the capitalist from

whom he buys the machine not only the necessary labour, but also the surplus labour. Or, if he had his own workers build the machine, he would have used a part of them for necessary labour only. In the case of machinery, thus, increase in surplus labour with absolute decrease of necessary labour time. It may be accompanied both by absolute diminution of the employed capital and by its growth.[74]

Marx reasons that even

the objective conditions of production which [capital] obtains from circulation remain unchanged in value, i.e. if the same amount of labour objectifies itself in the same amount of use value, then a lesser part of the capital can be laid out for living labour, or, there is a change in the proportion of the component part of capital.[75]

If a division of labour doubles the productive force of labour, the same labour using the same instrument can use up double the quantity of raw materials: if initial capital = 100 (40 raw materials + 40 labour + 20 instruments), capital would grow by 40, decreasing the proportion of labour from $\frac{40}{100}$ to $\frac{40}{140}$ (or keeping capital at 100, labour would go down to 20); but the share of raw materials would go up, possibly to 60. Concerning the use of raw materials, Marx distinguishes between three particular cases:

(i) With labour increasing its force of production (that is, increasing speed of work, increasing intensity of work), the better combination and division of labour may waste less raw material as a result of greater skill, whereby more instruments may be produced with the same value without buying more raw materials or requiring a greater advance in materials or instruments of labour. They perform a greater amount of work at the same maintenance cost, that is, labour's necessary labour time diminishes (relative to their surplus labour time); but the value of the product remains the same, of which, however, a larger surplus value goes to the capitalist, whose wages bill goes down because the same amount of living labour now costs him a smaller amount of objectified labour.[76]

(ii) With the growing productivity of labour, the extra raw material may not cost anything; capital does not have to lay out more value on raw materials and instruments.[77]

(iii) The increased productivity of labour does require a greater
outlay for raw materials and instruments, with a diminution of
the part of the extra surplus value going to the capitalist.[78]

In the first case, the increased productivity of labour processes a
greater amount of raw materials during the same time, but the
instruments remain the same; the part of capital exchanged for living
labour diminishes relative to the other components of labour (by an
amount equal to its own decline if the others remain the same or by
an amount equal to their growth if they increase; but this part of
capital can remain the same if absolute labour time increases,
whereby its proposition becomes smaller). In the second, the relation
of raw material rises in the same proportion as the relation of surplus
value rises. In the last, the growth of the population (which is
presupposed in all cases) presupposes additional accumulation (greater capital enters production).

Since the growing productivity of labour would lead capital to
encounter a barrier in the non-growing mass of raw materials and
machinery, industrial development, according to Marx, will take the
following course: the introduction of labour on a large scale, as well
as the employment of machinery, begins in the branches which are
the closest to being production of raw materials for industry, raw
materials both for the materials of labour and for the instruments of
labour.[79]

2. Is the Introduction of More Machinery Profitable for Capital?

The replacement of necessary labour by machinery ties in directly
with profit, suggests Marx when he goes on to review the contemporary reflections concerning the origin and the cause of profit. He is
not concerned (here) with merchants' profit,[80] but with the question
whether it is circulating capital or fixed capital which creates the
profit – whether, as claimed, profit is the 'product proper' of capital?

> As to profit . . . each part of the circulating capital which leaves
> and returns to the production process, i.e. contains objectified
> labour (the value of advances), necessary labour (the value of
> wages), and surplus labour – brings profit as soon as it passes fully
> through circulation, because the surplus labour which the product

contains is realized with it. But it is neither the circulating capital nor the fixed capital which create the profit, but rather the appropriation of alien labour which both of them mediate, hence at bottom only the part of circulating capital which enters into small-scale circulation. This profit is realized in practice, however, only through the entry of capital into circulation, hence only in its form as circulating capital, never in its form as fixed capital.[81]

Surplus value, as posited by capital itself and measured by its quantitative relation to the total value of the capital, is profit.[82]

But Marx is critical of the prevailing views that profit is the product of capital:

Because on one side the conditions of labour are posited as objective component parts of the capital, on the other side labour itself is posited as activity incorporated in it, the entire labour appears as capital's own process and the positing of surplus value is its own product, whose magnitude is therefore also not measured by the surplus labour which it compels the worker to do, but rather as a magnified productivity which it lends to labour. The product proper of capital is profit. To that extent, it is now posited as the source of wealth. . . . Since capital enters wholly into production, and since, as capital, its various component parts are only formally distinct from one another, are equally sums of value, it follows that the positing of value appears to be equally inherent in them.[83]

We are not concerned here with the illusion that *all parts of capital equally bring a profit*, an illusion arising out of the division of the surplus value into average portions, independently of the relations of the component parts of capital as circulating and fixed, and the part of it transformed into living labour. Because Ricardo half shares this illusion, he considers the influence of the proportions of fixed and circulating capital from the start of his determination of value as such, and the reverend parson Malthus stupidly and simple-mindedly speaks of profits accruing to fixed capital, as if capital grew organically by some power of nature.[84]

Marx looks around for examples and finds several in cotton manufacture:

Machinery is profitable for capital only in relation as it increases the surplus labour time of the workers employed in machinery (not in so far as it reduces it; only in so far as it reduces the relation of surplus labour time to necessary, so that the latter has not only relatively declined, while the number of simultaneous working days has remained the same, but has diminished absolutely).[85]

The increase in absolute labour time supposes the same or an increasing number of simultaneous working days; ditto the increase of the force of production by division of labour etc. In both cases the aggregate labour time remains the same or grows. With the employment of machinery, relative surplus labour time grows not only relative to necessary labour time and hence correlative with aggregate labour time; but rather the relation to necessary labour time grows while aggregate labour diminishes, i.e. the number of simultaneous working days diminishes (relative to surplus labour time).[86]

From these observations and his calculations of gross profit, Marx deduces the following conclusions:

At the same rate as the total ratio of the part of the capital laid out in wages declines relative to the part laid out in machinery and circulation capital, . . . the profit on the part laid out in wages must naturally rise, to allow the percentage point of profit to remain the same.[87]

The absolute decrease in aggregate labour, i.e. of the working days . . . can appear doubly. In the first-cited form, that one part of the hitherto employed workers is dismissed in consequence of the use of fixed capital (machinery). Or, that the introduction of machinery will diminish the increase of the working days employed, even though productivity grows and, indeed, at a greater rate (of course) than it diminishes in consequence of the 'value' of the newly introduced machinery. In so far as the fixed capital has value, it does not magnify, but rather diminishes the productivity of labour.[88]

What, asks Marx, are the long-run implications arising from the continuous replacement of living labour by capital (of 'subjective labour' by 'objective labour')?

First, less and less immediate labour is required for an increasingly greater product, and capital confronts labour with ever more power and independence:

in the development of the productive powers of labour the objective conditions of labour [*gegenständliches Arbeitsverhältnis*], objectified labour [*vergegenständlichte Arbeit*], must grow relative to living labour – this is actually a tautological statement, for what else does growing productive power of labour mean than that less immediate labour is required to create a greater product, and that therefore social wealth expresses itself more and more in the conditions of labour created by itself? – this fact appears from the standpoint of capital not in such a way that one of the moments of social activity – objective labour – becomes the ever more powerful body of the other moment, of subjective, living labour, but rather – and this is important for wage labour – that the objective conditions of labour assume an ever more colossal independence, represented by its very extent, opposite living labour, and that social wealth confronts labour in more powerful portions as an alien and dominant power.[89]

Second, this process of objectification appears as a process of dispossession:

To the extent that, from the standpoint of capital and wage labour, the creation of the objective body of activity happens in antithesis to the immediate labour capacity – that this process of objectification [*Vergegenständlichung*] in fact appears as a process of dispossession from the standpoint of labour or as appropriation of alien labour from the standpoint of capital – to that extent, this twisting and inversion [*Verdrehung und Verkehrung*] is a *real phenomenon* not a merely *supposed one* existing merely in the imagination of the workers and the capitalists. But obviously this process of inversion is a merely *historical* necessity, a necessity for the development of the forces of production solely from a specific point of departure, or basis, but in no way an *absolute* necessity of production; rather, a vanishing one . . . the result to suspend this basis itself, together with this form of process. [original emphasis][90]

Third, even though the workers' propertylessness and the ownership of labour by capital are fundamental conditions of the bourgeois mode of production, the more this contradiction develops, the more it becomes evident that the workers must themselves appropriate their own surplus labour. Once that happens, necessary labour time will be measured by the needs of the social individual, and the degradation of the worker will end:

> The worker's propertylessness, and the ownership of living labour by objectified labour, or the appropriation of alien labour by capital – both merely expressions of the same relation from opposite poles – are fundamental conditions of the bourgeois mode of production, in no way accidents irrelevant to it. These modes of distribution are the relations of production themselves, but *sub specie distributionis*. It is therefore highly absurd when e.g., J. S. Mill says (*Principles of Political Economy*, 2nd ed., London, 1849 Vol. I, p. 240): 'The laws and conditions of the production of wealth partake of the character of physical truths . . . It is not so with the distribution of wealth. That is a matter of human institutions solely' (p. 239, 240). The 'laws and conditions' of the production of wealth and the laws of the 'distribution of wealth' are the same laws under different forms, and both change, undergo the same historic process; are as such only moments of a historic process.[91]

It requires no great penetration to grasp that, e.g., where free labour or wage arising out of the dissolution of bondage is the point of departure, there machines can only *arise* in antithesis to living labour, as property alien to it, and as power hostile to it; i.e., they must confront it as capital. But it is just as easy to perceive that machines will not cease to be agencies of social production when they become e.g., property of the associated workers. In the first case, however, their distribution, i.e., that they *do not belong* to the worker, is just as much a condition of the mode of production founded on wage labour. In the second case, the changed distribution would start from a *changed* foundation of production, a new foundation first created by the process of history.[92]

It [capital] is thus, despite itself, instrumental in creating the means of social disposable time, in order to reduce labour time for the whole society to a diminishing minimum, and thus to free everyone's time for their own development. But its tendency always, on the one side, *to create disposable time, on the other, to convert it into surplus labour.* If it succeeds too well at the first, then it suffers from surplus production, and then necessary labour is interrupted, because *no surplus labour can be realized by capital.* The more this contradiction develops, the more it becomes evident that the growth of the forces of production can no longer be bound up with the appropriation of alien labour, but that the mass of workers must themselves appropriate their own surplus labour. Once they have done so – and *disposable time* thereby ceases to have an *antithetical* existence – then, on the one side, necessary labour time will be measured by the needs of the social individual, and, on the other, the development of the power of social production will grow so rapidly that, even though production is now calculated for the wealth of all, *disposable time* will grow for all. For real wealth is the developed productive power of all individuals. The measure of wealth is then not any longer in any way, labour time, but rather disposable time.[93]

NOTES AND COMMENTS

1. *Grundrisse*, p. 716.
2. Ibid., p. 722.
3. Marx outlines some of the complications in distinguishing between fixed and circulating capital: gold is fixed capital except in so far as it is consumed for gilding; ships are fixed but they float; foreign railways share in our markets, our railways in the markets of the world. *Approvisionnement* is circulating capital, which consists only of subsistence and other necessaries advanced to the workmen before the completion of the produce of labour: it is the only part of capital which circulates during the production phase itself (p. 643).
4. *Grundrisse*, p. 691.
5. Ibid., p. 703.
6. The gist of Marx's discussion of fixed capital is contained in Notebook VII, written end February–March and end May–beginning June 1858. This Notebook also contains his discussion of 'capital as fructiferous', the transfer of surplus value into profit, and miscellaneous other topics. In different places Marx also uses 'fluid' capital (for circulating capital) and 'variable value', as terms applicable to the current production process.
7. *Grundrisse*, p. 726.
8. Ibid., p. 678.
9. Ibid., p. 690.
10. Ibid., p. 686.
11. Ibid., p. 681.
12. Ibid., pp. 682–4.

13. Ibid., p. 686.
14. Ibid., p. 721.
15. Ibid., p. 680.
16. Let us recall Marx's definition of use value: the material character as a consumable product, a product entering directly into individual consumption (p. 678).
17. Marx makes at this point two interesting comments: the value of capital may change as its reproduction costs rise or fall, or as a consequence of a decline in profits (p. 649); and 'the profit of the capitalists as a class, or the profit of capital as such, has to exist before it can be distributed, and it is extremely absurd to try to explain its origin by distribution' (p. 684).
18. *Grundrisse*, p. 721. Marx states that 'natural agencies' – such as water, land, mines, etc. – possess *exchange* value and 'hence come as values into the calculation of production costs' (p. 715).
19. Ibid., p. 681.
20. Ibid., p. 682.
21. Ibid., p. 683.
22. Ibid., p. 685.
23. Ibid., p. 675.
24. Ibid., p. 695.
25. Ibid., pp. 686–7.
26. Ibid., pp. 766–7.
27. Ibid., pp. 720–3.
28. Ibid., p. 725.
29. Ibid.
30. Ibid.
31. Ibid.
32. Ibid., p. 727.
33. Ibid., p. 680.
34. Note that Marx classifies, in this context, raw materials as 'circulating capital'.
35. *Grundrisse*, p. 715.
36. Ibid.
37. Ibid., pp. 703–10.
38. Presumably, Marx means here a market with an adequate rate of return.
39. *Grundrisse*, p. 644. Marx proposes here that he will examine the question of the 'creation of markets' before 'he is done with circulation' (p. 644).
40. Note Marx's definition of 'circulation time': the time expended in large-scale circulation; the entire period from the moment when capital exits from the production process until it enters it again (*Grundrisse*, pp. 626–627).
41. *Grundrisse*, p. 741.
42. Ibid., p. 646. The size of the market and the velocity of turnover are not necessarily inversely related, claims Marx on p. 718: 'The fact that the velocity of turnover here [Marx uses examples] substitutes for the magnitude of the capital shows strikingly that it is only the amount of surplus labour set into motion, and labour generally, which determines the magnitude of the creation of value as well as the creation of surplus

value, and not the capital for itself. The capital of 100 has, during the year, set in motion successively as much labour as one of 400, and hence created the same surplus value.'

43. Ibid., p. 719.
44. Ibid., p. 623.
45. Ibid., p. 621.
46. Ibid., p. 739.
47. Ibid., p. 774.
48. Ibid., pp. 770–1.
49. Ibid., p. 742.
50. Ibid., p. 742, note.
51. Ibid., p. 739.
52. Ibid., pp. 729–30.
53. Ibid., pp. 739–40.
54. Ibid., p. 701.
55. Ibid.
56. Ibid.
57. Ibid.
58. Ibid., p. 702.
59. Ibid.
60. Ibid.
61. Ibid., p. 704.
62. Ibid., pp. 704–5.
63. Ibid., p. 705.
64. Ibid., pp. 705–6.
65. Ibid.
66. Ibid.
67. Ibid.
68. Ibid., p. 707.
69. Ibid., pp. 709–10.
70. Ibid., pp. 707–8.
71. Ibid., p. 711. Marx refers to 'the articles thrown into the consumption fund of which some are characterized as fixed capital because they are consumed slowly, and can be consumed by many individuals in series'. He says that these give rise to concern further determinations (e.g. renting rather than buying, interest, etc.) but that he is not concerned with them yet (p. 711).
72. Ibid., p. 819.
73. Ibid., p. 820.
74. Ibid., p. 821.
75. Ibid., p. 771.
76. Ibid., p. 772.
77. Ibid., p. 773.
78. Ibid.
79. Ibid., p. 775.
80. Ibid., p. 723. Marx does account for the fact that some forms of fixed capital figure initially as circulating capital and become fixed capital only when they become fixed in the production process, e.g. some machines, houses, which are circulating capital for the building trade but are fixed

capital as buildings for production (p. 723). He also adds that all parts of capital do not equally bring a profit 'as Malthus stupidly claims', but that the influence of the proportions of fixed and circulating capital is relevant.

81. Ibid., pp. 722–3.
82. Ibid., p. 821.
83. Ibid., pp. 822–3.
84. Ibid., p. 723, note.
85. Ibid., p. 828.
86. Ibid.
87. Ibid., p. 830.
88. Ibid., pp. 830–1.
89. Ibid., p. 831.
90. Ibid., pp. 831–2. Marx emphasises that in the development of the productive powers of labour, 'the emphasis comes to be placed not on the state of being objectified but on the state of being alienated, dispossessed, sold [*Der Ton wird gelegt nicht auf das Vergegenständlichtsein, sondern das Entfremdet-, Entäussert-, Veräussertsein*]; on the condition that the monstrous objective power which social labour erected opposite itself as one of its moments belongs not to the worker, but to the personified conditions of production, i.e. to capital' (p. 831).
91. Ibid.
92. Ibid., pp. 832–3.
93. Ibid., pp. 708–9.

9 Value, Surplus Value, and Profit

The question of the relation between value, surplus value, and profit and, specifically, of the transformation [*Verwandlung*] of surplus value into profit, commands Marx's attention throughout the *Grundrisse*, a major undertaking which arises from

(1) his review of the reflections on the nature of the *produit net* by the Physiocrats; his assessment of the propositions on value and profit of Adam Smith, David Ricardo, and Thomas Malthus; and from his critique of the 'simplifications' of some French economists and utopian socialists;
(2) his desire to fit the analysis of the relation between surplus value and profit and of the declining rates of profit into his reasoning concerning the evolution of capitalism.

Marx's lengthy deliberations will be covered in three subsections:

A. A restatement of Marx on value.
B. A summary of Marx's review and critique of the classicals *et al.* on value, surplus value, and profit.
C. A review, in concise form, of Marx's reflections concerning the transformation of surplus value into profit, including his definitions of profit, rate of profit, rate of surplus value, of the distinction between 'profit' and 'surplus value', and of the factors of which profit is a function.

A. MARX ON VALUE

Value is objectified direct labour time.[1]

Only toil gives value to things.[2]

Matter in its natural state is always *without value*. . . . Only through labour does it obtain exchange value, become element of wealth.[3]

As *use value*, labour exists only *for capital*, and is itself the use value of capital, i.e., the mediating activity by means of which it realizes [*verwertet*] itself. Capital, as that which reproduces and increases its value, is autonomous exchange value (money), as a process, as the *process of realization*. Therefore, labour does not exist as a use value for the worker; *for* him it is therefore not a *power productive of wealth*, [and] not a means or the activity of gaining wealth. . . . A *use value* for capital, labour is a *mere exchange value* for the worker, available *exchange value*. . . . The labour which the worker sells as a *use value* to capital is, for the worker, his *exchange value*, which he wants to realize, but which is already *determined* prior to this act of exchange and presupposed to it as a condition, and is determined like the value of every other commodity by supply and demand; or, in general, . . . by the cost of production, the amount of objectified labour, by means of which the labouring capacity of the worker has been produced and which he therefore obtains for it, as its equivalent.[4]

The exchange value of labour . . . is not determined by the use value of labour. It has a use value for the worker himself only in so far as it *is exchange value*, not in so far as it produces exchange values. It has exchange value for capital only in so far as it is use value. . . . The worker sells [his] labour as a simple, predetermined exchange value, determined by a previous process – he sells labour itself as *objectified labour* . . . in so far as its equivalent has already been measured, given; capital buys it as living labour, as the general productive force of wealth. . . .

By selling his labour to the capitalist, the worker obtains a right only to the price of labour, not to the product of his labour, nor to the value which his labour had added to it.[5]

In the exchange between capital and labour (that is, in developed circulation) two processes are involved, which are 'formally and qualitatively different', 'contradictory', and usually separated as to time:

(1) the worker sells his commodity, labour, which has a use value, and, as commodity, also a *price*, like all other commodities, for a specific sum of exchange values, specific sum of money, which capital concedes to him.
(2) The capitalist obtains labour itself, labour as value-positing activity, as productive labour; i.e. . . . multiplies capital, and

which thereby becomes the productive force, the reproductive force of capital, a force belonging to capital itself.[6]

The first process is usually completed before the second begins. It involves the payment of wages while the product is in the making; the second process ends with the completion of the product.

According to Marx, in *simple* (emphasis added) exchange, this 'double process does not take place'.[7] The difference consists in the fact that labour sells his 'commodity', his use value, for money, for a specific sum of exchange values (ordinary circulation, that is, no appropriation without full payment), whereas the second act of the exchange between capital and labour leads to the appropriation, by capital, of the surplus generated by labour. The capitalist thus obtains labour as productive labour, that is, the productive force which maintains and multiplies capital.[8]

In Marx's view, the economic concept of value does not occur in Antiquity but is peculiar to the most modern economy:

It has become apparent in the course of our presentation that value, which appeared as an abstraction, is possible only as such an abstraction, as soon as money is posited; this circulation of money in turn leads to capital, hence can be fully developed only on the foundation of capital, just as, generally, only on this foundation can circulation seize hold of all moments of production. This development, therefore, not only makes visible the historic character of forms, such as capital, which belong to a specific epoch of history, but also, [in its course] categories such as value, which appear as purely abstract, show the historic foundation from which they are abstracted, and on whose basis alone they can appear, therefore, in this abstraction; and categories which belong more or less to all epochs, such as e.g. money, show the historic modifications which they undergo. The economic concept of value does not occur in antiquity. Value distinguished only juridically from *pretium*, against fraud etc. The concept of value is entirely peculiar to the most modern economy, since it is the most abstract expression of capital itself and of the production resting on it. In the concept of value, its secret betrayed.[9]

Value supposes a common substance, a peculiar singular quality: precious metals, which are the natural substance of value because they have a uniform quality and because all relations reduce themselves to a specific quality of the metal. Labour, too, is distinct qualitatively as well, and also 'more or less intensive'.[10] These differences can be equalised and labour can thus be reduced to unskilled simple labour, whereby

> the higher kinds of labour are themselves appraised in simple labour . . . and the product of a higher sort of labour is reduced to an amount of simple labour. . . . Value supposes a common substance, and all differences, propositions etc. are reduced to merely quantitative ones. This is the case with precious metals, which thus appear as the natural substance of value.[11]

Labour time is the measure of value. This is so because 'equivalence is determined by the equality of labour time or of the amount of labour. It follows that the difference in value is determined by the inequality of labour time.'[12]

Since the value of a commodity is determined by the amount of labour it contains, the commodity exchanges for the same quantity of labour in every other form of use value. Therefore, if the labour time necessary for the production of A doubles, then now only half of the previous labour time is equal its earlier equivalent.[13]

Labour founded on machinery reduces necessary working time, employs fewer workers, and results in fewer necessary working days. The introduction of machinery arises out of competition and reflects the law of the reduction of production costs out of competition; but it affects the relation of capital to labour: If fifty workers are replaced by a machine, the capitalist experiences no change if the machine produces only as much as the fifty workers used to, if the machine has to be replaced in one year. But if the machine costs the capitalist less than the wages of the fifty workers in that year, he acquires part of the individual workers' surplus time.[14]

The total value created by capital in a certain time period is equal 'to the surplus labour it appropriates in one production phase, multiplied by the number of times this production phase is contained in the given time'.[15] If production time and labour time coincide and if circulation time = zero (the circulation cost is nil), the formula of the maximum value that can be produced in that time period is as follows:

$$\frac{ST}{p} \text{ or } Sq \quad (\text{where } q = \frac{T}{p}).[16]$$

Marx defines:

p – as the production phase of capital (labour time employed in production), as one turnover of capital on the assumption that circulation costs are zero, which time he takes as amounting to 60 days:

$$60 = 40 + 20$$

of which 40 is necessary labour time and 20 is surplus value (in one production phase of capital);

T – as the total period of time in which p can be repeated (360 days);

$\frac{T}{p}$ – the given number of production processes in which S can be repeated in that total time period (the number of turnovers of the capital in that time period);

q – the highest coefficient of S in a given T.

In this particular example, T = 360; S = 20; q = 6; therefore, qS = 120 days (in this total time period, of 360 days, the workers work 120 days for the capitalist, that is to say, total surplus value constitutes $\frac{1}{3}$ of the total value produced in 360 days.

Since $\frac{T}{p} = q$, therefore T = pq, that is, the entire duration of T is taken up by production (on the assumption that production time and turnover time are completely identical: that is, that none of T is taken up by circulation time.

But Marx then assigns a time magnitude to circulation = 30 days for each production period of 60 days, since 'circulation time has a definite magnitude, which can never become = zero.'[17] In consequence, the time period of one total turnover of capital ('the total time it requires before it can repeat the realization process – the positing of surplus value'[18]) now increases to 90 days:

$$1 R = p + c,$$

where R is one total turnover of capital;
     p is the production time in that turnover;
     c is the circulation time in that turnover.

Clearly, total surplus value in the entire time period T (= 360 days) will now be diminished:

$$\frac{ST}{p + c} = \frac{20 \times 360}{60 + 30} = 80$$

This result, 80 days, Marx calls S', 'value in second form'.[19]

In consequence of circulation – during which time, according to Marx, no value and no surplus value is created – the capitalist's total appropriation of surplus value decreased from the highest possible 120 days' worth (when production time equals turnover time and circulation time is zero) to 80 days' worth, down by $\frac{1}{3}$ because circulation time, in this particular case, is assumed to lengthen the total turnover of capital in one period by 50 per cent.

In seeking to formulate in more specific terms the relation between surplus value, production time and circulation time, Marx then engages in additional manipulation. He substracts the formula of value creation restricted by circulation from the maximum value creation formula:

$$\frac{ST}{p} - \frac{ST}{p + c} = \frac{ST}{p} - \frac{ST}{R} = \frac{STc}{p(p + c)} \text{ where } R = p + c.$$

This difference Marx rewrites: $\frac{ST}{p} \times \frac{c}{p + c}$ and subtracts:

$$\frac{ST}{p} - \frac{ST}{p} \times \frac{c}{p + c}$$

and obtains S', his 'value in second form', which he applies to his example:

$$S' = \frac{ST}{p} - \frac{ST}{p} \times \frac{c}{c + p} = \frac{360 \times 20}{60}$$

$$- 20 \frac{360}{60} \times \frac{30}{30 + 60} = 80.$$

This result 'signifies that value is equal to the maximum of value, i.e., to the value determined by the relation of production time to total time, minus the number which expresses how often the circulation time is contained in this maximum, plus $\frac{c}{p + c} = \frac{c}{R}$, the relation of circulation time to one turnover of capital.'[20]

Seeking to simplify, Marx replaces $\dfrac{T}{p+c}$ $(= \dfrac{T}{R})$ with q', where q' expresses the number of times production time, p, and circulation time, c, are contained in T, the total time:

$T = pq' + cq'$ where pq' is total production time in T and cq' is total circulation time in T.

Furthermore, he relabels cq' to C. But C = 4c (because q' = 4); and, since T = pq' + cq', therefore it is now = pq' + C.

He incorporates this change in the maximum value creation formula, to take into account circulation time: $S\,\dfrac{T-C}{p}$, and concludes:

since production time is no longer 360 days but 360 − cq', necessarily the total number of surplus value labour days will decrease:

$360 - 4 \times 30 = 360 - 120 = 240;$ therefore: $20\,\dfrac{360-120}{60} = 80,$

which gives the same result as with the S' formula.

Marx concludes: 'S' becomes smaller in the same degree as C grows, is inversely related to it, for the factor $\dfrac{c}{c+p}$ and $\dfrac{ST}{p}$ grows to the same degree.'[21]
He then shows that S' may be calculated with three different equations, and concludes as follows: the relation between S and S' is determined by

$$S : S' = \frac{ST}{p} : \frac{S(T-C)}{p} = T : (T-C) \; or$$
$$S : S' = pq' : (pq' - q'c) = p : (p-c).$$

'The maximum of value is to the real value as a given period of time is to this period of time minus total circulation time.'[22] The outer limit of the reproduction of capital, the reproduction of the production process of capital, is determined by the relation of the production period to the total period of time T in which the production period can be repeated. In Marx's example, T = 360 and p = 60; the reproduction process of capital can be repeated 6 times during the period of 1 year (360 days), which makes q = 6, the highest coefficient of S.

But since circulation time can never be zero, one turnover of capital now increases by 30 days, to 60 + 30: p + c = 90 days. The maximum value of q is decreased from 6 to 4, which means that the surplus value, S, of 20, can now be posited only 4 times during the period of 1 year. The number of turnovers is now smaller, as is total value.

Marx's concern about the relation between value, surplus value, and profit, and their measure becomes manifest in the *Grundrisse* subsection 'Capital as fructiferous [*fruchtbringend*]. Transformation of Surplus Value into Profit', as we can discern in the following extracts:

> In a definite period of time which is posited as the unit measure of its turnovers because it is the natural measure of its reproduction in agriculture, capital produces a definite surplus value, which is determined not only by the surplus value it posits in one production process, or by its reproductions in a specified period of time. . . . A capital of a certain value produces in a certain period of time a certain surplus value. Surplus value thus measured by the value of the presupposed capital, capital thus posits as self-realizing value – *is profit*. . . . and capital as capital, the producing and reproducing value, distinguishes itself within itself from itself as profit, the newly produced value. The product of capital is *profit*. The magnitude, surplus value, is therefore measured by the value-magnitude of the capital, and the *rate of profit* is therefore determined by the proportion between its value and the value of capital. . . . capital, grown by the amount of the profit, now begins the same process anew in larger dimensions. By describing its circle it expands itself as the subject of the circle and thus describes a self-expanding circle, a spiral.[23]

Marx reviews the 'general laws' having to do with all this:

> The real surplus value is determined by the relation of surplus labour to necessary labour, or by the portion of the capital, the portion of objectified labour, which exchanges for living labour, relative to the portion of objectified labour by which it is replaced.[24]

He then enunciates the 'law of the falling rate of profit':

> Presupposing the same surplus value, *the same surplus labour in proportion to necessary labour*, then the *rate of profit* depends on the relation between the part of capital exchanged for living labour and the part existing in the form of raw material and means of production. Hence, the smaller the portion exchanged for living labour becomes, the smaller becomes the rate of profit. Thus, in the same proportion as capital takes up a larger place as capital in the production process relative to immediate labour, i.e., the more the relative surplus value grows – the value-creating power of capital – the more *does the rate of profit fall.* . . . The wider the existence already achieved by capital, the narrower the relation of newly created value to presupposed value (reproduced value). *Presupposing equal surplus value, i.e., equal relation of surplus labour and necessary labour*, there can therefore be an unequal profit, and it must be unequal relative to the size of capitals. The rate of profit can rise although real surplus value falls.[25]

Indeed, the capital can grow and the rate of profit can grow in the same relation if the relation of the part of capital presupposed as value and existing in the form of raw materials and fixed capital rises at an equal rate relative to the part of the capital exchanged for living labour. But this equality of rates presupposes growth of the capital without growth and development of the productive power of labour. One presupposition suspends the other. This contradicts the law of the development of capital, and especially of the development of fixed capital. Such a progression can take place only at stages where the mode of production of capital is not yet adequate to it, or in spheres of production where it has assumed predominance only formally, e.g. in agriculture. Here, natural fertility of the soil can act like an increase of fixed capital – without the amount of necessary labour diminishing. (E.g. in the United States).[26]

Marx then speaks of 'gross profit' (sum of profit) and the 'rate of profit' and states 'the most important law of modern political economy':[27]

> If the profit rate declines more than its size increases, then the gross profit on the larger capital decreases relative to the smaller

one in proportion as its rate of profit declines. . . . It is the most important law from the historical standpoint. It is a law which, despite its simplicity, has never before been grasped, and, even less, consciously articulated.[28]

In this sequence of deliberations, Marx then develops his perception of the rising incompatibility of capital and labour, between the productive development of society and its hitherto existing relations of production and the violent destruction of capital – not by relations external to it, but rather as a condition of its self-preservation amidst a continuous decline in the rate of profit and leading to explosions, cataclysms, crises, and, ultimately, to the violent overthrow of capital:

Since this decline in the rate of profit is identical in meaning (1) with the productive power already produced and the foundation formed by it for new production, this simultaneously presupposing an enormous development of scientific powers; (2) with the decline of the part of the capital already produced which must be exchanged for immediate labour, i.e., with the decline in the immediate labour required for the reproduction of an immense value, expressing itself in a great mass of products, great mass of products with low prices, because the total sum of prices is = to the reproduced capital + profit; (3) [with] the dimension of capital generally, including the portion of it which is not fixed capital; hence intercourse on a magnificent scale, immense sum of exchange operations, large size of the market and all-sideness of simultaneous labour; means of communication etc., presence of the necessary consumption fund to undertake this gigantic process (workers' food, housing, etc.); hence it is evident that . . . the greatest conditions for the reproduction of wealth, i.e., the abundant development of the social individual – that the development of the productive forces brought about by the historical development of capital itself, when it reaches a certain point, suspends the self-realization of capital, instead of positing it. Beyond a certain point, the development of the powers of production becomes a barrier for capital; hence the capital relation a barrier for the development of the productive powers of labour. When it has reached this point . . . the last form of servitude assumed by human activity, that of wage labour on one side, capital on the other, is thereby cast off like a skin, and the casting off itself is the result of the mode of production corresponding to capital. . . . The growing incompatibility between the productive development of society and its hitherto existing relations of production expresses itself in bitter contradictions, crises, spasms. The violent destruction of capital not by relations external to it, but rather as a condition of its self-preservation, is the most striking form in which advice is given it to be gone and to give room to a higher state of social production. . . . Since this decline of profit signifies the same as the decrease in immediate labour relative to the size of the objectified labour which it reproduces and newly posits, capital will attempt every means of checking the smallness of the relation of living labour to the size of the capital generally, hence also of the surplus value, if expressed as profit, relative to the presupposed capital, by reducing the allotment made to necessary labour and by still more expanding the quantity of surplus labour with regard to the whole labour employed. Hence the highest development of productive power together with the greatest expansion of existing wealth will coincide with depreciation of capital, degradation of the labourer, and a most straitened exhaustion of his vital powers. . . . These contradictions lead to explosions, cataclysms, crises, in which by momentaneous suspension of labour and annihilation of a great portion of capital the latter is violently reduced to the point . . . where it is enabled [to go on] fully employing its productive powers without committing suicide. Yet, these regularly recurring catastrophes lead to their repetition on a higher scale, and finally to its violent overthrow.[29]

Marx does acknowledge that in this catastrophic evolution there are moments other than the lesser crises, which will delay the ultimate overthrow:

There are moments in the developed movement of capital which delay this movement other than by crises; such as e.g., the constant devaluation of a part of the existing capital; the transformation of a great part of capital into fixed capital which does not serve as agency of direct production; unproductive waste of a great portion of capital etc. (Productively employed capital is always replaced doubly, as we have seen, in that the positing of value by a productive capital presupposes a counter-value. The unproductive consumption of capital replaces it on one side, annihilates it on the other. That the fall of the rate of profit can further be delayed by the omission of existing deductions from profit e.g., by a lowering of taxes, reduction of ground rent etc., is actually not our concern here, although of importance in practice, for these are themselves portions of the profit under another name, and are appropriated by persons other than the capitalists themselves. The fall [in the rate of profit] likewise delayed by creation of new branches of production in which more direct labour in relation to capital is needed, or where the productive power of labour is not yet developed, i.e. the productive power of capital.) (Likewise, monopolies.) . . . Competition can permanently depress the rate of profit in all branches of industry, i.e., the average rate of profit, only if and in so far as a general and permanent fall of the rate of profit, having the force of a law, is conceivable *prior to* competition and regardless of competition. Competition executes the inner laws of capital; makes them into compulsory laws towards the individual capital, but it does not invent them. It realises them.[30]

In response to the debate (Ricardo *v.* Ramsay) concerning whether competition will level different rates of profit without lowering the average rate, Marx proclaims:[31]

Ramsay and other economists correctly distinguish between whether productivity grows in the branches of industry which make fixed capital, and naturally wages, or in other industries, e.g. luxury-goods industries. The latter cannot diminish necessary labour time. This they can do only through exchange for agricultural products of other countries, which is then the same as if productivity had increased in agriculture. Hence the importance of free trade in grain for the industrial capitalists.

B. A SUMMARY OF MARX'S REVIEW AND CRITIQUE OF THE CLASSICALS *ET AL.* VIEWS ON VALUE, SURPLUS VALUE, AND PROFIT

In his reflections on these issues, Marx makes direct reference to the following schools of thought or to individual writers:

1. Mercantilists (Monetary System as well as Mercantile System proper);
2. Physiocracy;

3. Smith, Ricardo, Malthus;
4. Others (Bastiat, Ramsay, etc.).

1. Mercantilists

The Monetary System considered value as money and made money the exclusive object of desire:

> The Monetary System had understood the autonomy of value only in the form in which it arose from simple circulation – money; it therefore made this abstract form of wealth into the exclusive object [*Objekt*] of nations which were just then entering into the period in which the *gaining of wealth* as such appeared as the aim of society itself.[32]

During the Mercantile System, industrial capital and wage labour emerged 'in antithesis to and at the expense of non-industrial wealth, of feudal landed property'.[33] Their notion of capital centres on money, the 'circulation of mercantile capital, of capital which transforms itself into money'.[34] But the notion of industrial capital gains increasing pre-eminence as a means towards the creation of mercantile capital and, ultimately, of money. Thus one form of wage labour, the industrial, and one form of capital, the industrial, were recognised as sources of wealth, but only in so far as they produced money. Exchange value itself therefore is not yet conceived in the form of capital; but the antithesis between labour in manufactures, as a source of wealth, *v.* labour in agriculture, as chiefly productive of use values, becomes clearly discernible.

2. Physiocracy

Faced with the tangible form of capital, the gift of nature – soil – and the tangible form of surplus value created in the act of production – *produit net* – they distinguish between capital and money and conceive of it as an autonomous exchange value which arises and grows out of production. But they view labour as productive only if it is applied to arable land such as to create more value than labour needs to consume, that is, labour which creates surplus value. In their simplistic view (viewing this process as a simple production process) surplus value arises not 'from labour as such, but rather from the natural forces which labour uses and conducts – agriculture'.[35]

This multiplication of use values, the excess of the product above that which has to serve as a means for new production – of which a part can therefore be consumed unproductively – appears tangibly only in the relation between the natural seed and its product. Only a part of the harvest has to be directly returned to the soil as seed; products found in nature, the elements of air, water, earth, light, and added substances such as fertilizer, then re-create the seed again in multiplied quantity as grain, etc. In short, human labour has only to conduct the chemical processes (in agriculture), and in part also to promote them mechanically, or promote the reproduction of life itself (cattle-raising) in order to obtain the surplus, i.e., to transform the identical natural substances from a useless into a valuable form. An over-abundance of agricultural products (grain, cattle, raw materials) is therefore the true form of general wealth. From the economic viewpoint, therefore, *rent* is the only form of wealth. . . . All other values merely represent raw material + labour; labour itself represents grain or other products of the soil, which labour consumes; hence the factory worker etc. adds no more to the raw material than he consumes in raw materials. Therefore, his labour as well as his employer create no additional wealth – but merely give it forms more pleasant and useful for consumption.[36]

But Marx agrees with the Physiocrats' view that land makes labour more productive, a contribution towards greater gain:

manufacture obtains this higher profit rate only through the employment of many workers at once. The greater surplus time can be gained only by collecting together the surplus time of many workers in relation to capital. Absolute, not relative surplus time predominates in manufacture. This is even more the case originally where the scattered, independent workers still realize a part of their own surplus labour for themselves. For capital to exist as capital, to be able to live off profit, as well as to accumulate, its gain must = the sum of the surplus time of many simultaneous living-workdays. In agriculture, the soil itself with its chemical etc. action is already a machine which makes direct labour more productive, and hence gives a surplus *earlier*, because work is done here at an *earlier* stage with a machine, namely a *natural* one. This is the only correct basis of the doctrine of the Physiocrats, which in this respect considers agriculture in comparison with a still quite undeveloped system of manufacture.[37]

3. Smith, Ricardo, Malthus

The questions of the relation between value and surplus value, surplus value and profit, the falling tendency of the rates of profit, and of the influence of competition in profit-rate equalisation, induced Marx to subject the classical economists (the 'Economists') to a critical review. His overall assessment: 'The Economists' absolute confusion in respect to the determination of value through labour time – something which is found on a basic defect of his own development – emerges very clearly with Mr. Ramsay.'[38]

Adam Smith

Adam Smith's view is incorrect: that capital is only command over alien labour, one which gives its possessor purchasing power; he is incorrect, since capital is the power to appropriate alien labour without compensation.[39]

Marx then extends his critique to Smith's views on labour and the relative price of commodities:

– an hour's work is an hour's work; once embodied as a definite amount of labour, equal quantities of labour must at all times and in all places have the same value for the worker because the price the worker pays (giving up his tranquillity) is always the same; but the price sometimes buys greater or lesser quantities of the essential commodities because their value changes;[40]
– work is not a pain, a sacrifice, since 'an individual needs a normal portion of work . . . the action of freedom is precisely, labour':[41] 'The natural price of things is not the sacrifice made for them . . . there has to be something besides sacrifice (the sacrifice of A is of no use to B) . . . . It is a positive, creative activity.'[42] 'Something that is merely negative, creates nothing.'[43]
– 'Labour is the only substance of products as values.'[44] Its measure is labour time, and presupposes equal intensity. Labour time does not depend on labour productivity because it is 'a unit of which the proportional parts of labour express a certain multiple.'[45] It follows that equal quantities of labour are the same measured magnitude.

The qualitative difference between workers, in so far as it is not natural, posited by sex, age, physical strength, etc. – , and thus basically expresses not the qualitative value of labour but rather the division and differentiation of labour – is itself a product of history, and is in turn suspended for the great mass of labour, in that the latter is itself simple, while the qualitatively higher takes its economic measure from the simple.[46]

An hour of work may always be an equal sacrifice for the worker. But the value of commodities in no way depends on his feelings; nor does the value of his hour of work.[47]

Products are objectified labour. Use value is not concerned with human activity at the source of the product . . . but with its being for mankind.[48]

– The aim of the capitalist is not to produce use value but to preserve his money and to add to it (money as the general form of wealth as wealth) through exchange with living labour. But the exchange of equivalents is not the exchange of capital for labour.[49]
– The difference in return depends not only on the longer or shorter labour time required to complete the article, but also, in certain branches of industry and agriculture, on the interruptions of the work which are due to the nature of the work itself.[50] The total capital's period of reproduction is determined by the total process, circulation included, including the time needed to be brought to the market, because it is destined for a more distant market.

But Marx agrees with Smith's proposition that as capital grows, competition will force the rate of profit down; except that, unlike Smith's explanation, competition is not imposed on capital from without, but rather is imposed by capitalist laws, the 'inner laws of capital'.[51]

David Ricardo

Marx is critical of Ricardo for his mixing up profit and surplus value:

Ricardo at once identifies profit directly with surplus value; he did not make this distinction at all. But whereas the rate of surplus value is determined by the relation of surplus labour employed by the capital to necessary labour, the rate of profit is nothing but the relation of surplus value to the total value of the capital presupposed to production. Its proportion falls and rises, hence, in relation with the part of the capital exchanged for living labour relative to the part existing as material and fixed capital. Under ALL circumstances, the surplus value regarded as profit must express a smaller proportion of the gain than the real proportion of the surplus value. For, under all circumstances, it is measured by the total capital, which is always larger than that employed for wages and exchanged for living labour. Since Ricardo simply mixes surplus value and profit together in this way, and since the surplus value can constantly decline, can *tendentially* decline only if the relation of surplus labour to necessasry labour, i.e., to the labour required for the reproduction of labouring capacity, declines, but since the latter is possible only if the productive force of labour declines, Ricardo assumes that the productive force of labour decreases in agriculture, although it grows in industry with the accumulation of capital. He flees from economics to seek refuge in organic chemistry.[52]

Marx cites Ricardo's statement that competition will reduce profits in the various branches of business to an average level, that the profit rate can be equalised but that the average rate itself cannot be depressed.[53] But he is critical of Ricardo for stating that 'no accumulation of capitals can permanently reduce profits unless and equally permanent cause raises wages', since Ricardo's view is based on one single case: the relatively growing unproductivity of agriculture, in which a great portion of necessary labour is required for the production of agricultural products, which constitutes 'a onesided view of conceiving of it'.[54] But then Marx quotes, without comment, Ricardo's statement that there is a natural tendency for profits to fall because in the progress of society and wealth, the additional food requires more and more labour, 'a tendency which may be delayed by improvements in machinery and . . . discoveries in the science of agriculture'.[55]

Marx further accuses Ricardo of misunderstanding the process and origin of reproduction, of not grasping the relationship between objectified labour and living labour, and of not comprehending the relation among the different parts of capital:

he misunderstands the process of its origins and reproduction . . .
[moreover] the distinction between *profit* and *surplus value* does

not exist for him, proof the he is clear about the nature of neither one.[56]

Since Ricardo does not grasp the relation between objectifed labour and living labour . . . and does not, therefore, grasp the relation among the different component parts of capital, it therefore seems with him as if the entire product were divided into wages and profits, so that the reproduction of capital is itself counted as part of profit. [original emphasis][57]

On the one hand, the capitalist counts wages and profit among the production costs and regulates the price accordingly; on the other, there is the contradiction between the determination of the value of the product by relative labour time and the *real determination of prices* (original emphasis) in practice; this contradiction comes about because 'profit is not grasped itself a derivative, secondary form of *surplus value.*'[58]

Marx then adds, in parentheses, the following comment:

From the possibility that profit may be *less than* surplus value, hence that capital [may] exchange profitably without realizing itself in the strict sense, it follows that not only individual capitalist, but also nations may continually exchange with one another, may even continually repeat the exchange on an ever-expanding scale, without for that reason necessarily gaining in equal degrees. One of the nations may continually appropriate for itself a part of the surplus labour of the other, giving back nothing for it in the exhange, except that the measure here [is] not as in the exchange between capitalist and worker.[59]

Marx spends some time on the question of the contradiction between the determination of the value of product by relative labour time and the real determination of prices, and comes up with interesting statements in seeking to substantiate his viewpoint, providing in this process some examples:

(1) what the capitalist acquires through exchange is labour *capacity*; this is the exchange value which he pays for living labour, the use value, from which springs the surplus value;[60]
(2) wages express the value of living labour capacity, but in no way

the value of living labour, which is expressed in wages and profits. Wages are the price of necessary labour and must be equal to the quantity of labour which the labourer must expend on his own reproduction, and 'the measure of this payment depends itself on the productivity of labour, for the latter determines the amount of necessary labour time.'[61]

(3) Surplus value is the source of profit for the capitalist. Profit is distinct from surplus value, as Marx attempts to show in comparison with the example put forth by Malthus:[62]

(a) Malthus's example:

Value of 363 000 lbs. twist spun	£16 000	
Interest on £10 000 fixed capital	500	
Interest on floating capital	350	
Sinking fund of $6\frac{1}{2}$%/yr for wear and tear of fixed capital	650	
Rents, taxes, rates	150	
	£1650	= surplus
Contingencies, carriage, coal, etc.	£1100	value
	£2750	
Wages and salaries	£2600	
	£5350	
For about 400 000 lbs. raw cotton at 6d.	£10 000	
	£15 350	
Malthus's profit (4.2%)	£ 650	
	£16 500	

(b) Marx calculates surplus value as follows:

2 interests	£ 850	which makes for a rate of
'profit'	£ 650	surplus value of
Rents, taxes	£ 150	£1650/£15 350 = 10.1%
	£ 1650	

Marx subtracts from annual advances which were made (£15 350), interest (£500, on 10 000), part of fixed capital which does not figure in the sinking fund ('floating capital' = £7000, of which annual interest equivalent is £350), which totals £850, leaving a net of

£14 500. Marx then submits that the capitalist sells £14 500 worth for £16 000, which leaves him with an annual profit of about 10 per cent (£1500), the advances to labour amounting only to $\frac{1}{6}$ of the total capital (£2600 for wages and salaries). But 10 on $16\frac{2}{3}$ amounts to a surplus value of 60 per cent, that is, Marx claims that the worker creates a surplus value of 60 per cent, which means that of the total labour time, 40 per cent is for necessary labour and 60 per cent amounts to surplus labour. Against a sum of £100, the advances are worth £$83\frac{1}{3}$, the wages are worth £$16\frac{2}{3}$; reproduction being worth £10, the profit amounts to £10.[63]

Marx suggests that

> in order to determine the size of real surplus value, one must calculate the profit on the advance made for wages; the percentage which expresses the proportion between the so-called profit and wages. . . . The examination of how far the rate of profit can decrease as capital grows, while the gross profit nevertheless increases, belongs to the doctrine on profit.[64]

Marx has three more bones to pick with Malthus. First he counters Malthus's claim that the value of labour is constant:

> The value of products is determined by the labour contained in them, not by that part of labour in them which the employer pays for. . . . Wages express only paid labour, never all labour *done*. The measure of this payment depends itself on the productivity of labour, for the latter determines the amount of necessary labour time. And since these wages constitute the *value of labour*, this value is constantly variable.[65]

> The fractional part of labour time which reproduces wages would vary with productivity; thus, with the productivity of labour, the *value of labour*, i.e. wages, would constantly vary. Wages would be measured both before and after by a definite *use value*, and since the latter constantly varies in its exchange depending on the productivity of labour, wages would change, or (in other words) the *value of labour*.[66]

Then he disagrees with Malthus's view that 'the quantity of labour which the product consists in is paid labour only . . . or that wages are the measuring rod of the value of the commodity', since 'where is the profit to come from if no unpaid labour is performed?'[67]

Finally, he attacks Malthus's view on population:

> Malthus's motley compilations . . . conception is altogether false and childish because he regards *overpopulation* as being *of the same kind* in all the different historic phases of economic development . . . and reduces these very complicated and varying relations to a single relation, two equations, in which the natural reproduction of humanity appears on the one side, and the natural reproduction of edible plants (or means of subsistence) on the other, . . . the former geometric and the latter arithmetic in progression. . . . He stupidly relates a specific quantity of people to a specific quantity of necessaries, Ricardo immediately confronted him with the fact that the quantity of grain available is completely irrelevant to the worker if he has no *employment*.[68]

In Marx's view, the development of capital shows that the conditions of the development of productive forces, of exchange, of division of labour, of co-operation, and so forth are all indentical with growth of population; that in addition to the necessary population (necessary labour), there should be a surplus population (which does not work – that is to say, in Marx's view, comprises the industrial capitalist part and the purely consuming part, the latter being the idlers who consume alien products and luxury products and who are treated, by some economists, as necessary population, necessary for consumption rather than for their labour capacity).[69] If the superfluous labouring capacity is supported, then this comes not out of the labour fund but out of the revenue of all classes, which secures its being kept intact as reserve for later use.[70]

4. Ramsay, Bastiat

Marx agrees with Ramsay and other economists, who

> correctly distinguish between whether productivity grows in the branches of industry which make fixed capital, and naturally wages, or in other industries, e.g. luxury industries. The latter cannot diminish necessary labour time, This they can do only through exchange for agricultural products of other countries,

which is then the same as if productivity had increased in agriculture. Hence the importance of free trade in grain the for industrial capitalists.[71]

Concerning the decreasing rate of profit, Marx ridicules Bastiat's 'law of unlimited decline which never reaches zero . . . and an endlessly decreasing multiplier.'[72] He suggests that Bastiat had been anticipated by Ricardo, quotes Ricardo's example, and says: 'Ricardo observed this tendency towards the decline of the rate of profit with the growth of capital; and since he confuses profit with surplus value, he was forced to make wages rise in order to let profits fall.'[73]

C. MARX ON SURPLUS VALUE AND PROFIT

1. Surplus Value

In Marx's view, there is a clear difference between surplus value and profit:

> While surplus value is measured directly by the surplus labour time which capital gains in the exchange with living labour, profit is nothing but another form of surplus value, a form developed further in the sense of capital. Thus the surplus value which capital posits in a given turnover period obtains the form of profit in so far as it is measured against the total value of the capital presupposed to production.[74]

Surplus value is absolute or relative. Absolute surplus value appears determined by the absolute lengthening of the working day above and beyond the necessary labour time. Necessary labour time is the time required for the production of the use value essential for the workers' subsistence. The remaining part of the working day represents surplus labour time, the time during which exchange value is produced, the time expended for the production of wealth. However, there is a natural limit to absolute surplus value: the number of simultaneous working days, each representing a living labour capacity, all, taken together, comprising the total working population. At a certain stage of the development of productive forces, surplus labour can be increased only by the transfer of a larger part of the population into the labour force,[75] whereby the number of simultaneous working days is increased: that is to say, an absolute increase in the working population is achieved. Clearly, therefore, the growth of the population is the essential requisite for all forms of surplus labour; it constitutes the basic source of wealth.[76]

Relative surplus value is the second form. It expresses the development of the productive power of labour and reveals itself as the 'reduction of necessary labour time relative to the working day and as the reduction of the necessary labouring population relative to the population'.[77]

The rate of surplus value has to do with the relation of surplus labour to necessary labour. It is determined by

(a) the magnitude of the surplus value itself;
(b) the relation of living labour to accumulated labour (the ratio of the capital expended as wages to the capital employed as such).

Marx proposes to 'examine separately' the causes which determine (a) and (b), but points out that the 'law of rent, e.g., belongs to (a)'.[78] He also mentions that in conducting this analysis (broadly speaking, 'to establish the laws of profit in so far as they are not determined by the rise and fall of wages or by the influence of landed property'[79]), he will suppose, for the time being, necessary labour as given: that is , that the worker always obtains the minimum of wages. He considers this supposition as necessary in seeking to establish the law of profit, because:

> All of these fixed suppositions themselves become fluid in the further course of development. But only by holding them fast at the beginning is their development possible without confounding everything. Besides it is practically sure that, for instance, however the standard of necessary labour may differ at various epochs and in various countries, or how much, in consequence of the demand and supply of labour, its amount and ratio may change, at any given epoch the standard is to be considered and acted upon as a fixed one by capital.[80]

2. Profit

Profit is a presupposition of capital as well as the result of capital:

> The product of capital, then, is profit. But the capitalist . . . has to

live, and since he does not live by working he must live from profit, i.e., from the alien labour he appropriates. Thus capital is posited as the source of wealth. Since capital has incorporated productivity into itself as its inherent quality, capital relates to profit as revenue. . . . Thus profit appears as a form of distribution, like wages. . . . While profit thus appears in one respect as the result of capital, it appears in the other as the presupposition of capital formation. . . . No longer regarded as surplus value exhanged for capital itself in the production process; not for labour; but as presupposed, produced value, relating to itself (capital) in its own process, the value posited by itself being called profit.[81]

Is profit included in the natural price, that is, is it part of production costs, asks Marx? What determines profit?

There is a 'mass confusion here', he claims,[82] referring specifically to the issue whether profit is realised [*ist verwirkicht*] in exchange or whether it arises from exchange? He admits that it can arise from exchange if one of the parties to the exchange does not obtain the equivalent, and then goes on to reason as follows:

Since the value posited in the production process realises its price through exchange, the price of the product appears in fact determined by the sum of money which expresses an equivalent for the total quantity of labour contained in raw materials, machinery, wages and in unpaid surplus labour. Thus price appears here merely as a formal modification of value; as value expressed in money; but the magnitude of this price is presupposed in the production process of capital. Capital thereby appears as a determinant of price, so that price is determined by the advances made by capital + the surplus labour realized by it in the product. We shall see later that price, *on the contrary*, appears as determining profit. And, while here the total *real* production costs appear as determining price, price appears later as determining the production costs. So as to impose the inherent laws of capital upon it as external necessity, competition seemingly turns all of them over, *inverts them*.[83]

Marx then engages, in a long paragraph, in a discussion of profit and its determination, including references to price, production costs, and equivalence. The following is the gist of his reflections:

(a) Profit on capital is realised ['*kann verwirklicht werden*'] only in the price that is paid for it, the use value created by it, which is possible only through exchange. In that realisation, 'profit is determined by the *excess of the price obtained over the price which covers outlays*'.[84]

(b) Profit realisation proceeds only through exchange; therefore 'the individual capital's *profit is not necessarily restricted by its surplus value*, by the surplus labour contained in it; but it is relative, rather, to the excess of price obtained in exchange. It can exchange *more than its equivalent, and then its profit is greater than its surplus value*'.[85]

(c) But one party obtains more than the equivalent only if the 'other party to the exchange does not obtain the equivalent'.[86] Nevertheless even though this kind of exchange does modify the distribution of surplus value among the different capitals, the total surplus value, as well as the total profit, 'which is only surplus value itself, computed differently, can neither grow nor decrease through this operation'.[87]

(d) Just as surplus value in the form of profit is measured against the total value of capital, it (surplus value) appears 'to be created by its different components [circulating capital and fixed capital] to an equal degree, [whereas] profit accrues to these component parts in proportion to their magnitude.'[88]

(e) In relation to profit, the value of capital presupposed in production appears as advances, production costs which must be paid for from price. But surplus labour (from which profit and interest are accounted for) costs capital nothing and cannot therefore figure as a cost item in the advanced capital (is not part of the value advanced by it); it does not therefore figure as production costs of capital, even though it forms the source of surplus value and hence of profit as well.

(f) Since surplus labour does not cost capital anything, production costs from the standpoint of capital are not the real production costs (Marx terms here 'real production costs' the whole of surplus labour set to work by capital[89]); therefore, the excess of the price of the product over the price of the production costs is its profit (because the *real* production costs are not accounted for). If the costs of the surplus labour were taken into account, argues Marx, profit, the excess over the advances made by capital, would be zero.

(g) Can profit so defined (the excess over the advances made by capital) be smaller than the surplus value? According to Marx, it can: 'If the surplus of living labour gained in exchange by capital is in excess of the objectified labour it has given in exchange for labour capacity. Also by separation of interest from profit, by which a part of surplus value is posited as production cost even for productive capital itself.'[90] However, risk plays no role in the surplus gain (even though economists claim it plays a role in the determination of profit), since risk does not increase the creation of surplus value. Risk cannot determine surplus value, even though capitalists view a part of their surplus gain as a compensation for risk. But interest becomes a cost of production as soon as profit and interest become separated as portions of the surplus gain.[91]

(h) The profit on capital does not depend on the magnitude of capital but rather, given an equal magnitude, on the relation between its component parts (the constant part and the variable part); on the productivity of labour (except that, with diminished productivity, the same capital could not work up the same material with the same portion of living labour); on the turnover time (which itself is determined by the different proportions between fixed and circulating capital, different durabilities of fixed capital, and so on).[92]

(i) Competition will tend to equalise unequal profits in different branches of industry with capital of equal magnitudes. This is so because the elements of capital, raw materials, instruments, and labour, all obtained through exchange, are already contained in them as prices. Through competition, the 'comparison of the market price of its product with the prices of its elements then becomes decisive for it.'[93]

3. Surplus Value and Profit; Rate of Surplus Value and Rate of Profit

According to Marx, the transformation of surplus value into profit yields 'two immediate great laws':

(a) Surplus value expressed as profit always appears as a smaller proportion than surplus value in its immediate reality actually amounts to. The surplus value must appear smaller when measured against $c + v$ than when measured against its real measure, v:

Profit [i.e. the rate of profit as expressed the relation in which capital has posited surplus value] never expresses the real rate at which capital exploits labour, but always a much smaller relation, and the larger the capital, the more false is the relation it expresses. The rate of profit could express the real rate of surplus value only if the entire capital were transformed solely into wages; if the entire capital were exchanged for living labour (i.e. if only *approvisionnement* alone existed), if not only the raw material costs were = 0 but the means of production . . . were also = 0. The latter case cannot occur on the basis of the mode of production corresponding to capital. If $A = c + v$, whatever the numerical value of s, then $\dfrac{s}{c+v} < \dfrac{s}{v}$ [94]

(b) The rate of profit declines to the degree that labour is already capitalised and hence also acts increasingly in the form of fixed capital in the production process, or to the degree that the productive power of labour grows. According to Marx, the growth of the productive power of labour is identical in meaning with the following:

   (i) the growth of relative surplus value or the relative surplus labour time which the worker gives to capital;

   (ii) the decline of the labour time necessary for the reproduction of labour capacity;

   (iii) the decline of the part of capital which exchanges for living labour relative to the part of it which participates in the production process as objectified labour and as presupposed value. [95]

The second law, the tendency of the profit rate to decline with the development of capital (that is the extent within which labour as well as productive power are capitalised), Marx ties in with other factors which reflects themselves, by depressing the rate of profit, for shorter or longer periods:

There are moments in the developed movement of capital which delay this movement other than by crises: such e.g. the constant devaluation of a part of the existing capital; the transformation of a great part of capital into fixed capital which does not serve as agency of direct production . . . [96]

But the fall in the rate of profit can be delayed by an increase in the labouring population, the action of fixed capital (the creation of new branches of production in which more direct labour in relation to capital is needed), more raw materials, increase in scientific power, the 'omission of existing deductions from profit, e.g. by lowering taxes, reduction of ground rent, etc . . .', large-scale increase in the population.[97]

Marx concludes his reflections concerning the rate of profit and the rate of surplus value with the following statements concerning their determination:

> The rate of surplus value is determined simply by the relation of surplus labour to necessary labour; the rate of profit is determined not only by the relation of surplus labour to necessary labour, but by the relation of the part of capital exchanged for living labour to the total capital entering into production. Profit as we still regard it here, i.e. as the profit of capital *as such*, not of an individual capital at the expense of another, but rather as the *profit of the capitalist class*, concretely expressed, *can never be greater than the sum of the surplus value*. As a sum, it is the sum of the surplus value, but it is this same sum of values as a proportion relative to the total value of the capital, instead of to that part of it whose value really grows, i.e. is exchanged for living labour. *In its immediate form, profit is nothing but the sum of the surplus value expressed as a proportion of the total value of the capital*.[98]

His views concerning the tendency of rates of profit to fall ties in with his theme concerning the fate of capitalism, including the long-run increase of capital to necessary labour, the increasingly frequent cycles, which cannot be remedied but only delayed by the various short-term and medium-term palliatives, and, ultimately, culmination in violent overthrow. His pessimism carries over into the realm of international trade in the subsection entitled: 'Two nations may exchange according to the law of profit in such a way that both gain, but one is always defrauded':,[99]

> From the possibility that profit may be *less than* surplus value, hence that capital [may] exchange profitably without realising itself in the strict sense, it follows that not only individual capitalists, but also nations may continually exchange with one another, may even continually repeat the exchange on an ever expanding scale, without for that reason necessarily gaining in equal degrees. One of the

nations may continually appropriate for itself a part of the surplus labour of the other, giving back nothing for it in the exchange, except that the measures here [is] not as in the exchange between capitalist and worker.[100]

NOTES AND COMMENTS

1. *Grundrisse*, p. 776.
2. Ibid., p. 846.
3. Ibid., p. 848.
4. Ibid., p. 305–6.
5. Ibid., p. 306–7.
6. Ibid., p. 274. Marx distinguishes here between 'productive labour' (as far as they increase the capital of their master) and 'unproductive labour' (when the worker sells his use value which does not increase capital).
7. Ibid., p. 274.
8. Ibid.
9. Ibid., p. 776.
10. Ibid., p. 846.
11. Ibid.
12. Ibid., p. 818.
13. Ibid.
14. Ibid., p. 777.
15. Ibid., p. 653. Interruptions of work within the production process itself may render unequal production time and labour time (labour time being the sum of stored-up labour and living labour). In consequence, 'value, and hence also surplus value, is not = to the time which the production phase lasts, but rather to the labour time, objectified and living, employed during this production phase. The living labour time alone . . . can create surplus value, because it creates surplus value time . . . capital creates no surplus value as long as it employs no living labour' (pp. 669–70).
16. Ibid., pp. 653–7.
17. Ibid., p. 654.
18. Ibid.
19. Ibid., p. 655.
20. Ibid., pp. 655–6.
21. Ibid., p. 656.
22. Ibid., pp. 656–7.
23. Ibid., pp. 745–6.
24. Ibid., p. 747.
25. Ibid.
26. Ibid., pp. 747–8.
27. Ibid., p. 748.
28. Ibid., p. 748. Marx provides an example, defines 'gross profit' as the 'surplus value', and declares that the sum of profit is directly related to

the value of capital, while the rate of profit is inversely related to the value of capital.

29. Ibid., pp. 748–750.
30. Ibid., pp. 750–2.
31. Ibid., p. 753.
32. Ibid., p. 327.
33. Ibid.
34. Ibid., pp. 327–8.
35. Ibid., p. 328.
36. Ibid., p. 329.
37. Ibid., p. 588.
38. Ibid., p. 549.
39. Ibid., pp. 614–15.
40. Ibid., pp. 610–11.
41. Ibid., p. 611.
42. Ibid., p. 613.
43. Ibid., pp. 613–14.
44. Ibid., p. 612.
45. Ibid., p. 613.
46. Ibid., pp. 612–13.
47. Ibid., p. 614.
48. Ibid.
49. Ibid., pp. 794–5.
50. Ibid., p. 602.
51. Ibid., p. 752.
52. Ibid., pp. 753–4.
53. Ibid., p. 751.
54. Ibid., p. 752.
55. Ibid., p. 753.
56. Ibid., p. 552.
57. Ibid., p. 553.
58. Ibid., p. 554.
59. Ibid., p. 872.
60. Ibid., p. 562.
61. Ibid., p. 571.
62. Th. R. Malthus, *Principles of Political Economy*, 2nd ed, 1836, p. 42.
63. *Grundrisse*, pp. 566–7.
64. Ibid., pp. 566–7.
65. Ibid., p. 571.
66. Ibid., pp. 571–6.
67. Ibid., p. 572.
68. Ibid., pp. 606–7.
69. Ibid., p. 608.
70. Ibid., pp. 609–10.
71. Ibid., p. 753.
72. Ibid., p. 755.
73. Ibid., p. 756.
74. Ibid., p. 762.
75. This statement is an example of Marx's awareness of the significance of an increase in the labour-force participation rate (p. 771).

76. Ibid., pp. 769–71.
77. Ibid., p. 769.
78. Ibid., p. 817.
79. Ibid.
80. Ibid.
81. Ibid., pp. 759–62.
82. Ibid., p. 761.
83. Ibid.
84. Ibid., p. 760.
85. Ibid.
86. Ibid.
87. Ibid.
88. Ibid., pp. 759–60.
89. Ibid., p. 760.
90. Ibid., p. 761.
91. Ibid., p. 722.
92. Ibid., p. 761.
93. Ibid., p. 762. Marx's treatment of the significance of competition is not as simple and straightforward as this statement seems to imply. First of all, his 'fundamental law of competition' reads as follows:

> The fundamental law in competition, as distinct from that advanced about value and surplus value, is that it is determined not by the labour contained in it, nor by the labour time in which it is produced, but rather by the labour time in which it can be produced, or, the labour time necessary for reproduction. By this means, the individual capital is in reality only placed within the conditions of capital as such, although it seems as if the original law were overtuned. Necessary labour time is determined by the movement of capital itself; but only in this way is it posited. This is the fundamental law of competition. Demand, supply, price (production costs) are further specific forms; price as market price; or general price (p. 657).

He then states that competition appears as the negation of the limits and barriers peculiar to the stages of production preceding capital (including lifting of blockades, prohibitions, protection in the world market); but that this merely negative side had never been examined; it is therefore absurd to regard it as the collision of unfettered individuals who are determined only by their own interest: 'nothing can be more mistaken . . .' (p. 649).

He suggests, however, that capital, having become strong enough, tore down historic barriers (e.g. the guild system) because they hindered free competition, and goes on to label competition as follows: 'Free competition is the relation of capital to itself as another capital, i.e. the real conduct of capital as capital. . . . Free competition is the real development of capital' (p. 650). He then lauds the role of competition: 'the reduction of the price as condition for conquest of the market belongs only to competition'; but he concludes by declaring that 'the assertion that free competition = the ultimate form of the development of the forces of production and hence of human freedom means nothing other than that middle-class rule is the culmination of world history . . .' (p. 652), a kind of freedom which is the most complete suspension of all individual freedom because it represents nothing more than the free development on the basis of capital, a limited basis indeed.

94. Ibid., p. 763. In the note on p. 763, the Marx-Engels-Lenin Institute inserted this particular expression, stating that the manuscript had $\frac{c + v}{c} < \frac{v}{s}$, which Marx had struck out and not replaced by anything else.
95. Ibid., p. 763.
96. Ibid., p. 750.
97. Ibid., p. 751.
98. Ibid., p. 767.
99. Ibid., p. 872.
100. Ibid.

Part III
Marx on Value and Prices

Introduction

In this final part, we shall assess Marx's views on value and on prices and pricing, as expressed mainly in both Chapters of the *Grundrisse*. In our discussion, Chapter I will treat in summary form Marx's own analysis of value, with particular emphasis on his critique of the propositions of Adam Smith and David Ricardo in the national context as well as internationally. In Chapter 2 we shall present a concise summary of Marx's treatment of prices and price determination, including his review of the classicals' propositions concerning price. We shall then conclude this assessment with an apropriate set of notes.

10 Marx, the Classicals, and the Theory of Value: Conclusion

In his assessment of the classical theory of value, Marx first lauds Adam Smith ('an immense step forward'[1]) for making labour not only an abstraction but also in reality 'the means of creating wealth in general'.[2] He accepts Smith's statement on labour being the real and money the nominal measure of value and that 'labour time is the original money with which all commodities are purchased.'[3]

But Marx then goes on to inquire more probingly into the relation between labour and labour time, on the one hand, and money, on the other, and their significance in the determination and measure of value. He starts by paying particular attention to the concept of exchange value. Exchange value arises from the creation of 'wealth in general', a process tantamount to a dissolution of all products and activities into exchange value, that is, into the dependence of each individual's production on the production of others, which is the end result of this process. This reciprocal dependence includes in particular the necessities of life and finds its expression in the constant need for exchange. In this process, each individual must produce a general product – that is, his own exchange value – which, in the form of exchange value or money, will enable him to exercise power over the activities of other individuals. Everyone gets involved, so that exchange value becomes the 'all-sided mediation', a social bond.[4] Of course, the individual must exchange his product, 'not only in order to take part in the general productive capacity but also to transfer his own product into his own subsistence'.[5]

This process of the creation of the 'all-sided mediation' is inherent in the evolution of the bourgeois society, of the society of free competition. In this evolution, the following transformations become clearly manifest:

– prices (an 'old concept' in Marx's eyes) are increasingly determined by the costs of production;
– exchange (also an 'old concept') exerts an increasing dominance

over all relations of production [*Produktionsverhältnisse*];
- exchange and division of labour reciprocally condition one another;
- and the pressure of general demand and supply on one another mediates the interconnecting linkages among mutually indifferent persons.

Since, in Marx's view, commodities are exchange values, they are therefore exchangeable for money, in a very specific proportion: 'The proportion in which a particular commodity is exchanged for money . . . is determined by the amount of labour objectified in the commodity. The commodity is an exchange value objectified in the commodity.'[7] Money is required in this transaction, with the task to express the labour time embodied in a particular product as a product equal to and convertible into all other products of an equal labour time.[8]

But then Marx's review of Adam Smith's initial propositions takes on a perceptibly critical attitude. First of all, 'as Ricardo had pointed out',[9] Smith leaves a fallacious conclusion when he claims that from the standpoint of exchange alone, the worker's pay would have to equal the value of the product: that the amount of labour in objective form which the worker obtains in pay would be equal to the amount of labour in subjective form which he expends in labour. This conclusion is fallacious because the value of the worker's product is not equal to his pay.[10] Secondly – and contrary to Smith's proposition that capital is command over alien labour only in the sense that every exchange value is that since it gives its possessor buying power – capital is also 'the power to appropriate alien labour without exchange, without equivalent, but with the semblance of exchange'.[11] Thirdly, in reflecting on Smith's view that labour is the real and money the nominal measure of value, Marx proposes that labour *alone* produces and that it is therefore the *only substance* of products *as values* (emphasis added). The measure of labour, labour time (presupposing equal intensity), is therefore the measure of values.

From these critical reflections on Adam Smith, Marx goes on to develop his own perception of value, repeatedly declaring in the *Grundrisse* that labour *time* (emphasis added) is the measure of value; this being so because 'equivalence is determined by the equality of labour time or of the amount of labour. It follows that the difference in value is determined by the inequality of labour time.'[12]

At this point Marx does not seem concerned about the issue of the relation between value and qualitative difference between workers, on the one hand, and value and labour productivity, on the other:

> The qualitative difference between workers, as far as it is not natural, posited by sex, age, physical strength, etc. – and thus basically expresses not the quantitative value of labour, but rather the division and differentiation of labour – is itself a product of history, and is in turn suspended for the great mass of labour, in that the latter is itself simple; while the qualitatively higher takes its economic measure from the simple. . . . [13]

> The measure of labour-time – of course does not depend on labour's productivity; its measure is precisely nothing but a unit of which proportional parts of labour express a certain multiple. . . .' The equivalent expresses the condition of the products reproduction, as given to them through exchange, i.e., the possibility of repeating productive activity anew . . . [14]

Neither is production time necessarily equal to labour time:

> Interruptions of work within the production process itself . . . may render unequal production time and labour time [labour time is stored-up labour and living labour together]. . . . Value, hence also surplus value, is not equal to the time which the production phase lasts, but rather to the labour time, objectified and living, employed during this production phase. The living labour alone . . . can create surplus value, because [it creates] surplus labour time. . . . The point to remember here is only that capital creates no surplus value as long as it employs no living labour. [15]

Marx's own analysis of value comprises several definitions:

> The real value of a product expresses the labour time objectified in it. It contains the constant part of capital, the wage part (the part of objectified labour necessary to reproduce living labour capacity) and the surplus value. [16]

> Only toil gives value to things. [17]

> The economic concept of value does not occur in antiquity. Value distinguished only juridically from *pretium*, against fraud, etc. The

concept of value is entirely peculiar to the most modern economy, since it is the most abstract expression of capital itself and of the production resting on it.[18]

The higher kinds of labour are themselves appraised in simple labour . . . and the product of a higher sort of labour is reduced to an amount of simple labour. . . . Value supposes a common substance, and all differences, propositions, etc. are reduced to merely quantitative ones. This is the case with precious metals, which thus appear as the natural substance of value.[19]

Value is determined in production but realised in circulation. Circulation costs can never increase value.[20]

The value of commodities as determined by labour time is only their *average value* . . . an external abstraction if it is calculated out as the average figure of an epoch . . . but it is very rest real if it is at the same time recognised as the driving force and the moving principle of the oscillations which commodity prices run through during a given epoch.[21]

Marx also views value in aggregate terms: the total value created by capital in a certain time period is equal to the 'surplus labour it appropriates in one production phase, multiplied by the number of times this production phase is contained in the given time'.[22]

If production time and labour time coincide and if circulation time = 0 (that is, circulation cost is nil), the formula of the maximum value that can be produced in that time period is as follows:

$$\frac{SP}{p} \ or \ Sq \ (where \ q = \frac{T}{p}).$$

Marx defines his terms as follows:

p : the production phase of capital (labour time employed in production), as one turnover of capital on the assumption that circulation costs are zero: 60 days (of which 40 are necessary labour time and 20 constitute surplus-value days);

T : the total period of time in which 'p' can be repeated (360 days);

$\frac{T}{p}$: the given number of production processes in which S can be repeated in that total time period (the number of turnovers of capital in that time period);

q : the highest coefficient of S in a given T;

S : the surplus value produced in one production phase of capital.[23]

Marx distinguishes clearly between use value and exchange value. Whereas exchange value arises in the course of the production process which rests on the division of labour and expresses the social form of value, use value does not represent the economic form of value but only the significance (the 'being') of the product for mankind.[24] If the worker produces and consumes a product for which only he has use value, this act of production and consumption does not produce exchange value. Exchange value emerges when the worker's product has use value for someone else, and the worker is willing to part with his product in exchange for something he has use value for. It is his own use value that the worker offers to the capitalist, 'as his specific, productive, capacity',[25] which capitalist solicits. The use value contained in this 'value creating, productive, labour',[26] becomes specific exchange value when 'the common element of use values – labour time – is applied to it as an external yardstick. This exchange value the worker obtains in money.'[27] Labour is 'unproductive' when they render, in exchange for money, a service, a use value which does not increase their user's capital; labour is 'productive' when the workers increase the capital of their master.[28]

Marx gives serious consideration to the question of how wealth (wealth = the sum of values) can be increased?

Wealth grows with the growth of productive forces, and the increase in values is the result of the self-realisation of capital. The production of wealth depends more on science and technology and less on labour time.[29]

Marx then goes on to analyse the effect of an increase in productivity: an increase in exchange values arises from an increase in productivity, the latter being the result of the following three phenomena:

(a) an increase in the population leads to a subsequent increase in the productive force of labour;

(b) this increase in the productive force of labour is due to a greater division of labour, which expresses itself in different combinations of labour;

(c) the process of capital accumulation and growth in savings.

The increase in the productivity of labour (that is, the improvement in the mode of production) will, according to Marx, increase capital, expand the labouring population, and lead to the accumulation and growth of property. With capital accumulation and the subsequent increase in savings (because the capitalists will eat up only part of their extra surplus value while saving the other part, towards investment) exchange values will eventually increase because of the growth of the money supply.[30]

However, two barriers become manifest as capital emerges from the production process:

(1) consumption capacity: that is, the number of consumers times the magnitude of their needs (which amounts to the use value of the commodities produced);
(2) the capacity to consume surplus value: that is, the availability of the 'surplus equivalent', in the form of 'new money'.

In sum, the manifestation of this barrier is linked to the capacity to produce new consumption. In Marx's view, the production of new consumption may derived from:

(a) the constant expansion of sphere of circulation, which is a moving magnitude expanded by production itself;
(b) the production of more gold and silver or of more money;
(c) the production of new needs and the creation of additional needs over a larger area;
(d) the discovery and creation of new use values;
(e) the development of different kinds of labour;
(f) the engagement in universal exchange by the development of a world market;
(g) science, discoveries, development of qualities as social human being.[31]

Marx then asks if products can be 'devalued'? He declares that products are subject to devaluation. He views 'devaluation' from two vantage points, one essentially micro-economic, the other clearly macro-economic. In the former sense, he terms a product devalued when it is sold below its value (even though it may still be sold at a price which leaves its owner with a profit). In the latter sense devaluation means a general depreciation of prices, a general devaluation of capital.[32]

An individual product is devalued when the amount of objectified labour contained in it does not obtain, for itself, an equal quantity of objectified labour contained in the other commodity, but a smaller quantity (which expresses itself in a reduced quantity of the other commodity). If silver worth 180 Thalers buys a value of 200 Thalers' worth of twist, then the silver producers obtain a surplus of 20 Thalers' worth of twist, so that the silver producer retains 20 Thalers' worth of silver, even though the absolute value of both silver and twist remains the same (because each already contains an equivalent quantity of objectified labour).

In Marx's view, devaluation can be absolute or relative. This is because values expresses more than just the relation between one commodity and another (as does price): value is also the relation between the price of the commodity and the labour objectified in it; but it is also the relation between one amount of objectified labour and another, of the same quality.[33]

Value can also decrease from production interruption which is linked to market distance,[34] but such decrease should be distinguished from the subtraction, from surplus value, of money costs and of *faux frais de production*.[35]

General devaluation occurs in general crises. Marx terms this 'general devaluation of prices or the general devaluation of capital'.[36] This type of situation comes about when the sum of the quantities of products is sold at less than their total value (of value measured in terms of objectified labour: if 200 Thalers' worth of silver exchange for a value of 200 Thalers' worth of twist, then a full-value exchange takes place. If, however, it takes only 180 Thalers' worth of silver to purchase 200 Thalers' worth of twist, then a general depreciation of capital takes place, from a total value of 400 Thalers down to a value of 380 Thalers. This happens because the silver producer exchanges less objectified labour contained in his silver for a higher quantity of labour time embodied in the twist. But Marx then observes that the capitalist in twist does not suffer the consequence of his loss because he is able to pass on this loss to the workers, whose value he then obtains at a lower price (which is, in Marx's view, the same as if the real value of labour had decreased – possibly by an increase in the productive force of the labour in twist). General devaluation is tied to developed exchange and, in particular, to overproduction.[37]

How does Marx view the effect on value of an increase in the productive force of labour? He reflects on several circumstances in which such a situation may arise:

(1) Value can go up when higher-finish labour is added in manufacturing; as a consequence, the use value of the commodity increases in quality and the exchange value increases by the extra labour added.[38] The exchange value of labour goes up because the value of a special skill has to show itself in the costs necessary to produce a similar labouring skill.[39]

(2) An increase in the productive force of labour increases use values for the capitalist and leads therefore to an increase in the value of capital; but it diminishes the value of the worker, since the quantity of necessary labour is decreased.[40] An increase in the productive force of labour will increase the surplus labour: that is to say the relation of living labour to that objectified in the worker, whereby the relative surplus day time increases over the necessary labour time, even though absolute labour time remains unchanged.[41]

(3) The effects of an increase in the productive power of force of labour are expressed with reference to both simple exchange and developed exchange and eventually involve external trade:[42]

(a) With respect to the effect in simple exchange, Marx starts with the postulate that there is no exploitation in simple exchange (recall that in his view, exploitation can occur only in production not in circulation). In simple exchange, Marx postulates the following situation:

> 100 Thalers' worth of a commodity is produced in 4 hours, and the value components are as follows:
> 100 Thaler = 50 Th. cotton + 10 Th. instruments + 40 Th. wages.

This total value is retained by the worker-producer, and equal value is obtained in exchange for it from the fellow worker-producer. If then the productive force of the worker-producer doubles, he can now achieve in two hours what he used to expend on four hours of work. But his increase in productivity will enable him to reduce by one half the amount of labour time he needed in order to feed himself, and he will in fact feed himself at one half of the previous cost (2 hours and 20 Thalers v. 4 hours and 40 Thalers). The increase in the productive force of the worker-producer will decrease the Thaler-value of the commodity, even though the quantity of the commodity will remain unchanged; but the worker-producer now works only half as much as before and still retains, in exchange, the full value of his product.

(b) In developed exchange the effects are significantly different; developed exchange involving capitalist production and capitalist exchange. In this system, Marx views the production process as follows: at first, a total of 4 + 4 hours are worked by labour, for the total value of 140 Thalers, containing the following value components, during an 8-hour day:

$$140 \text{ Thalers} = 50 \text{ Th. cotton} + 10 \text{ Th. instruments} + 40 \text{ Th.}$$
$$\text{wages} + 40 \text{ Th. surplus value.}$$

Of this total value, value in circulation amounts to 80 Thalers (40 + 40), of which the capitalist retains the surplus value of 40 Thalers.

When the productive force of labour doubles in developed exchange, the absolute working time remains unchanged (is not decreased) at 4 + 4 hours, and the value of the commodity also remains the same. But the workers' use value diminishes and the exchange value of their (*enhanced*) *Arbeitskraft decreases* (emphasis added):

$$140 \text{ Th.} = 50 \text{ Th. cotton} + 10 \text{ Th. instruments} + 20 \text{ Th. wages}$$
$$+ 60 \text{ Th. surplus value.}[43]$$

In this situation capital pockets an extra 20 Thalers' worth of product, even though it throws into circulation an unchanged quantity of capital. Again Marx supposes that the increasing productivity of *Arbeitskraft* will result in the provision of the same quantity of workers' needs, with the commensurate decrease of 50 per cent in the exchange value of the workers' labour power; again he suggests that the new, autonomous ('liberated') value will be transferred to the owner of capital. He concludes that the increase in the productive force of labour in developed circulation will increase capital and wealth, but not wages. However, he states later in the *Grundrisse* that wages will vary with the productivity of labour.[44]

(c) Changes in the value of gold coins and silver coins are also tied to

increases in the productivity of labour plus other factors, which Marx
treats as follows, naming four reasons which will cause such coins to
change their value:[45]

(i) the changing value of other commodities over time, requiring
    that more or fewer gold coins or silver coins be given up in
    exchange;
(ii) the gold and silver content in these coins is the product of more
    or less labour time;
(iii) restriction on the exportation of gold;
(iv) an increase in grain prices, which amounts to a decrease in the
    price of all other commodities, including gold coins and silver
    coins, because their purchasing power will have changed (will
    have become more 'deficient'). However, Marx considers this
    changes as a change in price *relatives* and suggests that the price
    of grain increases above the value of grain while the price of
    everything else devalues below their values (where 'value' is
    determined by the 'normal costs of production': that is, by the
    quantity of labour time embodied).[46]

Marx ties in the question concerning the change in the value of gold
coins and silver coins with the broader issue of convertibility: 'To be a
value-symbol, money, the general equivalent, must be convertible
and must be equated with a third commodity.'[47] In his view, convertibility can be assured only in conditions of equivalent exchange, which
occurs when a specific amount of labour time which is embodied in a
commodity exchanges for the same amount of labour time embodied
in the other commodity. But convertibility is threatened in conditions
of non-equivalent exchange, which occurs when a specified quantity
of a commodity, worth so many hours of embodied labour, can
obtain in exchange for itself either a greater or a lesser quantity of
labour time which is embodied in the other commodity. This happens
when, for example, a specified quantity of gold can obtain, in exchange for itself, a greater (or a lesser) amount of labour than the
quantity of labour embodied in this particular gold coin. This can
happen even though the quantity of gold embodied in the currency
and the quantity of historically embodied labour time in the gold coin
remain unchanged. In this sense, a currency will appreciate when it
can buy, in exchange for itself, a greater amount of labour than it
contains; it will depreciate when it obtains only a lesser amount of

embodied labour in exchange for itself. Both these types of exchange amount to non-equivalent exchange.

Looking over this problem in its historical setting, Marx finds that the increasing productivity of labour in gold production (as substantiated, in his view, by the general economic law that costs of production constantly decline), will lead to the constant depreciation of gold money (its 'inevitable fate'), and will, consequently, result in 'great revolutions between the different classes of a state':[48]

> it is well known that the depreciation of gold and silver, due to the discovery of America, depreciated the labouring class and that of the landed proprietors; raised that of the capitalists (specially of the industrial capitalists) . . . . In the Roman republic, the appreciation of copper turned the plebeians into the slaves of the patricians. . . . This great revolution in the exchange value of the monetary substance, to the measure it proceeded, most cruelly worsened the lot of the unfortunate plebeians, who had obtained the depreciated copper as a loan, and, having spent or used it at the rate it then had, now owed, by the letter of their contracts, a five times greater sum than they had borrowed in reality.[49]

In summary form, Marx's propositions concerning gold as money and changes in the relative value of gold are as follows:

(1) The increased productivity of gold-producing labour leads to the production of more gold (coins) during the same period of labour time, reducing the real value of the gold coin (on account of the reduction of the labour time contained in it);

(2) in consequence, it now takes more (newly minted) gold coins to purchase commodities which contain a higher proportion of labour time relative to the amount contained in these newly minted coins (even though the labour time contained in these commodities is equivalent to the labour time contained in the old coins);

(3) the coins used in the gold standard system will depreciate in terms of other commodities, whereby the convertibility of gold (which presumes equivalence between the quantities of labour time embodied) will be endangered.

Seeking a solution to the problem of the historical tendency of gold coins to depreciate, Marx proposes the following solutions:

- keep constant the productivity of labour in gold production (which includes minting);
- switch to the paper currency system.

The latter, he claims, would be of advantage to the workers, even though it would have some drawbacks: for example, if the paper standard were composed of labour money – time-chits – representing the productivity of one hour's labour, the increased productivity of labour would lead to a constant appreciation of this labour money, the new chits as well as the accumulated ones, which would also benefit the non-workers.[50]

MARX ON VALUE: CONCLUSION

It appears that Marx had three concepts of value:

(1) a static theory;
(2) a dynamic theory;
(3) a theory relating to international trade and the international division of labour.

The static theory is based on the assumption that the productive force of labour and the mode of production are constant and unchanging, in all realms of production, including that of money metals. In its essence this analysis of value reflects a pre-capitalist economy, a situation of equal exchange: a period during which costs of production remain unchanged and no devaluation or revaluation, absolute or relative, is possible. In this interpretation, each commodity obtains 'full value' in payment for its number of labour hours embodied, the metal content of currency has mint-parity purchasing power, and the flows of C-M-C and M-C-M represent the two, mutually balanced flows in the economy. In this interpretation, the use value of commodity equals its exchange value, and the use value of labour contained in the commodity obtains full payment in the form of exchange value (of the owner-worker). The static theory of value does not allow for (unsold) surpluses (devaluations). This particular Marxian version of the definition of value may be referred to as the 'equilibrium-value theory' because it postulates that:

(a) the total value of the product = the total value of the money metal;

(b) total use value = total exchange value;
(c) the goods market and the (sole) input market (labour) are in equilibrium;
(d) the supply of the money metal (gold) is a constant, whereby the money metal can serve as the measure (the universal equivalent) of the value of any commodity whatsoever.

The dynamic theory of value involves two concepts and emanates directly from Marx's reflections concerning the evolution of capitalism:

(a) a continuous increase in the productivity of labour, including, in particular, the productivity of labour in gold and silver production; this increase in labour productivity leads to the devaluation of the social product;

(b) a continuous increase in the capital – labour ratio, whereby the coefficient of $\dfrac{c}{c + v}$ is rendered higher, while the 'v'-part in the value equation becomes increasingly smaller, which results in the diminution of the relative purchasing power of the increasing percentage of the population, leading to underconsumption, induced crises, and the eventual downfall of capitalism. A particularly interesting analytical proposition by Marx in this rendition of the theory of value concerns the necessity that surplus value (as a macro-magnitude which is produced in the capitalist circulation of production) can be realised only by making available a 'super-equivalent' of an equal magnitude: that is, the purchasing power that is required to realise the commodities' full value in the circulation phase.

The value theory involving the dimensions of international trade and the international division of labour are linked to Marx's proposition that market prices oscillate around the value of the commodity and that values constitute the driving force and the moving principle of these oscillations. This proposition applies to the circulation of production in general and involves the international sphere, the worldwide market in which commodities are produced for exchange. At the base of this inquiry into value is his view that it is production itself which expands the sphere of circulation, a moving magnitude which derives from the production of more gold and silver, both in commodity form and in money form, the discovery and creation of new use values, science and discoveries, and the development of different kinds of labour and different kinds of markets on a universal scale. In the *Grundrisse*, Marx does not propose specifically just how values will tend to equalise on an international scale; but he implies that there will be a tendency towards equalisation – a view which he had discussed in one of his earlier writings (*Address on the Question of Free Trade*, 9 January 1848) in which he assessed the effect of free trade on values and prices and on the relative earnings of workers on land and workers in industry.

Marx's view on the evolution of the world market contains seminal ideas on a world general equilibrium, a situation in which the total use value of commodities produced equals their total exchange value, and the total exchange value equals the total purchasing power (= the total use value of the means of exchange) in money form (gold and silver). His concept of devaluation hails from the increasing productivity of labour in gold and silver and entails a lack of purchasing power on a worldwide scale (that is, of use values in money form) relative to the available quantity of exchange values which are contained in the commodities offered for sale on an expanding world market.

NOTES AND COMMENTS

1. *Grundrisse*, p. 104.
2. Ibid.
3. Ibid., p. 167, p. 861.
4. Ibid., p. 158.
5. Ibid.
6. Ibid.
7. Ibid., p. 167.
8. Ibid.
9. Ibid., pp. 160–1.
10. Ibid.
11. Ibid., p. 551.
12. Ibid., p. 818.
13. Ibid., p. 612.
14. Ibid., p. 614.
15. Ibid., p. 668–670.
16. Ibid., p. 136–7.
17. Ibid., p. 846–7.
18. Ibid., p. 776.
19. Ibid., p. 846.
20. Ibid., p. 632.
21. Ibid., p. 137.

22. Ibid., p. 653.
23. Ibid., pp. 653–67.
24. *MEGA*, IV/2, p. 758. Apparat.
25. *Grundrisse*, pp. 269–72.
26. Ibid.
27. Ibid., p. 269.
28. Ibid., pp. 272–3.
29. Ibid., pp. 210, 224, 226–8.
30. Ibid., p. 157
31. Ibid., pp. 159–60.
32. Ibid., p. 167.
33. Ibid., pp. 168–69.
34. Ibid., p. 204.
35. Ibid., p. 193.
36. Ibid., p. 169.
37. Ibid.
38. Ibid., p. 164.
39. Ibid., pp. 127, 147.
40. Ibid. Marx adds here the phrase: 'and not because the increase in the productive force increases the quantity of products or use values created by the same labour.'
41. Ibid., p. 147.
42. Ibid., pp. 146–53.
43. Ibid., p. 148.
44. Ibid., p. 246, fn. 19.
45. Ibid., p. 149.
46. Ibid., p. 134.
47. Ibid.
48. Ibid., p. 805.
49. Ibid.
50. Ibid., p. 806.

11 Marx on Prices and Price Determination: Conclusion

In the *Grundrisse*, Marx's deliberations concerning price are found in his Chapter On Money; his critical assessment, in the Chapter On Capital, of the classicals' and some socialists' (Proudhon) views concerning value, surplus, and price; and his own preoccupation with value, exchange value, surplus value and profit, and price.

Overall, his treatment of price divides quite distinctly into a macro-economic-monetary approach and a micro-economic consideration, including, as the components of price, costs of production, circulation costs, profit, interest, and rent.

Like most of his other deliberations concerning other major economic issues, Marx's treatment of prices, pricing, and price levels is discontinuous in that it is spread over both the major Chapters as well as over many of the Sections. In many instances his views are declaratory, but at times they are also profoundly analytical. In a general sense, his presentations incorporate many aspects of a general theory of price. Thus, in the macro-sense, he deals with Say's Law, the quantity theory, price ratios between precious metals (in their quality as commodities as well as money) and other commodities and staples, a treatment in which he clearly emphasises the role of relative scarcity and from which he deduces his definition of devaluation and revaluation, depreciation and appreciation. In the macro-sense, his treatment of price levels and of price-level determination may be termed orthodox but innovative in that it encompasses the assessment of effects of free gold-flows across national boundaries, including gold discoveries and subsequent inflows of gold into worldwide commodity circulation, of their effects upon savings and investment and a universal expansion of production. As we shall demonstrate below, in the *Grundrisse*, Marx had no problems adducing price changes (absolute as well as relative) to shifts in effective demand on the one hand, and to the expansion of supply capacity arising of an increase in accumulation and productivity of labour on the other.

Treating prices and price levels in the macro-sense, Marx assumes a free flow of capital and a free flow of gold as a means of international settlement; recognises the role of central banking (Banque de France) in seeking to stem the outflow of gold and describes the effect of that role on bills of exchange and the cost on domestic currency; implies the existence of a system of worldwide free competition; points to an immediate effect, on international as well as national prices, of crop failures; speaks of longer-term effects from foreign investment with long gestation periods; and, finally, makes reference to monopolies.

Also in the macro-sense, he ponders about Say's Law (which he refers to as a 'simple-exchange situation' and therefore a 'truism' because it keeps everything else constant, including price levels, and because it assumes away savings and accumulation) and then goes on to review the relations, in the equation, arising from changes in each of its four magnitudes while holding the other three constant.

In his macro-treatment, nothing revolutionary becomes even remotely visible – except, perhaps, for his suggestion to abolish exchange value in order to rid society of the evil and exploitatory system of prices. Instead, he adds insights of his own to the then prevailing orthodox-classical interpretations: de-pricing and devaluations; price-level effects arising from overproduction; relation between price levels and circulating media; and, finally, the suggestion that not even central banks are exempt from the general laws of supply and demand.

In the micro-sense, Marx's analysis of prices is undertaken mainly in response to two initiatives: first, in his seeking to reply to his predecessors' and contemporaries' propagations as regards the relation between price and its component parts – costs of production and profit – and secondly, his own attempts to clarify the relation between value and price, surplus value and 'gross profit', equivalent v. non-equivalent exchange, and the unequal sharing in surplus value (profit).

Even in his micro-treatment he assumes free competition, which includes the market for productive factors; free mobility, including that of secondary goods; shifts in demand and shifts in supply; an institutionalised framework (banking and central bank, government, public means of transport and public investment v. users' fees), exchange, and agents involved in the circulation of production as well as in the circulation of commodities. Within all these, he presumes the existence of the tendency towards equalisation (rates of profit, but not rates of surplus value, rates of interest, and subsistence levels for unskilled labour).

In his micro-treatment of pricing he recognises the significance of scarcity, as a factor over and beyond labour as determinant of value; of different intensities of labour (the exchange amongst which is unequal but is rendered possible either by a recalculation in reference to simple labour or by the payment, in money, of the difference, a situation which also applies to the exchange between countries at different levels of development). He struggles with the question of the equality of profit and surplus value, an account in which he lists several component parts of surplus value for example, *faux frais de production*, road-building costs, and, lastly, the costs of engaging in an unfavourable deal owing to lack of information or, simply, be cause of cheating), any and all of these component parts causing a reduction of the accrued surplus value, In addition, Marx also suggests that because of competition goods or excessive production may at times be sold at prices which are lower than the values of the goods at the end of the production phase, a situation which, if prolonged, could lead to bankcruptcy or to an overall economic depression.

In his view, at the base of pricing is the requirement that the commodity be (a) produced by labour, and (b) have use value to the buyer. His prices are set in the market (commodity market and, respectively, input markets, especially for labour) in conditions of free competition (except when he refers to monopoly situations). Four laws rule pre-eminently in the price-setting scenario: the law of supply and demand (in reference to which he repeatedly emphasises the significance of effective demand); the law of the diminishing rate of profit; the law of rent (which makes itself visible in diminishing returns on land); and the law of the progressive devaluation of capital owing to the increase in the productive force of labour.

In our specific analysis of Marx on prices and price setting, we shall commence with his macro-economic treatment of these concepts. Before we engage in this analysis, however, we wish to present a selection, from the *Grundrisse*, of Marx's comments regarding price and price setting:

A merchandise is not offered simply because one is able to produce it, but because it is in demand.[1]

If, by a change in fashion, the demand for silks goes up and that for wool products down, the market price of silks will go up and that of woollens down, but their natural price will remain the same; however, the change in market price will increase the profits in silk above the average rate of profit, and that of woollens will drop below this average: eventually, this change will reflect itself on wages.[2]

Supply and demand constantly determine the prices of commodities. But it is the costs of production . . . which determine the oscillations of supply and demand.[3]

It is not the costs of production, i.e. the real value, but the market prices which determine production. If the market price is higher than the costs of production, capital will flow in and more will be produced.[4]

In modern society, market price always surpasses real price.[5]

Competition among capitalists who seek to employ their capitals most profitably, will tend to push market price towards the level of real price.[6]

An import duty on wheat will continually increase price and therefore rent because it will push cultivation to worse lands.[7]

If the market price of wheat is increased by one tenth because of an import duty or a difficulty of production, wheat consumption could still remain unchanged if everyone needed a specific quantity of wheat and he will consume it as if he had the extra money to buy it at the higher price.[8]

If in the course of unfavourable development, a country does not export sufficient precious metals, its currency will depreciate as it receives an undue surplus of precious metals.[9]

Gold and silver are transferred from countries in which they are the most expensive (where the price of merchandise has fallen to the lowest level) towards countries in which they are the least expensive (where merchandise prices are relatively high).[10]

Prohibition of exportation of *numéraire* can affect the price of wheat and of labour.[11]

Perhaps Marx's most significant statement in the *Grundrisse* concerning price and price setting is found in the following extracts:

Price is the exchange value of commodities, expressed in money. [If measured] in labour money denominated in labour time, the real value (the exchange value) of commodities would be equal to their nominal value (value, price).[12]

But the value of commodities as determined by labour time is only their average value . . . the average figure of an epoch . . . the median price average. . . . The *market value* is always different, is always below or above this average value of the commodity. . . . The price of a commodity constantly stands above or below the value of the commodity, and the value of the commodity itself exists only in this up-and-down movement of commodity prices. Supply and demand constantly determine the prices of commodities; never balance, or only coincidentally; but the cost of production, for its part, determines the oscillations of supply and demand. The gold or silver in which the price of a commodity, its market value, is expressed is itself a certain quantity of accumulated labour, a certain measure of materialized labour time. On the assumption that the production costs of a commodity and the production costs of gold and silver remain constant, the rise or fall of its market price means nothing more than that a commodity, $= x$ labour time, constantly commands $>$ or $< x$ labour time on the market, that it stands above or beneath its average value as determined by labour time.[13]

Price can fall *below* the value, and capital can still make a gain: . . . if the relation of labour to raw material etc. is 1:5, then he can sell at e.g. only $\frac{1}{10}$ above the constant value, since the surplus labour *costs* him *nothing*. He then makes a present of $\frac{1}{10}$ of the surplus labour to the consumer and realises only $\frac{1}{10}$ for himself. This is very important in competition; overlooked in particular by Ricardo. The determination of prices is founded on the determination of values, but new elements enter in.[14]

A. MARX ON PRICES: THE MACRO-ECONOMIC APPROACH

In the *Grundrisse*, Marx's macro-economic treatment of price is found in his analysis of the following subjects: gold exports and prices; money, value, and price; money as a means of payment; precious metals as money, and coin and world money.

His first involvement with the question of price occurs in The Chapter On Money, in his critique of Darimon's reasoning concerning the outflow of gold from France. Marx refutes Darimon's argumentation as too simplistic, and substitutes instead the following explanation: the outflow of gold decreases circulation at home and leads to an unlimited increase in bank drafts, in consequence of which domestic prices of products, of raw materials, and of labour increase, while the price per bank draft decreases, which results in a devaluation of the country's paper.[15] In addition, in consequence of the run on the central bank's (Banque de France) supply of gold (because the demand for grain exceeded the supply of grain, which drove up the price of grain), the Bank increased the cost of its services because it is not exempt from 'these general laws, i.e. the disproportion of demand and supply'.[16] Moreover, since a rise in the price of grain was equal to the fall in the price of all other commodites, including gold and silver, all these prices, including that of labour, depreciate in terms of grain.[17] Furthermore, the law of supply and demand acts far more sharply – on a national scale – within the sphere of primary needs than in all others.[18] A domestic crop failure presupposes a rise in the price and greater imports at a higher price.[19] The extra spending on wheat imports leaves a deficit in the purchase of all other products, which leads to a decline in their prices, even below their values (the latter having been determined by their normal cost of production).

The law of supply and demand applies as well to gold and silver in their relation to other commodites: in prosperity, a temporary general rise in prices occurs, when gold and silver appreciate relative to other commodites (whereas, in a crisis, there is a general decrease in prices, when gold and silver depreciate relative to other commodites)[20]; an increase in the productivity of labour in gold and silver will depreciate the prices of gold and silver relative to other prices, but will also lead to a contradiction between exchange value and price.[21] Money, too, comes under the laws of supply and demand: the price of money is brought down by a general rise in demand for commodities against money (unless there is an equivalent increase in the production cost of gold).[22]

However, the proposition that prices are determined by the quantity of money is more complex than its simple expression implies:

> The quantity of money which is required for circulation is determined initially by the level of prices of the commodities thrown

into circulation. . . . Secondly, by the quantity of commodities at specified prices. . . . Thirdly, . . . on the rapidity with which money circulates.[23]

This much is clear, that prices are not high or low because much or little money circulates, but that much or little money circulates because prices are high or low.[24]

If the value of the currency is given, as is the quantity (the mass of transactions) and the velocity of circulation, then only a specific quantity of money can circulate; if prices, quantity of transaction, and velocity are given, then the quantity of circulating money depends on the value of the currency; if the value of the currency and velocity are given, then the quantity of money in circulation depends exclusively on prices and the quantity of transactions. However, if money in circulation is representative money (mere value-symbols), then the quantity that circulates depends on the standard this money represents (for example, fewer pounds sterling than shillings will circulate).[25] Clearly, prices must fall because the commodities are estimated to be worth so many ounces of gold and the amount of gold in this country is diminished.[26]

These general reflections include a treatment of convertibility: two commodities are convertible into each other when both contain an equal amount of labour time, that is, when exchange value = market value = real value = price.[27] If this relation is disturbed – for example by a greater productivity of labour in gold production – inconvertibility will emerge because a good containing less quantity of labour will seek to exchange itself for a good containing a higher quantity of labour; in consequence, the former will depreciate in terms of the latter and the original quantity ratio involved in the original exchange will have to be adjusted (that is, an extra quantity of gold will be offered).[28] In this sense, prices express only proportions in which commodities are exchanged for one another, their reciprocal value.[29]

This proportionality also applies to exchange rates: exchange rates reduce the measuring units of the different countries with different fractional parts of an ounce of gold, to the same unit of weight in gold or silver with the same quantity of labour objectified in it.[30] However, Marx emphasises that the coincidence of price and value presupposes an equality of demand and supply and the exchange solely of equivalents – the exchange of capital for labour constituting non-equivalent exchange because the price of labour (= wage) is less than the value of labour (to the capitalist).[31]

Since denominations such as pounds, shillings, dollars, and so forth are, as accounting units, merely arbitrary points of comparison which do not themselves express value (since the value in the commodity money is determined by its labour content, for example the labour content in producing one ounce of gold), to consider any of these denominations as a 'fixed price of gold' amounts to nonsense. This is so because, as commodities, gold and silver, too, reflect their own – different – labour times, which may be changed over time (the process of the constant devaluation of gold and silver metals). From an initial equal reciprocal exchange of one commodity for another, if their labour-content equality changes over time, 'in order to cover the excess of one value over another in exchange, in order to liquidate the balance, the crudest barter, just as with international trade today, requires payment in money', money being the balancing item, the universal equivalent. In international trade, payment in money equalises the imbalance in the exchange of unequal values. Naturally, no money payment is required if there is no difference between two values (that is, if real value equals price).[32] This is so because gold and silver, as the universal commodity, are the universal equivalent for everything, as they are the materials representative of general wealth. In this character, gold and silver play an important role in the creation of the world market: in developed trade they no longer appear for the purpose of exchanging the excess production but to balance it out as part of the total process of international commodity exchange. In money form, they serve as world coin.[33]

Marx also views gold and silver as commodities *per se*, and ties the price of these two commodities to their costs of production, which is essentially a micro-economic consideration: the value of the money metal is determined by the quantity of labour embodied in its production; but the price of the money metal (its exchange value) may fluctuate, depending on the productivity of labour which produces it or on the cost of production of commodities which this money metal will buy:

> [Gold and silver] values are determined, in the first place, by their cost of production in the country of production . . . in other words: on the quantity of gold and silver which is directly or indirectly obtained from the mining countries in exchange for a given quantity of labour (exportable products).[34]

As a medium of exchange between the nations . . . gold and silver, as . . . the universal commodity, . . . are the material representative of wealth . . . But even beyond Mercantilism, in periods of general crisis, gold and silver, . . . a universal equivalent for everything, also become the measure of power between nations. . . . In this character, gold and silver play an important role in the creation of the world market . . . In developed trade it no longer appears for the purpose of exchanging the excess production but to balance it out as part of the total process of international commodity exchange. It is coin, now, only as world coin.[35]

Marx's treatment of general price levels ties in directly with his propositions concerning capitalist accumulation and crises: the universality towards which capitalism irresistibly strives encounters barriers in its own nature.[36] On the one hand, the process of the realisation of capital includes the real possibility of new and larger values; on the other, the opposite tendency becomes clearly manifest: overproduction, followed by crises, when the new and larger values are neither consumed by the capitalist nor laid out for new labour. The general overproduction would take place because too many of those commodities had been produced by capital in proportion to that part of capital going to the workers, or too much relative to the part of capital consumable by the capitalists:

> It is clear here that D and E, where E represents all commodities consumed by the workers and D all those consumed by the capitalist, would have produced too much . . . that *general overproduction* would take place, not because relatively *too little* had been produced of the commodities consumed by the workers or too little of those consumed by the capitalists, but because too much of *both* had been produced – *not* too much for *consumption*, but too much to retain *the correct relation between consumption and realisation*; *too much for realisation*.[37]

This extra value requires a surplus equivalent, if it is to be consumed.[38]

Overproduction leads to a general depreciation of prices or a general devaluation or destruction of capital. Overproduction is due to a sudden general increase in the forces of production and will lead to crises unless the 'barriers to consumption' are overcome.[39] These barriers are artificial checks to production and they include the following:

On the supply side: necessary labour as the limit of the exchange value of living labour capacity; surplus value as the limit of surplus labour and of the development of the forces of production; the restriction of the production of use value by exchange value; capital accumulation as barrier to production.

On the demand side: money and the entire credit system, including overtrading, overspeculation, lending to foreign nations; outflow of gold payment for grain imports in case of crop failures;[40] the extraction, from labour, of an equivalent-plus;[41] the failure to increase consumption capacity or to secure additional purchasing power; the increasing scarcity of purchasing power (gold and silver).[42]

Whereas Marx considers the tendency of the forces of production to grow (which includes the growth of the industrial population) to be inherent in capitalism (interestingly, he does not advocate slowing down or putting a stop to accumulation[43]), he does specify conditions which must be met if the surplus equivalent is to be provided, whereby the equilibrium between the increasing productivity of labour and its increasing output of surplus value (the supply side) and the required purchasing power (the demand side) would permit this expanded circulation of capital to realise itself. He names three such conditions: the constant expansion of the sphere of circulation, which includes the creation of the world market; the production of more gold or silver; the addition of more money, through commerce.[44]

If this surplus equivalent is not provided, overproduction will ensue, with its inevitable result of devaluation and de-pricing, even of capital and of living labour.[45]

B. MARX ON PRICES: THE MICRO-ECONOMIC APPROACH

In the *Grundrisse*, Marx's micro-economic treatment of price and price determination begins in The Chapter On Money, in which he reviews the concept of 'chit-money': the concept of price had to be developed before that of circulation, since circulation was the posting of prices, the process in which commodities were transferred into prices.[46] It is in this Chapter that he makes his first major pronouncement with respect to price, when de gets involved in his review of paper labour money; this review compels him, once again, to juxtapose value and price. He starts by defining both value and price:

> The value (the real exchange value) of all commodities (labour included) is determined by their cost of production, in other words by the labour time required to produce them. Their *price* is this exchange value of theirs, expressed in money.[47]

He then becomes very specific about value being only 'average value', while 'price' constantly stands above or below the value of the commodity, the latter constituting the 'median price average':

> Price is different from value . . . the two are constantly different and never balance out, or balance only coincidentally and exceptionally. . . . The price of a commodity constantly stands above or below the value of the commodity, and the value of the commodity itself exists only in this up-and-down movement of commodity prices. Supply and demand constantly determine the prices of commodities; never balance, or only coincidentally, but the cost of production, for its part, determines the oscillations of supply and demand.[48]

> . . .the value of commodities as determined by labour time is only their *average value* . . . an external abstraction if it is calculated out as the average figure of an epoch . . .but real if it is at the same time recognised as the driving force and the moving principle of the oscillations which commodity prices run through during a given epoch.[49]

The sum total of these prices (the prices of commodities thrown into circulation) follows from Marx's definition of price:

> The sum total of these prices is determined firstly: by the prices of the individual commodities; secondly: by the quantity of commodities at given prices which enter into circulation.[50]

In Marx's view, prices express the relations in which commodities are exchanged for one another, the proportions in which they are exchanged for one another. In this sense the reciprocal value of, say, potash to cocoa to iron bars is defined as their relative prices: 35s/ton to 60s/ton to 145s/ton. Once these proportions are given, commodities become commensurable magnitudes and their ratios amount to exchange rates, even without any reference to fixed quantities of gold or silver.[51] However, once each commodity is expressed in terms of a common, particular, measuring unit, this measuring unit (gold or fraction thereof) marks the proportion of the values of these commodities; it marks their relative value.

Why, asks Marx, are prices and values different at all? In commodity exchange, the coincidence of price and value presupposes the equality of demand and supply as well as the exchange of equivalents, a situation which is possible only in simple exchange. However, this condition does not apply to the exchange of capital for labour in developed exchange, since such an exchange is a non-equivalent one, exchange values and prices not being the same (the exchange value of labour being less than the price of what labour produces).[52]

The value of gold and silver depends on the production time they cost.[53] This value is variable, since the same quantity of labour is not always contained in the same quantity of gold.

As a measure, money is an element in price determination,[54] but its price ratio to commodities at which it exchanges is also subject to variation.[55] This is so because even though money is a general commodity, it is also a particular commodity; as such, it too comes under the laws of supply and demand. Not only does the value of gold and silver depend on the production time they cost,[56] but the price of money is brought down by a general demand for commodities against money. An exception exists when an equivalent increase in the cost of production (that is, the exchange value) of gold brings up the price of gold relative to the prices of commodities, in which case the price ratio of gold to commodities remains unchanged.[57]

For money to realise prices, it must be full-bodied: that is to say, its intrinsic worth must equal the equivalent of the exchange value of the other commodity. If money is a subsidiary medium of exchange, its intrinsic worth is much less than the equivalent (less than its nominal value), in which case it is not the quantity of the circulating medium that determines prices but prices that determine the quantity of the (subsidiary) circulating medium.[58]

Apart from its relation to supply and demand, rarity is also an element in exchange value (price). This is so because for something to become an object of exchange, to have exchange value, it must not be available to everyone without the mediation of exchange; it must not appear in such an elemental form (for example common pebbles) as to be common property: it must be produced. But if a commodity cannot be transferred into money (because the demand for it is not backed by money) it will appear de-priced, since its price will not be realised.[59]

Marx attributes the increasing difference between the price of gold (high) and the price of silver (low) to the increasingly greater scarcity of gold, on the one hand, and to the more abundant and cheaper labour in silver production, on the other – a complete changeover from Ancient Persia. But he notes that the consumption of gold and silver is not inversely proportional to their cost of production (as is the consumption of other commodities) but that they are consumed more in proportion as wealth in general increases.[60]

With reference to the supply of commodities, Marx emphasises the following determinants of supply:

– costs of production, which include wages, rent, interest, and profit (and their price setting);
– depreciation costs, which involve capital intensity and rate of depreciation (time factor);
– labour productivity (a doubling in labour productivity will, other things being equal, reduce by one-half the living-labour equivalent);
– labour intensity (more intensive labour is higher-quality labour, which adds to value and therefore to exchange value);[61]
– costs of transportation and distribution (even though some of these are referred to as *faux frais de production* and are rendered payable from surplus value);[62]
– interest costs, which are made payable from surplus value;[63]
– the costs of the capitalist's own upkeep, which are also made payable from surplus value: these costs must be met if the capitalist is not to devalue or even destroy his capital;[64]
– the costs of risk, also payable from surplus value;[65]
– the costs of money (printing, minting, and so on), payable from surplus value;[66]
– profit, as an embedded, added-on cost at the various stages of production;[67]
– rarity, an element of value which calls for the production of a commodity;
– distance and time, which form an aspect of the costs of circulation and result in a postponement of the realisation of capital, whereby the process of the complete turnover of capital is impeded; all circulation costs are subtracted from the sum of values (individual

values times the number of production times in a complete production period), where the sum of values is determined in the production phase;[68]
- the cost of the continuous devaluation of gold and silver, as well as of capital, both of which arise from the increasing productivity of labour over time (the law of the reduction of production cost);[69]
- the law of diminishing returns.[70]

Marx's treatment of the demand side of price and pricing is dispersed all over the *Grundrisse*, but he makes a basic distinction between the equilibrium in simple exchange (demand = supply and exchange value = price) and the equilibrium (or lack of it, since non-equivalent exchange is involved in the market for labour) in developed exchange, where additional price-determining factors must be accounted for.

The following are typical references to the significance of demand in setting a market price, a situation which occurs in the circulation part of the total turnover of capital ('the price realization of capital' in developed exchange, in which the market price may be set either above or below the value of the commodity):[71]

Supply and demand constantly determine the prices of commodities; never balance, or only coincidentally, but the cost of production, for its part, determines the oscillations of supply and demand;[72]

the value of commodities as determined by labour time is only their average value . . . an external abstraction if it is calculated out as the average figure of an epoch . . . but real if it is at the same time recognized as the driving force and the moving principle of the oscillations which commodity prices run during a given epoch.[73]

Money . . . is demanded because of its exchange value, . . . whereas the commodities are demanded because of their natural properties, because of the needs for which they are the desired object.[74]

the sum of money exchanged for a commodity is its realized price, its real price. . . . The commodity requires not simply demand, but demand which can pay in money. Thus, if its price cannot be realized, if it cannot be transferred into money, the commodity appears as *devalued, de-priced*.[75]

[The notion that] to accumulate it [money] is to increase it, [since] its own quantity is the measure of its value, turns out again to be false. If the other riches do not [also] accumulate, then it loses its value in the measure in which it is accumulated. What appears as an increase is in fact its decrease. Its independence is a mere semblance; its independence of circulation exists only in view of circulation, exists as dependence on it. It pretends to be the general commodity but because of its natural particularity it is again a particular commodity, whose value depends both on demand and supply, and on variations in its specific costs of production.[76]

Rarity (apart from supply and demand) is an element of value in so far as its opposite, the non-rare as such, the negation of rarity, the elemental, has no value because it does not appear as the result of production. . . . To this extent, rarity is an element of exchange value and hence this property of the precious metal is of importance, even apart from its further relation to supply and demand.[77]

It is less true of gold and silver than of any other commodities that their consumption can grow only in inverse proportion to their costs of production. . . . Apart from their use as money, silver and gold are consumed more in proportion as wealth in general increases. When, therefore, their supply suddenly increases, even if their costs of production or their value does not proportionately decrease, they find a rapidly expanding market which retards their depreciation. A number of problems which appear inexplicable to the economists – who generally make the consumption of gold and silver dependent solely on the decrease in their costs of production – in regard to the California – Australia case, where they go around in circles, are thereby clarified.[78]

Institutions emerge whereby each individual can acquire information about the activity of all others and attempt to adjust his own accordingly, e.g. list of current prices, rates of exchange, interconnections between those active in commerce through the mails, telegraphs, etc. . . . (This means that, although total supply and demand are independent of the actions of each individual, everyone attempts to inform himself about them, and this knowledge then reacts back in practice on the total supply and demand). . . . In the case of the *world market*, the *connection of the individual* with all, but at the same time the *independence of this connection from the individual*, have developed to such a high-level that the formation of the world market already at the same time contains the conditions for going beyond it.[79]

Commenting on the outflow of capital (money) in payment for extra imports owing to crop failures at home, Marx points to an increased demand (for the importable) and specifies the effect of the (increased) scarcity on price, in an international context:

> This part, the capital part [of the monetary outflow which involves gold and silver as capital]. . . . does not stand in a simple arithmetical relation to the loss, because the deficient product rises and must rise on the world market as a result of the decreased supply and the increased demand.[80]

The extra spending on wheat imports leaves a deficit in the purchase of other products, which leads to a decline in their prices, with the result that the price of the outputs will drop below their value, which is determined by the normal cost of their production; the same holds true, in the opposite, of the grain price/value relation (i.e., the price rises above the value).[81]

In Marx's view, 'the demand of the labourer can never be adequate demand.'[82] In such a market situation, the product will be devalued because it cannot sell:

> A product is devalued [when] it has been sold *below* its real value, even though it may still be sold at a *price* which leaves him [the capitalist] a profit, . . . when part of the objectified labour becomes valueless because it cannot sell.[83]

The workers' lack of adequate purchasing power (towards buying up the fruits of their labour) is caused not by their being overcharged but by their being underpaid:

> The capitalist's profit does not come from over-charging the worker but from the fact that in the whole of the product he sells a fractional part which he had not paid for, and which represents, precisely, *surplus labour time*.[84]

In his view, no devaluation will take place and wealth will continue to increase if the capitalist will expend as follows the extra value which arises from an increase in the productivity of labour:

- if he buys more *productive* labour;
- if he exchanges this extra value (in money form) for other commodities, whereby the latter's exchange value will increase by that amount;
- if he adds this extra value to his capital;
- if he puts this extra money back into circulation, whereby the prices of the commodities bought with them will rise.[85]

Finally, Marx proposes that the determination of prices is founded on the determination of values. However, new elements enter, since price, which originally appears as value expressed in money, becomes further determined as a specific magnitude, as follows:

- the total quantity produced becomes decisively important in the determination of price;
- fraud and reciprocal chicanery: one party can gain part of the surplus value which the other party loses;
- supply and demand;
- competition.[86]

The price of labour itself is first set by convention (tradition), but is then determined economically:

> [The price of labour] which begins as conventional and traditional [e.g. in old communities, when the pay of the common soldier is reduced to a minimum – determined solely by the production costs necessary to procure him] is thereafter increasingly determined economically, first by the relation of demand and supply, finally by the production costs at which the vendors themselves of these services can be produced.[87].

Nevertheless, Marx admits that 'necessary labour' may differ from epoch to epoch and from country to country, but that in any given epoch, the 'standard of necessary labour' is considered fixed by capital:

> However the standard of necessary labour may differ at various epochs and in various countries, or how much, in consequence of

the demand and supply of labour, its amount and ratio may change, at any given epoch the standard is to be considered and acted upon as a fixed one by capital.[88]

C. MARX ON PRICES: THE COMPONENTS OF PRICE

Marx's discussion of wages, rent, interest, and profit follows his critical review, in the *Grundrisse*, mainly of Malthus, Ricardo, Bastiat, Carey, and Proudhon. However, his treatment of the price components follows in the footsteps of his previous analysis, in *Wage Labour and Capital* (1849) and in *Poverty of Philosophy* (1847), of the relation of wages and profit (in the former) and of rent and interest (in the latter).

Wages: Marx first distinguishes between wages (= the price of *necessary* labour) and the value of *living* labour (= wages + profit):

> Wages . . . express the value of living labour *capacity*, but in no way the *value* of living labour, which is expressed, rather, in wages + profit. Wages are the *price* of *necessary labour* . . . The wages command . . . a much greater quantity of labour than they consist of, and a given quantity of living labour actually exchanges for a much smaller one of accumulated labour. . . . The wages of any quantity of labour must be equal to the quantity of labour which the labourer must expend upon his own reproduction.[89]

> Competition among workers could press down a higher wage level, etc. but the general standard of wages, or as Ricardo puts it, the natural price of wages, could not be explained by the competition between worker and worker, but only by the general relation between capital and labour.[90]

Marx counters Malthus's claim that the value of labour is constant:

> The value of products is determined by the labour contained in them, not by that part of labour in them which the employer pays for. . . . wages express only *paid labour*, never all labour *done*, The measure of this payment depends itself on the productivity of labour, for the latter determines the amount of necessary labour

time. And since these wages constitute the *value of labour*, this value is constantly variable.[91]

The fractional part of labour time which reproduces wages would vary with productivity; thus, with the productivity of labour, the *value of labour*, i.e. wages, would constantly vary. Wages would be measured both before and after by a definite *use value*, and since the latter constantly varies in its exchange depending on the productivity of labour, wages would change, or (in other words) the *value of labour*.[92]

Marx disagrees with Malthus's view that 'the quantity of labour which the product consists in is paid labour only . . . or that wages are the measuring rod of the value of the commodity', since 'where is the profit to come from if no unpaid labour is performed'.[93]

Marx's treatment of wage determination in the *Grundrisse* reflects his deliberations in *Wage Labour and Capital*:[94] wages are determined like any other commodity price: 'by the competition between buyers and sellers, the relation between demand and supply, of the want to the offer'.[95] Competition among sellers will tend to depress the price; competition among buyers will drive up the price; the end result will depend on which of the two parties is the stronger and on the degree of infighting within each of the two parties. Colluding sellers will drive up the price, while a dearth of buyers will decrease it.[96] In his view, the costs of production serve as the measure of high prices or low prices, as well as the measure of profit. The costs of production are determined by labour time, and it is thus labour time that determines prices.

In general market, a rise in the price of a particular product will lead to massive capital inflows, which will continue until profits sink back to normal levels or until the price drops below the costs of production. The market price [*der courante Preis*] is usually higher than or lower than the long-run price.[97] In the longer run, which includes the expansion and contraction of the industry, the alternation between price above costs of production and price below costs of production will ultimately set the price at the cost of production.

The laws which set commodity prices in general also determine the price of labour, the wage: the interaction between buyers and sellers. The wage is paid for the commodity *Arbeitskraft*. Here too, the interaction between buyers and sellers will cause deviations in price from costs of producing the *Arbeitskraft*. But ultimately, the price of *Arbeitskraft* is determined by the cost of producing it, that is, by the socially necessary labour time.

Marx names these costs:

- the price of the provisions which are required to keep the workers capable of working; the costs of producing a worker will be the lower, the simpler the task and the lower the educational requirements; in the case of unskilled workers, the costs of their production is limited to their food costs;[98]
- other considerations: the reproduction costs of the 'race of labour'[99] must be added to the cost of producing the simple *Arbeitskraft*, since it is by incurring these costs that the 'workers will multiply and used up workers will be replaced by new ones; the depreciation of the worker will be accounted for in the same manner as will the depreciation of the machines.'[100]

He recognises that the workers' real wage will go down when the price of labour remains the same while the prices of foodstuffs rise, but real wages will go up if produce prices and prices of manufactures decrease owing to good weather or the use of new machines, respectively, while the money price of labour remains unchanged.[101]

Marx submits that special skills cost more to produce[102] and that the equalisation of different qualities and intensities of labour and higher and lower kinds of labour can be resolved by expressing the product of a higher sort of labour as a multiple of simple labour.[103]

Concerning the relation between wages and profits, he states:

First of all, there is a difference between the 'relative wage' (the price of immediate, direct labour to the price of accumulated, stored labour; which means the value of wage labour relative to the value of capital) and the 'real wage' (the price of labour relative to the prices of the commodities which labour needs for its survival).

Second, wages and profit stand in an inverse relation to one another: if food prices decrease and the wage of labour (the price of labour) falls, then the ratio of the share of capital to the share of labour rises and profit goes up; and inversely. Profit rises to the extent that the wage falls, and falls to the extent that the wage rises.[104]

But Marx acknowledges that an increase in profit may be due to factors other than the decline in wages:

- an increase of demand in the domestic market;
- the opening up of new markets;
- an improvement in the instruments of labour;
- new utilisation of natural forces, and so forth.

Any or all of these may increase (or decrease, if considered in the reverse) a capitalist's profit independently of the fall (or rise) in the wages of labour, that is, in the exchange value of *Arbeitskraft*. However, so long as the capitalist goes on purchasing a higher sum of exchange values with the same sum of labour without paying more for this labour, the ratio of wage labour will keep on changing to the detriment of labour (the relative share of the workers' wages to the capitalists' net revenue will keep on decreasing).[105]

Rent: In the *Grundrisse*, Marx touches upon the question of rent in his assessment of Ricardo's view of value determination,[106] but it may be appropriate at this point to portray Marx's own view on rent as expressed in his *Poverty of Philosophy*, in a section in which he seeks to distinguish between the price of products in manufacturing as against the price of produce in agriculture.

Thus, in manufacturing, price is determined by the costs of production (the expended labour time) and includes the industrial profit. In manufacturing, assuming that production can be multiplied indefinitely, the market price is the common price for all the products of the same kind; this price includes the minimum labour costs and the cheapest and most productive instruments of production.[107]

In agriculture, on the contrary, the price of all produce of the same kind is regulated by the produce obtained with the greatest amount of labour. This is so because, as population increases, inferior lands are brought into cultivation at higher labour cost or new capital is applied to the same plots of land under conditions of diminishing returns ('proportionally less productive than used before').[108] At the going market price, the product of the better soil is paid for as dearly as is that of the inferior soil.

Marx's definition of rent then follows: rent is the excess of the price of the produce of the better soil over the cost of the production on that soil.[109]

Marx appears basically in agreement with Ricardo's explanation of rent; but he feels compelled to qualify the latter's rent doctrine:

For the Ricardian doctrine to be generally true, it is essential that capital should be freely applicable to different branches of industry; that a strongly developed competition among capitalists should have brought profits to an equal level; that the farmer should be no more than an industrial capitalist claiming for the use of his capital on inferior land, a profit equal to that which he would draw from his capital if it were applied in any kind of manufacture; that agricultural exploitation should be subjected to the regime of large-scale industry; and, finally, that the landowner himself should aim at nothing beyond the money return.[110]

He also suggests that often, the payment of land rent includes the rate of interest which the landowner may claim for his invested capital; but he adds that the interest on capital invested in land is generally lower than the interest on capital invested in manufacture or commerce.

Finally, Marx comments negatively on Ricardo's inclination to consider as immutable his own main economic principles:

> Ricardo, after postulating bourgeois production as necessary for determining rent, applies the conception of rent to the landed property of all ages and all countries. This is an error common to all the economists, who represent the bourgeois relations of production as eternal categories.[111]

Interest: In the *Grundrisse*, Marx's treatment of interest arises from his reply to Darimon;[112] his consideration of the question of 'interest-bearing capital';[113] his account of the evaluation of money and the history of usury;[114] and his assessment of others' (Bastiat, Carey, J.W. Gilbart, *et al.*) propositions concerning the nature and forms of interest.

First he defines interest: 'for the industrial capitalist, interest is among his direct expenses, his *real* costs of production; . . . the payment of interest shows that capital as such is not the mere addition of value-components.'[115]

Interest arises from the laws of the exchange of values: 'Proudhon grasps neither how profit, nor, therefore, how interest, arises from the laws of exchange of values.'[116]

Countering Darimon's critique of the Banque de France, policy of raising increase the cost of its services because the system is based on the rule of gold and silver, but that the cost went up because demand for grains exceeded supply, driving up the price; in consequence, there was a run on the Banque's supply of gold as the means of payment for the grain imports, inducing Marx to ask: 'And the bank should be made an exception to these general economic laws i.e. the disproportion of demand and supply? *Quelle idée!*'[117] We can clearly deduce from this statement Marx's view concerning the setting of the rate of interest (discount): the law of supply and demand.

Then he refers to the question of interest-bearing capital: interest ties in with surplus value and is rendered, as real cost of production, in payment for borrowed capital:

> Interest on borrowed capital makes tangible the truth that what is meant by the *cost of production* – even by economists who make this assertion – is not the sum of values which enter into production. For the industrial capitalist, interest is among his direct expenses, his *real* costs of production. But interest itself already presupposes that capital emerges from production as surplus value, since interest is itself only *one form* of this surplus value. Therefore, since, from the standpoint of the borrower, interest always enters into his *direct production costs*, it is apparent that capital enters as such into the cost of production, but that capital as such is not the mere addition of its value-components. –As interest, capital itself appears again in the character of a *commodity*, but as a commodity *specifically* distinct from all other commodities; . . . The demand raised by Mr. Proudhon, that capital should not be loaned out and should bear no interest, but should be sold like a commodity for its equivalent, amounts at bottom to no more than the demand that exchange value should never become capital, but always remain simple exchange value; that *capital* should *not exist as capital*.[118]

Marx fits the notion of interest-bearing capital into the (macro) circumstances of the realisation of capital. Interest constitutes the minimum limit between that part of capital which is produced for the capitalist and consumed by him: 'too much relative to the proportion by which they must increase their capital; and this proportion later obtains a minimum limit in the form of interest.'[119]

Marx's account of the history of usury follows his description (by paraphrasing others) of the evolution of money, especially of gold and silver coins:

> Usury originally unrestricted in Rome. The law of the 12 tables

(303 A.U.C.) had fixed the interest on money at 1% per year
(Niebuhr says 10). These laws promptly violated. . . . lending at
interest was absolutely forbidden by a plebiscite engineered by the
tribune, Genucius. . . . This situation lasted 3 years, until the
capture of Carthage. 12% then: 6% the average annual rate of
interest. . . . Commercial interest in Egypt, 146 B.C., was 12%
. . . The involuntary alienation of feudal landed property develops
with usury and with money.[120]

Marx makes reference to the ecclesiastical prohibition of interest and
accounts for the widely differing rates of interest rates in medieval
Europe, keeping his elaboration, in this context, strictly historical.

In Marx's view, both interest and profit express relations to
capital.[121] The unity of interest and profit (which 'the English call
"gross profit" '[122]) reveals, on closer look, an antithetical linkage: the
difference becomes perceptible as soon as a class of monied capitalists comes to confront a class of industrial capitalists.[123] Of the two
forms, interest is older than profit: historically, the form of industrial
profit arises only after capital no longer appears alongside the independent worker. Profit thus appears originally determined by interest. But in the bourgeois economy interest is determined by profit
'hence profit must be large enough to allow of a part of its branching
off as interest. Historically, interest must have become so depressed that
a part of the surplus gain could achieve independence as profit.'[124]

Marx also refers to that form of interest which arises from lending
capital for consumption: 'the other form of interest is lending of
capital to wealth which is engaged in consumption . . . whereby
income of landed proprietors often accumulates and becomes capitalised in the pockets of the usurer.'[125]

Profit: Throughout the *Grundrisse*, Marx is preoccupied with the
question of the difference between surplus value and profit. Profit
arises in developed exchange, and surplus value is the source of
profit.[126] Profit is surplus value, the product proper of the capital.[127]
Profit comes from the fact that the whole value contains a fractional
part which is not paid, and hence a fractional part of surplus labour is
paid in each fractional part of the whole (when the product is sold).[128]

Marx's attempt to distinguish clearly between surplus value and
profit takes a very specific form in his critique of Malthus's calculation of profit.[129] Malthus's example is fully cited in the *Grundrisse*,
with Marx's own commentary:

Capital sunk in building and machinery   £10 000
Floating capital   £ 7 000
     £500 interest on £10 000 fixed capital
     350 interest on floating capital
     150 rent, taxes, rates
     650 sinking fund of $6\frac{1}{2}$% for wear and tear of the
         fixed capital
   £ 1 650
   £ 1 100 Contingencies, carriage, coal, oil
    2 750
    2 600 Wages and salaries
    5 350
   10 000 for about 400 000 lb. of raw cotton at 6d.
   15 350
   16 000 for 363 000 lb. twist spun. Value £16 000.

Marx's explanation follows:

Capital laid out in labour is 2600; the surplus value = 1650 (850 interest + 150 rents etc., makes 1000 + 650 profit). In Marx's view, the rate of surplus value = 63 $\frac{6}{13}$% (1650/15 350), which is nearly 10.1%.

Malthus's measure of profit is 650 or about 4.2%. Marx disagrees: To the amount of 650 must be added the interest (5% on 17 000, since it is possible that capitalist A does not pocket the interest, but capitalist B). Marx then subtracts 850 from the total outlay of £15 350, and is left with £14 500. Of this net total, wages and salaries make up 16 $\frac{2}{3}$%, the other advances, 83 $\frac{1}{3}$%. The capitalist sells 14 500 worth for 16 000, for a profit of 1500 (10 $\frac{2}{3}$%). In short, he advances a sum of 100% and reproduces a total 100% (the latter includes the profit of about 10%). However, since labour makes up only $\frac{1}{6}$ of the annual advances (2600 of the total of 14 500), of the total labour time, 40% are for necessary and 60% are for surplus labour.

From his review of this example, Marx draws the following conclusions:

(1) in order to determine the size of the real surplus value, one must calculate the profit on the advance made for wages: the percentage which expresses the proportion between so-called profit and wages;

(2) the relatively smaller percentage made up by the proportion between the outlay on living labour and the total outlay presupposes a greater outlay on fixed capital, machinery, and so on, and a greater division of labour; the percentage of labour being smaller (with the greater capital), the mass of labour set in motion must be significantly greater;

(3) the profit from capital working with machinery is absolutely smaller than that from the capital working with living labour.[130]

On the general nature of profit, Marx declares:

- a general rate of profit as such is possible only if the rate of profit in one branch of business is too high and in another too low: that is to say, a part of the surplus value – which corresponds to surplus labour – is transferred from one capitalist to the other;[131]

- it is impossible for rates of profit on the same capital of 100 to be equal, since the relations of surplus labour are altogether different, depending on the productivity of labour and on the relation between raw materials, machinery and wages, and on the overall volume in which production takes place;[132]

- competition among capitalists may well even out or equalise the level of profit, but in no way creates the measure of the level;[133]

- competition among capitals can change only the relation in which they share the total profit, but cannot alter the relation between total profit and total wages. The general standard of profit is this relation between total profit and total wages, which is not altered through competition;[134]

- the alteration in the relation between total profit and total wages is due to an alteration in wages, whose necessary costs may rise (theory of the progressive deterioration of the soil in agriculture) in consequence of a decrease in the productive force of labour due to natural causes: the rate of profit falls, as a result not of a decrease but rather of an increase in the productive force;[135]

- the capitalist class to a certain extent distributes the total surplus value so that, to a certain degree, it shares in it evenly in accordance with the size of its capital, instead of in accordance with the surplus values actually created by the capitals in the various branches of business. The larger profit – arising from the real surplus labour within a branch of production, the really created surplus value – is pushed down to the average level by competition, and the deficit surplus value in the other branch of business is raised up to the average level by withdrawals of capital from it, that is, the favourable relation of demand and supply. Competition cannot lower this level itself, but merely has the tendency to create such a level. This is realised (in competition) by means of the relation of prices in the different branches of business, which fall below the value in some, rise above it in others. This makes it seem as if an equal sum of capital in unequal branches of business created equal surplus labour or surplus value.[136]

In concluding our review of Marx on prices in the *Grundrisse*, let us once again emphasise his recognition of the influence of demand and supply and of factors making for changes in both. Let us also attempt to name and add up the various price components:

wages and salaries + raw materials + contingencies + energy +
+ transportation + rent, taxes, rates + interest on fixed capital +
+ interest on floating capital + depreciation (sinking fund) +
+ profit.

In Marx's view, profit will be (a) higher than surplus value; (b) lower than surplus value; (c) only coincidentally equal to surplus value. However, let us note that he had difficulties placing the several components of *faux frais de production* (do they add to the value of the commodity or only to the overall costs of production?) and of the several transaction costs (for example shipping costs: do they represent a real cost of production, and therefore an increase in the value of the commodity, or do they constitute a subtraction from the surplus value?).

Last but not least, let us also remind ourselves that Marx did, implicitly and explicitly, allude to the notion of opportunity cost, when he spoke of the frequency of production periods in a given time span (his concept of the production multiplier) and expressed concern about the distance of markets and the postponement of the realisation of capital.

NOTES AND COMMENTS

1. *Grundrisse*, pp. 402–5, 407, 418.
2. *Werke*, vol. 6, 'Wage Labour and Capital', p. 404.
3. *Grundrisse*, p. 138.
4. Ibid., pp. 138, 413–4. *Werke*, vol. 6, 'Wage Labour and Capital', p. 404.
5. *Grundrisse*, pp. 137, 192–3.
6. Ibid., p. 657.

7. *Werke*, vol. 4, 'Address on the Question of Free Trade', p. 447.
8. Ibid., pp. 444–5.
9. *Grundrisse*, p. 134, 169, 880.
10. Ibid., pp. 872–3.
11. Ibid., pp. 147–9.
12. Ibid., p. 137.
13. Ibid., p. 137–8.
14. Ibid., p. 432.
15. Ibid., pp. 122–3.
16. Ibid., p. 120.
17. Ibid., pp. 131–2.
18. Ibid., p. 130.
19. Ibid., p. 129. Note Marx's allusion to the effect of increasing scarcity on price.
20. Ibid., p. 134.
21. Ibid., pp. 139–40.
22. Ibid., p. 200.
23. Ibid., pp. 194–5.
24. Ibid., p. 195.
25. Ibid., p. 878.
26. Ibid., p. 869.
27. Ibid., p. 140.
28. Ibid.
29. Ibid., pp. 791–2.
30. Ibid.
31. Ibid., pp. 794–5.
32. Ibid., pp. 142–3, 147, 791–6.
33. Ibid., pp. 226–7.
34. Ibid., pp. 207–12.
35. Ibid., p. 226.
36. Ibid., pp. 409–10.
37. Ibid., pp. 442–3.
38. Ibid., p. 405.
39. Ibid., pp. 410–11.
40. Ibid., pp. 416–17.
41. Ibid., p. 405.
42. Ibid., pp. 407–10.
43. Ibid., pp. 410–11.
44. Ibid., pp. 408–10.
45. Ibid., p. 446.
46. Ibid., pp. 139, 187.
47. Ibid., p. 137.
48. Ibid., pp. 136–8.
49. Ibid.
50. Ibid., p. 194.
51. Ibid., pp. 791–2.
52. Ibid., pp. 206–7.
53. Ibid., pp. 794–5. Also, see note on p. 407.
54. Ibid., pp. 206–7.

55. Ibid., p. 793.
56. Ibid., p. 796.
57. Ibid., p. 200.
58. Ibid., pp. 111–13.
59. Ibid., p. 198.
60. Ibid., p. 169.
61. Ibid., pp. 126–7, 226.
62. Ibid., pp. 186, 188.
63. Ibid., pp. 107, 125.
64. Ibid., pp. 124–5.
65. Ibid.
66. Ibid., p. 193.
67. Ibid., pp. 129, 218–19, 233.
68. Ibid., p. 184.
69. Ibid., p. 182.
70. Ibid., p. 227.
71. Ibid., p. 130.
72. Ibid., p. 138.
73. Ibid., p. 137.
74. Ibid., p. 147.
75. Ibid., p. 198.
76. Ibid., p. 234.
77. Ibid., p. 176.
78. Ibid., pp. 169–70.
79. Ibid., pp. 160–1.
80. Ibid., pp. 127–8. Note Marx's allusion to the effect of scarcity on a change in international prices.
81. Ibid., p. 129. Note Marx's clear perception as to the effect, on other commodities, of the rise in price of a particular staple (wheat).
82. Ibid., p. 420.
83. Ibid., pp. 444–5.
84. Ibid., p. 427.
85. Ibid., p. 346.
86. Ibid., pp. 432–5.
87. Ibid., p. 467.
88. Ibid., p. 817.
89. Ibid., p. 570.
90. Ibid., p. 552.
91. Ibid., p. 571.
92. Ibid., p. 575.
93. Ibid., p. 572.
94. Marx, Karl, *Wage Labour and Capital*, 1849. *Werke*, VI.
95. Ibid., p. 402.
96. Ibid., p. 403.
97. Ibid., pp. 403–5.
98. Ibid., p. 406.
99. Ibid.
100. Ibid.
101. Ibid.

102. *Grundrisse*, pp. 323–5.
103. Ibid., pp. 845–6.
104. Ibid., p. 318.
105. Ibid., pp. 414–15.
106. Ibid., p. 267.
107. Marx, Karl, *Poverty of Philosophy* (Moscow), p. 151.
108. Ibid.
109. Ibid., p. 152.
110. Ibid.
111. Ibid., p. 154.
112. *Grundrisse.*, pp. 115–27.
113. Ibid., p. 318.
114. Ibid., pp. 836–9.
115. Ibid., p. 318.
116. Ibid., p. 312.
117. Ibid., p. 120.
118. Ibid., p. 318.
119. Ibid., p. 442.
120. Ibid., pp. 836–8.
121. Ibid., p. 852.
122. Ibid., p. 851.
123. Ibid.
124. Ibid.
125. Ibid., p. 854.
126. Ibid., p. 427.
127. Ibid., p. 822.
128. Ibid., p. 427.
129. Ibid., pp. 564–6.
130. Ibid., p. 566.
131. Ibid., p. 435.
132. Ibid.
133. Ibid., p. 552.
134. Ibid., p. 557.
135. Ibid., p. 558.
136. Ibid., p. 446.

Bibliography

Anonymous, *The Source and Remedy of the National Difficulties* (London, 1821).

DARIMON, ALFRED, *De la réforme des banques* (Paris, 1856).

FULLARTON, J., *On the Regulation of Currencies*, 2nd edn. (London, 1845).

HODGSKIN, THOMAS, *Popular Political Economy* (London, 1827).

HUBBARD, J.G., *The Currency and the Country* (London, 1843).

KOHLMEY, GÜNTHER, 'Karl Marx Theorie von den internationalen Werten', *Jahrbuch des Instituts für Wirtschaftswissenschaften*, Band 11 (1962).

MALTHUS, THOMAS, *Principles of Political Economy* (1836).

MARX, KARL, *A Contribution to the Critique of Political Economy* (1859).

—— *Class Struggles in France* (1850).

—— *Das Kapital* (1867).

—— *Grundrisse* (Harmondsworth: Penguin, 1973)

—— *Paris Manuscripts* (1844).

—— *Poverty of Philosophy* (1847).

—— *Wage Labour and Capital* (1849).

MARX, K. and FRIEDRICH ENGELS, *Werke*, Band 7 (Berlin: Dietz, 1957).

MCLELLAN, D. (ed.), *The Grundrisse Karl Marx* (New York: Harper Torchbooks, 1971).

MILL, JOHN STUART, *Principles of Political Economy*, 2nd edn, vol. I (London, 1849).

PROUDHON, PIERRE JOSEPH, *Philosophie de la misère*, vol. I (Paris, 1846).

RICARDO, DAVID, *Principles of Political Economy and Taxation* (1821).

RUBEL, M. and M. MANALE, *Marx Without Myth* (Oxford: Basil Blackwell, 1975).

SENIOR, NASSAU, *Three Lectures On the Cost of Obtaining Money* (London, 1830).

STEUART, SIR JAMES, *An Inquiry into the Principles of Political Economy*, vol. I (Dublin, 1770).

STORCH, HEINRICH FRIEDRICH. *Considérations sur la nature du revenu national* (Paris, 1824).

TOWNSHEND, REVEREND J., *A Dissertation on the Poor- laws* (1817).

XENOPHON, *Scripta Minora* (London, 1925).

Index